5/15

Citizens' Rights and the Right to Be a Citizen

Developments
in International Law

VOLUME 66

The titles published in this series are listed at brill.com/diil

Citizens' Rights and the Right to Be a Citizen

By

Ernst Hirsch Ballin

BRILL

NIJHOFF

LEIDEN | BOSTON

Cover illustration: 'The Arrival'. Artwork and photograph by Joel Bergner.

This book is partially based on the author's inaugural address "Burgerrechten" (2011). The extended version of this lecture was translated into English by UvA Vertalingen, Amsterdam.

Library of Congress Cataloging-in-Publication Data

Hirsch Ballin, E. M. H., author.
 Citizens' rights and the right to be a citizen / By Ernst Hirsch Ballin.
    p. cm. -- (Developments in international law volume 66)
 Includes bibliographical references and index.
 ISBN 978-90-04-22318-9 (hardback : alk. paper) -- ISBN 978-90-04-22320-2 (e-book) 1. Citizenship.
2. Constitutional law. 3. Human rights. 4. Civil rights. 5. Emigration and immigration law. I. Title.
 K3224.H58 2014
 323.6--dc23

                                        2013048040

This publication has been typeset in the multilingual "Brill" typeface. With over 5,100 characters covering Latin, IPA, Greek, and Cyrillic, this typeface is especially suitable for use in the humanities. For more information, please see www.brill.com/brill-typeface.

ISSN 0924-5332
ISBN 978-90-04-22318-9 (hardback)
ISBN 978-90-04-22320-2 (e-book)

Copyright 2014 E.M.H. Hirsch Ballin, University of Amsterdam.
Koninklijke Brill NV incorporates the imprints Brill, Brill Nijhoff, Global Oriental and Hotei Publishing.

Printed by Printforce, the Netherlands

To Maurits and Marianne

CONTENTS

PREFACE

This book springs from the inaugural address I gave at the University of Amsterdam on 9 September 2011 as the newly appointed Professor of Human Rights Law. Many of those who attended the lecture or read it on the University's website encouraged me not to let the topic rest there, sometimes because they felt that my text advanced the constitutional understanding of actual perplexities, or because they identified with my argumentation from their own experience. This response confirmed to me that it is worthwhile discussing citizenship in the context of internationalized relationships and the dynamics inherent in them.

When my inauguration was announced, people were at first surprised that I would take as my subject the rights associated with citizenship. Surely citizens' rights are not universal human rights but merely the rights of citizens of this or that state? This is certainly true, but without such rights there would be something essential missing from the connection between human rights and democracy under the rule of law. It is for this reason that the right to a nationality is recognized as a human right under Article 15 of the Universal Declaration of Human Rights. This inevitably leads to the objection that private individuals cannot choose the state of which they are citizens. This objection, however, cannot be the last word in a world where people's lives are increasingly lived in the setting of more than one nation.

Those to whom these questions occurred had actually grasped the issue addressed in my lecture before I delivered it. Nonetheless my discourse was also intended as a personal statement. When I gave my lecture, indeed, it was only six months since I had resumed my academic work. In October 2010 – earlier than foreseen – the formation of a coalition government supported partly by a right-wing political movement put an end to my long-standing involvement in political life, the beginnings of which dated back to 1989, when Ruud Lubbers, having employed me as an adviser on constitutional and legal policy questions for some years, asked me, as an outsider, to be Minister of Justice in his third government. During the years that followed I was involved variously in academia, the administration of justice – for six years at the judicial division of the Council of State – and politics, from 2006 to 2010 again as Minister of Justice.

That was a period when issues of migration and citizenship became increasingly important. The collapse of the communist system, the ensuing civil wars in the Balkans and the Caucasus, and the conflicts in Sri Lanka, Somalia, Afghanistan and Iraq brought large numbers of asylum seekers to Western Europe. The decades-old antagonism with communist ideology made way – already before 9/11/2001, but with even greater vehemence thereafter – for a new antagonism with an anti-Western movement which is – wrongly – identified with Islam. It was in precisely that period that I was one of the people responsible for the infrastructure of the rule of law, a political principle that has been corroborated by human rights and therefore opposes prejudice or discrimination based on belonging to a particular group.

This period of my working life is in sharp contrast to the decades in my father's life that led up to the point in 1959 when he delivered his inaugural address to the Law Faculty of the University of Amsterdam, at the same age as I did in 2011. The preceding thirty years were very much different for my father and for me. Having spent his formative years in an environment rich in culture, in 1929 my father appeared to be at the start of a career as an already esteemed attorney and notary in his home city of Wiesbaden (Germany). When I had the same age I started working as Professor of Constitutional and Administrative Law in Tilburg, midway between Amsterdam and Brussels. In 1933, owing to his Jewish parentage, his world and German democracy collapsed for my father and all other right-minded Germans. My generation has been spared this, but I have learned from boyhood how much depends on whether political and state powers subject themselves to the rule of law or are made subservient to lust for power and the obsessions of people who are not willing to recognize others as equals. This book is about one aspect of these constitutional issues. I wish such insights and the experiences of past and present to be beneficial to future generations. Therefore I dedicate this book to Pauline's and my children.

September 8, 2013   HB

ACKNOWLEDGEMENTS

The author is grateful to his colleagues at the Faculty of Law of the University of Amsterdam, especially Roland Pierik, Annette Schrauwen, and Tamar de Waal, for their valuable comments on various parts of the manuscript, and to dean Edgar du Perron for encouraging and facilitating the publication of this book. He wishes to thank his research assistants at the Law School of Tilburg University Caia Vlieks for composing the bibliography and collecting documents on statelessness and European citizenship, and Eva van Vugt for composing the index and revising the footnotes.

CHAPTER ONE

CITIES AND CITIZENS

1.1 Introduction

The history of law and the state is part and parcel of the history of mankind: it is determined by the way in which people coexist and their needs are met. In retrospect we can say that the regimes of sedentarized nations – who had moved to arable areas where they were better able to supply their needs[1] – grew into political systems in which rulers no longer held sway solely over their own peoples but subjected foreign peoples where their military power permitted.[2] The development of science and technology has played a major role here. The positions of heavenly bodies as a function of time were calculated using the astrolabe, a Hellenistic invention that reached the Christian world in the eleventh century via the then Arabic city of Toledo.[3] Once reality could be measured and mapped,[4] navigation enabled European nations to sail the high seas and make not only the natural resources in other parts of the world but also the people who lived there subservient to their desire for ever greater riches.

As a result of scientific and technological development, flourishing cities striving for self-rule started to develop in the late Middle Ages – first in Lombardy and then north of the Alps – with an image marked by prestigious town halls and burghers' houses.[5] In the Netherlands these cities – to quote Wim Blockmans – became "centers of cultural output", "North Sea Metropolises".[6] Their connections with the ocean enabled

---

[1] J.M. Roberts, *A History of Europe* (Allan Lane/The Penguin Press 1996) 10–11.

[2] Siep Stuurman, *De uitvinding van de mensheid. Korte wereldgeschiedenis van het denken over gelijkheid en cultuurverschil* [The Invention of Mankind. A Short World History of Ideas on Equality and Cultural Difference] (Bert Bakker 2009) 183ff.

[3] Jerrilynn D. Dodds, María Rosa Menocal and Abigail Krasner Balbale, *The Arts of Intimacy. Christians, Jews, and Muslims in the Making of Castilian Culture* (Yale UP 2009) 57.

[4] Alfred W. Crosby, *The Measure of Reality. Quantification and Western Society, 1250–1600* (CUP 1997).

[5] *Putzger Atlas und Chronik zur Weltgeschichte* [Atlas and Chronicle of World History] (2nd edn, Cornelsen Verlag 2009) 102–3.

[6] Wim Blockmans, *Metropolen aan de Noordzee. De geschiedenis van Nederland, 1100–1560* [North Sea Metropolises. The History of the Netherlands 1100–1560] (Bert Bakker 2010) 636ff.

unprecedented economic growth to take place.[7] Amsterdam and the other Dutch cities secured freedom of trade for themselves in the Dutch Revolt against the Habsburg rulers. During the Golden Age of the Netherlands they continued to expand, both economically and demographically, thanks to what Jan Lucassen describes as "mass immigration". As a result of the influx from home and abroad the population of Amsterdam grew from 30,000 in 1560 to 219,000 in 1680.[8] The seventeenth century was "the century of the cities", in the words of Geert Mak. At the turn of the century Western Europe numbered only forty cities with more than 40,000 inhabitants, six of which were in France, seven in Spain and seven in the much smaller Holland; by the end of the century there were dozens more.[9]

The development of political structures in Europe under the influence of economic and social change was neither unique nor without precedent: there were forms of political rule in the Far East that had both differences from and similarities with those in Europe.[10] In the centuries before Christ a dynamism characterized by seafaring, trade and warfare had developed around the Mediterranean, resulting in the formation of cities (πόλεις).[11] Phoenicians, Greeks and Romans established colonies – in the original sense of overseas settlements – in other countries, but their metropolises in turn became places of settlement for the subjected peoples: the Jewish diaspora dates back to this era.[12]

The countries around the Mediterranean continued to provide the backdrop for cultural exchange. Centuries later, a Catholic nun at the court of Emperor Otto the Great was overheard describing the Umayyad

---

[7] Ibid. 649ff.

[8] Leo Lucassen and Jan Lucassen, *Winnaars en verliezers. Een nuchtere balans van vijf-honderd jaar immigratie* [Winners and Losers. A Rational Review of Five Hundred Years of Immigration] (Bert Bakker 2011) 191.

[9] Geert Mak, *Een kleine geschiedenis van Amsterdam* [A Short History of Amsterdam] (Uitgeverij Atlas 2005) 126.

[10] Francis Fukuyama, *The Origins of Political Order. From Prehuman Times to the French Revolution* (Farrar, Straus and Giroux 2011).

[11] Cf. Christian Meier, *A Culture of Freedom. Ancient Greece and the Origins of Europe* (OUP 2009) 9: "For several centuries these [i.e. ancient Greek] communities evolved in clusters and constant competition among each other, expanded their world through the foundation of a great number of new *poleis* along the coasts of the Mediterranean and Black Sea areas, interacted intensively with the more highly developed cultures to the east and south (from Anatolia and the Levant to Mesopotamia and Egypt) but lived outside the sphere of direct control by the great powers of the time. As a people, they thus were free, not ruled by others."

[12] Fik Meijer, *De Middellandse Zee. Een persoonlijke geschiedenis* [The Mediterranean Sea. A Personal History] (Athenaeum – Polak & Van Gennep 2010).

Caliphate in Córdoba as "the ornament of the world".[13] The pomp and circumstance of the court was the outward symbol of this, but the real jewel in the crown of Andalusia (al-Andalus) at that time was the unprecedented cultural and economic dynamism that had been brought about by different peoples, cultures and religions coexisting. The intellectual fruits of this – the rediscovery of Aristotle by Islamic, Jewish and Christian scholars, for instance – survived subsequent periods of harsh repression. The rediscovery also led to a reinterpretation. In the light of Christian revealed faith, Thomas Aquinas reinterpreted the cosmocentric philosophy in the work of Aristotle, which he studied in dialogue with the Córdoban Arab Ibn Rushd (Averroes), whom Aquinas respectfully dubbed 'the Commentator'. This intellectual encounter was the starting point for a philosophy based on the principle of man as his own subject, the 'anthropocentrism' that came to permeate all areas of human knowledge in the ensuing centuries.[14] This turnaround, which developed in interaction between cultures, eventually resulted in 'natural justice' – a concept that links Aristotle, Aquinas and Hegel with twentieth-century figures such as Radbruch – no longer being regarded as an order reflecting cosmology but as a set of legal principles that respect the spiritual nature of mankind.[15]

The relationships between people have socio-economic and politico-legal dimensions that are intertwined and interlinked, as in both respects we are concerned with the patterns by which coexistence is organized – spontaneously or by force. Solidarity within a single tribe or people (ἔθνος) was the 'normal' pattern worldwide[16] and remained so as long as

---

[13] María Rosa Menocal, *The Ornament of the World. How Muslims, Jews, and Christians Created a Culture of Tolerance in Medieval Spain* (Little, Brown & Company 2002) 32.

[14] Johann Baptist Metz, *Christliche Anthropozentrik* [Christian Anthropocentrism] (Kösel-Verlag 1962); David Novak, 'Maimonides and Aquinas on Natural Law' in John Goyette and others, *St. Thomas Aquinas and the Natural Law Tradition. Contemporary Perspectives* (The Catholic University of America Press 2004) 55: "The Judeo-Christian-Islamic idea that nature is the lawful creation of the divine creator/lawgiver gives a new and more satisfying grounding to the process whereby ethics presupposes metaphysics and metaphysics entails ethics".

[15] Cf. Paul Sigmund, 'Law and Politics' in Norman Kretzman and Eleonore Stump (eds.), *The Cambridge Companion to Aquinas* (CUP 1993) 229: "Recognizing that many of Aquinas' views on society and politics that are unacceptable today (...) were historically conditioned or the result of an uncritical acceptance of Aristotle, the modern reader (...) can still find relevant Aquinas's belief in the human capacity to identify goals, values, and purposes in the structure and functioning of the human person that can be used to evaluate and reform social, political, and legal strucures (...). This belief (...) is really a faith that the meaning of human life is, at least in part, accessible to human reason (....)."

[16] The parable of the Good Samaritan (Gospel of St Luke, 10:25–37) tells the story of Jesus's solidarity going beyond tribal restrictions.

tribes – initially living more or less nomadically, with no fixed place of
temporary or permanent residence, then becoming mainly sedentarized
once arable farming developed – supplied their needs. 'The law' was that
of a particular people, a particular tribe, that had been handed down and
eventually set down in writing.[17] The rulers of these peoples were warriors
who led them in the battle for grazing areas and fertile land and settled
disputes between them; when they converted to a new faith they did so on
behalf of their entire people.[18]

Scope for personal freedom widened in the cities.[19] It did not develop
once and for all and simultaneously throughout the world. In classical
antiquity we find examples in Athens, Alexandria and Rome, in the Middle
Ages in a host of Western European cities. Rome developed in the direction of greater liberty and back to a closed society several times. Serfs who
sheltered for a year and a day in a medieval city became free citizens in
line with the dictum *'Stadtluft macht frei'* (city air makes you free).[20] In
Europe the rise of the mercantile class was due mainly to the growth of
cities: "merchants were inseparably linked with the most dynamic element in medieval European civilization, the towns and cities which
increasingly fostered within their walls so much of the future history of
Europe."[21] The cities developed various forms of independence from monarchs, who granted increasing legal and personal freedoms to their male
citizens. "The burgher – the *bourgeois*, the dweller in bourg or borough –
was a man who stood up for himself in a universe of dependence, a citizen
in the making, as well as a subject."[22]

This explains the genesis and development of citizenship in terms of a
transition from tribal means of supplying needs and political organization

---

[17] See e.g. the edition of early Frisian texts, Jelle Hindriks Brouwer and others, *Specimina linguae Frisiae veteris* (Brill 1950).

[18] Such as in 985 István, King of the Magyars, honored as St Stephen of Hungary.

[19] Sir Paul Vinogradoff, 'Historical Types of International Law' in *Bibliotheca Visseriana Dissertationum Ius Internationale Illustrantium. Tomus primus* (Brill 1923) 5ff, describes the genesis of a – potentially – reciprocal humane legal culture in the "law of the city" of the classical Greek and Italian republics between "citizens making use of their close cohesion to establish a more or less exclusive civil law."

[20] Heinrich Mitteis, 'Über den Rechtsgrund des Satzes "Stadtluft macht frei"' [On the Legal Foundation of the Dictum 'Stadtluft macht frei'] in Erika Kunz (ed.), *Festschrift Edmund E. Stengel zum 70. Geburtstag am 24. Dezember 1949 dargebracht von Freunden, Fachgenossen und Schülern* [Festschrift in honour of Edmund E. Stengel presented by friends, colleagues and pupils on the occasion of his 70th birthday on 24 December 1949] (Böhlau 1952) 342–58.

[21] Roberts (n. 1) 142.

[22] Ibid.

to urbanization processes – nowadays worldwide –, which result in peoples living increasingly less separated from one another.[23] Western Europe played a major role in this trend owing to the rise of an urban bourgeoisie in the Low Countries, Northern Italy and the Hanseatic cities; in Eastern Europe, on the other hand, as Fukuyama points out, cities were far less independent, as in ancient China, and they were governed by local rulers as administrative-cum-trade centers.[24]

With industrialization and the tremendous growth in productivity in the urban areas, there developed – at different times and rates worldwide – a civil society that demanded democratic legitimacy and the rule of law.[25] In 1950 29% of the world's population lived in towns and cities; since 2008 it has been the majority, and by 2030 the proportion will have risen to 60%.[26] Migration to urban areas has caused them to be populated by people with diverse cultural, religious and ethnic identities. In the individualizing socio-cultural climate of the towns and cities their inhabitants have increasingly shown themselves to be free subjects who wish to be in command of their own destiny and are less and less defined by a single ethnic identity characteristic of their community.

The response to this genuine ethnic diversity has differed, and still differs today. On the one hand, many attempts have been made to put a lid on urban diversity and ensure the dominance of the ruling class through persecution, enforced 'conversion' or ghettoization. On the other hand, regimes that have accepted the principle of tolerance – as a calculated ploy or out of conviction – have defined their nation (δῆμος), composed of people with different origins and beliefs, in non-ethnic terms. Under those regimes, diversity within the nation goes hand in hand with equal treatment as a feature of the social order.

In the first case the exclusional dimension of nationality predominates: 'full enjoyment' of citizens' rights is confined to those who belong to the ruling class in terms of ethnicity or religion, as was the case in the United States before the civil rights movement prevailed and in South Africa

---

[23] Kenneth Jackson, 'Cities' in Richard Bulliet (ed.), *The Columbia History of the 20th Century* (Columbia UP 1998) 528–42; Randall Lesaffer, *European Legal History. A Cultural and Political Perspective* (CUP 2009) 136–137.

[24] Fukuyama (n. 10) 376, 410–11.

[25] Ibid. ch. 30.

[26] United Nations Department of Economic and Social Affairs (UNDESA) Population Division, 'World Urbanization Prospects: The 2005 Revision – Fact Sheet 1: World Urban Population' (2005) UNDESA <www.un.org/esa/population/publications/WUP2005/2005 WUP_FS1.pdf> accessed 4 February 2012.

when its non-white inhabitants were demoted to aliens with the dubious status of citizens of the 'homelands'. This exclusional implementation of citizenship is found in a host of different forms. They are often less overt than the historical examples just mentioned, but they can nevertheless have far-reaching effects on those concerned, especially when legal exclusion is combined with socio-economic deprivation or removal of residence rights.

In the second case a legal foundation is created for the integration of people in a single δῆμος irrespective of their origin. Herein lies the legal significance of citizenship without limitations based on ethnicity, culture or religion; but here too it is important to look at its true value in socio-economic terms. Where divisions remain in terms of language or participation, for example, equal enjoyment of citizens' rights misses the target. The purpose of citizens' rights is to place involvement in the political system and society on a footing of reciprocal responsibility: in other words, citizens also have civil duties, such as sharing the burden of public expenditure, participating in elections and in some countries performing other public duties, e.g. serving in the military, acting as a dike warden or sitting on a jury.

1.2   The Nature of Citizens' Rights

This brings us to a significant tension for the Dutch society and many others. The concept of 'citizen' refers to ties with a political community, whereas that of 'person' refers to the dignity of every human being, for which we demand universal recognition.[27] As a framework for social order we find that the state remains indispensable, either independently or in broader contexts such as the European Union. The nation-state, however, is permanently challenged by ideals of world citizenship, with rights that are supposed to be granted to everyone without distinction. While achieving such ideals lies far over the horizon, the challenge they present is significant:[28] what actually justifies the fact that states set and guard

---

[27] Cf. Linda Bosniak, 'Persons and Citizens in Constitutional Thought' (2010) 8 *International Journal of Constitutional Law* 9.

[28] For the tension between the moral ideals of cosmopolitanism and the need to have a variety of functioning national and international institutions, see Roland Pierik and Wouter Werner, 'Cosmopolitanism in context: an introduction' in Roland Pierik and Wouter Werner (eds.), *Cosmopolitanism in Context. Perspectives from International Law & Political Theory* (CUP 2010) 1–15.

limits, denying citizens' rights to some people who make their contribution to a community – rights that others do enjoy even if they neglect their duties to society?[29] The key question I wish to pose, then, is how – in a twenty-first century European society such as the Netherlands – citizens' rights can once more bridge the gap between the universality of human rights without distinction and the political and social setting in which people participate in a democratic society.

To answer this question we need – as Nils Butenschøn writes – to take as our starting point the connection between a citizen and the state referred to as 'citizenship': "what does it mean to belong tot a state?".[30] He notes the "'Janus-faced' nature of citizenship", whose function "to exclude people is just as important as the function to include [them]."[31] His analysis of the meaning of 'citizenship' starts as it were at a point antecedent to any "normative model of governance", namely (1) the function "to distribute people between state territories (thereby contributing in forming 'peoples' or 'nations')" and (2) by regulating "people's access to public resources and institutions" in combination with other criteria.[32] Over three centuries – as Butenschøn notes, following in the footsteps of T.H. Marshall and Asbjørn Eide – this basic citizenship has been armed with three kinds of rights: civil rights in the eighteenth century, political rights in the nineteenth century and social rights in the twentieth century.[33] The increasing importance of citizenship meant that the relationship between the state and the citizen, which was taken for granted in the Christian nations of pre-French Revolution Europe and arbitrarily granted to people or withheld from others – for instance Jews in the diaspora – became the object of political struggle.

This inevitably raises the question of whether citizenship in the twenty-first century can still be discussed in terms of an exclusive relationship with a particular state. This question touches upon the legitimacy of restricting rights to nationals. Let us not be in too much of a hurry to assume that this restriction unfavorably differentiates the concept of

---

[29] Seyla Benhabib points this out and establishes a connection with Habermas' discussion of the Janus-headed nature of the modern state in *Another Cosmopolitanism* (OUP 2006) 19, 32.

[30] Nils A. Butenschøn, 'Citizenship and Human Rights. Some Thoughts on a Complex Relationship' in Morten Bergsmo (ed.), *Human Rights and Criminal Justice for the Downtrodden. Essays in Honor of Asbjørn Eide* (Martinus Nijhoff Publishers 2003) 556.

[31] Ibid. 558.

[32] Ibid. 559.

[33] Ibid. 562.

citizens' rights from that of human rights, however. After all, the historical purpose of citizens' rights was to permit a positive relationship between citizens and their state. The recognition of citizens' rights was inextricably linked with political human rights (in particular freedom of expression and freedom of association and assembly) and the democratic order, which gave people the right – and the moral duty – to participate in the functioning of the constitutional system. Citizens' rights came into being in the era of the French Revolution. The citizens of the towns and cities had come to see themselves as lawful *subjects of their own destiny*, free of feudal and other traditional ties. The *Déclaration des droits de l'homme et du citoyen* of 26 August 1789[34] marked a fundamental political turning point: the recognition of the rights of man and of the citizen put an end to subjection to the sovereignty of the monarch.[35] That became the essence of citizenship: this is what the struggle for the recognition of citizens' rights (*droits du citoyen*) was – and is – about.

The civil revolutions at the end of the eighteenth century bore the unmistakable character of a struggle for political and economic freedom: the 1776 American Revolution against the British motherland's self-serving domination of the colonies, the 1789 French Revolution against the class system. The idea that inspired them, however, went beyond this, lying in a universalist notion of everyone being born free and equal – a view of humanity that in the United States tended to be tinted by Christianity and in France more by the rationalism of the Enlightenment but in both cases was egalitarian and universalist, as the result of a

---

[34] This declaration marked the beginning of the recognition of human rights in Europe; in America it was the Declaration of Rights of 12 June 1776. The body of ideas from which these declarations sprang has developed classical antiquity. As early as "in classical Roman law legal notions [are] to be found that are similar to modern human rights", notes Jacob Giltaij, *Mensenrechten in het Romeinse recht?* [Human Rights in Roman Law?] (Wolf Legal Publishers 2011) 161. The beginnings here of the recognition of persons as having legal rights, the notion of natural justice starting with Thomas Aquinas that gave human reason a place in Christian culture, and English documents such as Magna Carta (1215), the Petition of Right (1628), the Habeas Corpus Act (1679) and the Bill of Rights (1689) are part of the 'prehistory' of human rights. This is also true e.g. of the Dutch *Akte van Verlatinghe,* cf. Paul Brood and Raymond Kobben, *The Act of Abjuration. Inspired and Inspirational* (Wolf Legal Publishers 2011). For this prehistory of the Declarations see Peter C. Kop, *Mens en Burger. Een geschiedenis van de grondrechten* [Man and Citizen. A History of Fundamental Rights] (Walburg Pers 2009) 17–51.

[35] Francesca Raimondi, 'Einleitung' [Introduction] in Christoph Menke and Francesca Raimondi (eds.), *Die Revolution der Menschenrechte. Grundlegende Texte zu einem neuen Begriff des Politischen* [The Human Rights Revolution. Basic Texts for a New Concept of the Political] (Suhrkamp 2011) 96.

deepening sacralization of the person.[36] "We hold these truths to be self-evident, that all men are created equal, that they are endowed by their Creator with certain unalienable Rights, that among these are Life, Liberty and the pursuit of Happiness", to quote the second sentence of the United States Declaration of Independence of 4 July 1776; "Les hommes naissent et demeurent libres et égaux en droits" (Men are born and remain free and equal in rights), to quote the opening sentence of Article 1 of the Déclaration des droits de l'homme et du citoyen of 26 August 1789. Thus guaranteeing fundamental rights involved a tension – which already developed in the late eighteenth century and inevitably persists today – between their politico-social focus on the relationship between the state and the citizen and their ideological focus on universal respect for human beings in all places and at all times.

At the time of their formulation, *droits du citoyen* were seen with great optimism as the political armament of those who made up French society. Under the 1793 Constitution (Article 4, *De l'État des citoyens*) these included not only everyone aged 21 and over who was born and resident in France; an adult *étranger* who had been domiciled in France for at least one year also enjoyed the rights of a *citoyen français*, provided he was able to support himself, or owned property, or married a Frenchwoman, or had adopted a child, or looked after an elderly person – in short, provided he behaved like a right-minded *citoyen*. The legislature could also make anyone else a *citoyen* who had performed services to mankind, *l'humanité*.[37]

The fundamental rights guaranteed by the *Déclaration* – which still form part of the French Constitution – are not divided up (as would nowadays probably be the case) between two chapters, one on universal human rights and one on citizens' rights. Their joint treatment makes the

---

[36] Stuurman (n. 2) 323; Hans Joas, *The Sacredness of the Person. A New Genealogy of Human Rights* (Alex Skinner trans., Georgetown UP 2013). Originally published as *Die Sakralität der Person. Eine neue Genealogie der Menschenrechte* (Suhrkamp 2011).

[37] Claude Mazauric, 'La Déclaration des Droits de l'Homme et du Citoyen et la Révolution Française' [The Declaration of Human Rights and Citizens' Rights and the French Revolution] in Guy Braibant and Gérard Marcou (eds.), *Les Droits de l'Homme. Universalité et Renouveau 1789–1989* [Human Rights: Universality and Renewal 1789–1989] (Éditions l'Harmattan 1989) 86–87; cf. the broad admission of aliens to political rights in the *Staatsregeling voor het Bataafsche Volk* [Batavian Constitution] (1798) art. 11. After the Batavian (i.e. Dutch) Revolution of 1795, national citizenship, based on the principle of equality, replaced the former distinction between the citizens of the cities and the rural population. No sharp distinction between human rights and citizens' rights was made at that time. See Mart Rutjes, *Door gelijkheid gegrepen. Democratie, burgerschap en staat in Nederland 1795–1801* [Seized by Equality. Democracy, Citizenship and State in the Netherlands 1795–1801] (Vantilt 2012) 161.

connection between them clear, but also the distinction. Equal protection of the *"droits naturels de chaque homme"* (Article IV) encompasses the right to do anything not forbidden by law (Article V), but participating in the creation of these laws is the sole province of *Citoyens* (Article VI). Freedom of thought and belief is a human right (first half of Article XI), but freedom of expression as a participatory right of *citoyens* follows in the second half. As the political philosopher Lucien Jaume points out, the *Déclaration*, drawing upon the philosophical and legal tradition of natural justice, articulates three concepts, those of man, sovereignty and citizen.[38] *La citoyenneté*, citizenship, comprises rights and duties; it is an *"activité vivante"* which demands that people engage in the joint exercise of sovereignty so as to produce laws that apply equally to everyone.[39]

Citizenship, then, is the status that forms the bridge between the universal right of every human being to live freely in equality and the political and social setting this requires, that of a *constitution* that protects everyone equally under the law and enables them to contribute to public life. *Citizens' rights* are rights that developed historically along with human rights, but they are set apart by a special requirement – apparently a restriction – namely a specific relationship to the state that qualifies people as *citizens of that state* (i.e. nationals). Article 2 of the Dutch Constitution leaves it to the ordinary statute law to stipulate who is a citizen of the state (Dutch national). Under the Constitution such citizenship is the decisive factor when it comes to certain fundamental rights guaranteed in the chapter on constitutional rights, namely the equal appointability of all Dutch nationals to public office (Article 3), the right to vote and to stand for election (Article 4), the free choice of work (Article 19 (3)), and entitlement to social security benefit, which the Constitution restricts to Dutch nationals resident in the Netherlands who are unable to provide for themselves (Article 20 (3)). Although the words "citizenship" (French: *citoyenneté*, German: *Staatsbürgerschaft*, Dutch: *staatsburgerschap*) and "nationality" (French: *nationalité*, German: *Staatsangehörigkeit*,

---

[38] Lucien Jaume, 'Préface aux droits de l'homme' [Preface to Droits De L'Homme] in Lucien Jaume, *Les Déclarations des Droits de l'Homme (Du débat 1789–1793 au Préambule de 1946)* [The Declarations of Human Rights (from the 1789–1793 debate to the 1946 Preamble)] (Flammarion 1989) 29; Marcel Gauchet, *La Révolution des droits de l'homme* [The Human Rights Revolution] (Éditions Gallimard 1989). See also Mazauric (n. 37) 75–89.
[39] Jaume (n. 38) 31, 39. This explains the *légicentrisme* (see Jaume (n. 38) 58) of French constitutional thought, which had a strong influence in the Netherlands (cf. the present author's *Het grondrecht op vrijheid en de wet* [The Fundamental Right to Freedom and the Law] (Samsom H.D. Tjeenk Willink 1989).

Dutch: *nationalitieit*) have different origins and in some contexts may have different connotations, they refer to the same legal situation, i.e. a specific legal bond between a state (or other public entity) and a person, entailing rights and obligations. In accordance with international usage but also for reasons of conceptual clarity (see in detail § 3.1), I will not try to write any substantive legal difference into the juxtaposition of the two words. The notion of citizenship has a wider field of application, though, than that of nationality, since the latter in common use is related to a state ("nation" in the sense of country), whereas citizenship can also be related to infrastatal entities like the Swiss cantons or supranational entities like the European Union. In a sociological context, one might regard every person who is an active participant in a community, especially a city, as a citizen.

It is standard practice for a constitution to restrict rights such as these to nationals. Not everyone has the right to vote and occupy public office in the state where he or she lives. Even if the person has a residence permit at the time, his or her right to enter the country can be withdrawn. This right, then, differentiates between nationals of the country and 'aliens', in the Netherlands just as in other countries. Aliens may be socially, economically and culturally integrated, but they are not nationals, so they do not enjoy the citizens' rights associated with nationality, or only to a limited extent. Citizens' rights are the fundamental rights guaranteed to *nationals* that enable them to take a full and active part in the public life of their state. This is what distinguishes them from the fundamental rights that we refer to as 'human rights', which are enjoyed by *everyone without distinction*. What rights these are is thus determined by the relationship with the state.

1.3 *Transformations of Citizens' Rights*

It has been a long road from the end of the eighteenth century to the turn of the twenty-first century. The rights granted to citizens since 1789 in many European states following the French example were partially rescinded in 1814–15 on the Restoration of the European monarchies.[40] The genie was already out of the bottle, however: a full return to the old feudal system was inconceivable, and in 1848 revolutionary movements in large parts of Europe enshrined fundamental rights more firmly in the constitution.[41] Meanwhile, the emancipation of the Jews was a painful

---

[40] Kop (n. 34) ch. 3.
[41] Ibid. ch. 5.

slow process with repeated setbacks.[42] In their colonies various European states maintained the system of slavery until well into the nineteenth century – the Netherlands until 1863–, a system that deprived people of even the most elementary status of a free person having legal rights.

The essential openness of nationality remained restricted throughout the nineteenth century and at the beginning of the twentieth – and burdened in its moral pretensions – by the exclusion from suffrage of men whose wealth or education was considered inadequate and of women in general. This tension between the essential significance of citizenship and socially and economically motivated exclusion was noted early as 1844 by J.R. Thorbecke in an address to the Royal Institute of Sciences in Amsterdam "On Present-Day Citizenship". In the opinion of many, Thorbecke was the greatest Dutch statesman of the nineteenth century, occupying the post of Prime Minister several times between 1849 and his death in 1872. His lecture begins with a sentence that rings out like a clarion call: "We can characterize our century politically as the century of citizenship." Citizenship means "cooperation or suffrage by virtue of membership of the State".[43] At the time Thorbecke not only advocated direct elections – which were introduced four years later, in the revolutionary year of 1848 – but also called into question the linking of suffrage to requirements of material wealth: "The requirement of a certain amount of capital has become the principal means of *exclusion*, while it is not a fortune of a certain size but personal membership of a State in general that forms the basis of entitlement to citizenship."[44] As capital holdings "with their increasing confluence are strengthened by a daily growing dominion over nature", "the inequality grows ever greater".[45] The result – as described by Thorbecke in phraseology more reminiscent of nineteenth-century social movements than liberalism – is that citizenship once again signifies "a part of the people, a class", in breach of its very principle.[46]

The Dutch Constitution continued to restrict citizens' rights on the basis of class and sex until 1917, in other words for some considerable time

---

[42] Michael Goldfarb, *Emancipation. How Liberating Europe's Jews from the Ghetto Led to Revolution & Renaissance* (Simon & Schuster 2009); Ernst M.H. Hirsch Ballin, *A Mission for his Time. Tobias Asser's Inaugural Address on Commercial Law and Commerce, Amsterdam 1862* (Asser Press 2012) 1–14.

[43] J.R. Thorbecke, 'Over het hedendaagsche staatsburgerschap' [On Present-Day Nationality] in K.H. Boersema, *Johan Rudolf Thorbecke. Een historisch-critische studie* [Johan Rudolf Thorbecke, A Historical-Critical Study] (E.J. Brill 1949).

[44] Ibid. 478 ('exclusion' is italicized by the present author).

[45] Ibid. 479, 480.

[46] Ibid. 480.

after the rise of labor movements and other equal rights movements. In spite of the essential recognition of citizenship as a principle of political organization, it thus took many decades of political struggle to put an end to exclusion – the word used by Thorbecke back in the day – on socio-economic grounds. This battle was fought citing the equality of people as nationals, in contrast to feudal class distinctions, and it shows how close the link between human rights and citizens' rights originally was. At the same time, during the nineteenth century, with the invention and the growth of European nationalism[47] there was increasing emphasis on the 'national' element in citizenship, however. As a result the connection between human rights and citizens' rights during the nineteenth and twentieth century in Europe became looser, reflected in the separate development of human rights on the one hand – first as a line of defense against the authorities, later as entitlements to certain forms of government welfare – and the democratic system on the other, in which only nationals eligible to vote could in principle take part. The right to nationality became a separate area, in some cases in relation to migration law.

The erosion of the historical link between human rights and citizens' rights enabled citizenship to be used as a legal tool for demarcation and exclusion. This is connected with the rise, in the nineteenth century and the first half of the twentieth, of the idea of the nation-state and the nationalism associated with it, which ultimately became destructive.[48] Nowadays we need to realize how dangerous it is to regard 'identity' – national identity for instance – as a means of demarcation, a characteristic by which other people can be excluded and turned into enemies. This attacks the principle of citizenship and threatens the coexistence of people in peace and freedom.

Little by little the right to citizenship has thus become further removed from political human rights – the right to participate in the democratic system being linked more and more to immigration policy. States that did not want immigrants have used descent (*ius sanguinis*) as their criterion, whereas states that have welcomed immigration have awarded citizenship generously, in particular to immigrants' children born there (*ius soli*). In this respect the Netherlands has developed in the decades after the Second

[47] Cf. Philip Spencer and Howard Wollman, 'Blood and Sacrifice. Politics Versus Culture in the Construction of Nationalism' in Kevin J. Brehony and Naz Rassool (eds.), *Nationalisms Old and New* (Macmillan Press 1999) 88.
[48] Cf. E.J. Hobsbawm, *Nations and Nationalism since 1780. Programme, Myth, Reality* (CUP 1992).

World War towards greater acceptance of integrated aliens as Dutch citizens, but with twists and turns in its policy.

The demand for the protection of fundamental rights for all has come more and more to the fore, amidst a history of humanity with indelible tragedies carved into the collective memory: slavery and the slave trade continued until well into the nineteenth century by various European states; the industrialized mass murder of European Jewry; the genocides that have been a by-product of many civil wars, with the systematic rape of women as a recent manifestation of inhumanity.

What all these crimes have in common is the fact that they were committed citing a difference between people based on a single all-embracing characteristic that supposedly determines their identity and decides whether it is their destiny to gain the upper hand or to be cast out. Amartya Sen has written about this in *Identity and Violence*[49] – the one book that should suffice for any jurist to understand what his profession should and should not be used for, for what purposes he should and should not make himself available. It is important and necessary, however, to examine how the recognition of citizens' rights *can* contribute to dignified coexistence within a state, also beyond the borders of states. Where people are mobilized in eras of migration, bringing growing cultural political or religious diversity based on a specific distinguishing feature of "identity", this unavoidably tests the reciprocity needed for a community, i.e. the ability and willingness to see others, although different, as equals and thus dissociate solidarity from tribal reference points. Yet, generally speaking, socio-economic and politico-legal structures worldwide have developed – and need to develop – towards greater acceptance of diversity; however, these trends are non-synchronous and dissimilar.

Various constitutional means of accommodating diversity democratically have developed. We know from the Dutch experience that relatively closed groups distinguished by religious or ideological characteristics can coexist if their respective leaderships are able to reach peaceful arrangements guided by common interests.[50] Other countries such as Belgium have developed federal models with a similar aim. These presuppose a pre-existing geographical division of population groups; achieving this by force, as in Bosnia-Herzegovina, always goes hand in hand with unspeakable human suffering and violations of human rights.

---

[49] Amartya Sen, *Identity and Violence. The Illusion of Destiny* (W.W. Norton & Company 2006).

[50] Arend Lijphart, *Thinking about Democracy. Power Sharing and Majority Rule in Theory and Practice* (Routledge 2008).

Where – partly as a result of urbanization – the population groups are indistinguishable (or no longer clearly distinguishable), a type of citizenship based on individual recognition of human rights develops. From a Western European perspective this is the ideal type of democratic constitutional state, with freedom through peaceful deliberation as the ideal.[51] There is another model of organized solidarity, however, where a single-party regime tries to prevent ethnic and interest groups reacting against one another with a combination of economic development, strict oversight and welfare measures, in essence the Chinese political model.[52] Nowadays these differences are more important in constitutional theory than traditional scenarios such as the dichotomy between federal states and unitary states, monarchies and republics, and parliamentary and presidential democracies. On top of this, other types of organization emerge – e.g. by international organizations, and non-state forms of governance – which also require constitutional interpretation.[53]

Owing to socio-economic and technological developments, migration is playing a decisive role in these constitutional changes. It has developed from a collective process in which – as in the fourth to sixth centuries – entire peoples moved home, to a movement of groups such as families or extended families, and individuals. This change in migration patterns is again a process that is non-synchronous and dissimilar.

In the context of multiethnic cities the dominant people's forms of rule are no longer taken for granted. When city-dwellers have gained self-confidence and wish to take their destiny into their own hands, the freedom of citizens gains the upper hand – or conversely the rule of the dominant people is reinforced by the ultimately violent repression of minorities and anyone deemed to be inferior. Here the development of the law and society diverges into two separate paths. Where other people are recognized and respected as 'different', human rights take on political significance and they can be the driving force behind development to full participation.[54] It is not ethnicity but citizenship that is the deciding

---

[51] Oliver Gerstenberg, *Bürgerrechte und deliberative Demokratie. Elemente einer pluralistischen Verfassungstheorie* [Citizens' Rights and Deliberative Democracy. Elements of a Pluralist Constitutional Theory] (Suhrkamp 1997).

[52] Cf. Henry Kissinger, *On China* (Penguin Press 2011). Martin Jacques views this as a different modernity: *When China Rules the World. The End of the Western World and the Birth of a New Global Order* (Penguin Press 2009) ch. 12.

[53] Daniel Halberstam, 'Local, global and plural constitutionalism. Europe meets the world' in Gráinne de Búrca and J.H.H. Weiler (eds.), *The Worlds of European Constitutionalism* (CUP 2012) 150–202.

[54] For social difference as a resource for the development of inclusive democracy cf. Iris Marion Young, *Inclusion and Democracy* (OUP 2000) 115–20.

factor when it comes to having a voice in the state. Where one single identity is associated with claims of supremacy, however, we embark upon a
path that has led to inhuman violence on many occasions and still does
so today.

People's settlement patterns and the development of citizenship and
citizens' rights are inextricably linked, then. The amount and intensity of
migration differs, depending on the physical infrastructure to meet people's needs and means of transport. The pattern that developed two thou-
sand years ago in the Mediterranean basin, from the second century before
Christ to the modern era along the Silk Route,[55] and in the Hansa area in
the Middle Ages, has now become a complex, world-encircling process.

Everywhere where citizenship prevails over distinguishing characteristics such as religion, culture and ethnicity, people engage with one another
based not on their origins but on their share in a common future. The
status of citizen (πολίτης) of a city (πόλις), which in our Western culture
we are familiar with as a product of the Hellenic city states, provides an
anthropological model for man as a πολιτικόν ζωιον and legally stands for a
person whose dignity should be respected. Citizenship, however, albeit
stripped of ties to origin, is not a universal category, as it relates to the polity, i.e. historically the city state, which has developed into the national
state and in our era into supranational polities as the European Union.

Migration, urbanization and the development of political structures
thus provide the background to the analysis of transformations in *citizenship* in the ensuing chapters, with which I try to answer the question of
how this category, related to specific polities, relates to the universal recognition of *human rights*. Legal thinking has increasingly focused on individual rights and freedoms rather than *auctoritas* and subjection. This
trend can be only explained by the relationship of people to the means
by which they meet their needs, increasingly led by *ratio* and *voluntas*.[56]
At this juncture, however, we are seeing political forces in many places
whose aim is to cut that solidarity back to a closed community that marks
itself off against other communities. Restricting citizens' rights to one's
own group – however it may be defined – ineluctably impacts the
equal recognition of human rights. This book is therefore concerned not
only with understanding the law but also with issues that actually affect
people's lives.

---

[55] Christopher I. Beckwith, *Empires of the Silk Road. A History of Central Eurasia from
the Bronze Age to the Present* (Princeton UP 2009).
[56] Lesaffer (n. 23).

CHAPTER TWO

CITIZENSHIP AND MIGRATION

2.1 *Citizenship and Identity*

In the previous chapter I defined citizenship as a legal category related to a polity such as the πόλις of yesteryear and the modern state. The fact that people participate in the community organized by that particular polity is the social basis for citizenship. Social science treatises often discuss citizenship in this sense. 'Integration' used to be regarded mainly as a natural process, but in the Netherlands, since the Integration Act came into force on 1 January 2007,[57] it has been organized as a cognitive process, in courses leading to examinations. Passing the examination is a requirement for the granting of a residence permit in the case of aliens who are not EU citizens or subjects of European Economic Area countries, Switzerland or Turkey[58] and also for naturalization.[59] The last section of Chapter 1 mentioned the rise of nationalism in the nineteenth century, which demanded a state 'of their own' for the 'own' people. To some extent this was a way of wresting independence from repressive 'foreign' rulers, but nationalism also concealed a denial of the universalism of the French Revolution. In the first quarter of the nineteenth century Ludwig van Beethoven composed *Alle Menschen werden Brüder*; in the last quarter ethnomusicologists such as Béla Bartók and Zoltán Kodály carefully transcribed Hungarian and other Eastern European folk music. This trend started during the nineteenth century, eventually resulting in destructive nationalism in the first half of the twentieth.[60] The exercise of citizens' rights (and the fulfillment of the associated obligations) came to be seen in a monocultural perspective.

---

[57] Wet inburgering (*Stb* [Bulletin of Acts and Decrees] 2006, 625).

[58] National legislation has to comply with European law concerning so-called third-country nationals. See Catherine Barnard, *The Substantive Law of the EU. The Four Freedoms* (OUP 2010) ch. 14. With respect to the rights of Turkish citizens, the importance and scope of the EEC-Turkey Association Agreement of 1963 have often – sometimes deliberately for domestic political reasons – been overlooked.

[59] The term "naturalization" originates from a procedure in 16th-18th century France. The King issued a "lettre de naturalité", thus granting French nationality to a stranger who was not a Frenchman by nature, i.e. not born in France. See 'Guide de Généalogie. Naturalisations' [Guide on Genealogy. Naturalizations] <www.guide-genealogie.com/guide/naturalisations.html> accessed 20 July 2013.

[60] Cf. Hobsbawm (n. 48).

This trend has turned the meaning of legal citizenship on its head. Instead of legally *recognizing* actual participation (being integrated) it became a legal tool for *delimiting* who is and is not entitled to participate fully in political and social life. 'Nationality' – often defined in terms of elusive criteria such as descent and culture – became a way of defining people's 'identity', thus taking on heavier associations than just citizenship of the state. Amartya Sen has described how risky it is to deny the multiplicity of everyone's identity – the author of this book, for example, is a man, an 'Amsterdammer', a Catholic, a music lover, a 'Tilburger', a European, an academic lawyer, a humanist, a Dutchman – in order to classify people on the basis of a single criterion deemed to be superior.[61] 'Identities' do not necessarily have to be in tension with one another. The oft-cited contention of a "Clash of Civilizations" – the title of a book by Samuel Huntington, about which later more – is untenable according to Sen, for one thing because of the absence of a workable definition of what makes a 'civilization' a more or less homogeneous opposing force.[62] It is true that chauvinist affirmation of a distinguishing 'identity' is by no means always a bad thing. There are international football matches that pass off without riots, for example, and in the Eurovision Song Festival nothing much worse happens than the commercial exploitation of national pride, insofar as there is any justification for it. Where political or religious leaders use their group's 'own' identity to consolidate or extend their power base, however, the seed is sown for violence and oppression. Once that violence starts it takes on a dynamic of its own, whipping up nationalist sentiment that barely existed originally into emotions that lead to even more violence.[63]

The starting point for identity politics is always marking off your own group from people who were previously regarded primarily as fellow citizens. Carl Schmitt even accepted – and justified – the use of ethnicity as a distinguishing criterion for *enmity*, which he took to be a characteristic of politics.[64] The statutory regimes of nationality and suffrage are – and are

---

[61] Sen, *Identity and Violence* (n. 49).

[62] Ibid. 40–43. See also Dieter Senghaas, 'Die Wirklichkeiten der Kulturkämpfe' [The Realities of Cultural Conflict] in Hans Joas and Klaus Wiegandt (eds.), *Die kulturellen Werte Europas* [The Cultural Values of Europe] (Fischer 2005).

[63] Michael S. Neiberg, *Dance of the Furies. Europe and the Outbreak of World War I* (The Belknap Press of Harvard UP 2011).

[64] Carl Schmitt, *Der Begriff des Politischen. Text von 1932 mit einem Vorwort und drie Corollarien* [The Concept of the Political. 1932 text with a preface and three corollaries] (8th edn, Duncker & Humblot 2009) 35.

often made into – a tool for restricting the full enjoyment of citizens' rights to those who possess the privileged national identity. Examples of this are not confined to the Nuremberg Race Laws[65] or the imposing of 'homeland' nationality on black South Africans. Far more recently the European Court of Human Rights was called upon to give a ruling on laws that deprived the petitioners of the right to stand for election for reasons of ethnic identity. On 22 December 2009 the Court ruled that the European Convention for the Protection of Human Rights and Fundamental Freedoms (ECHR) had been contravened in that two citizens of Bosnia-Herzegovina who were leading figures in public life had been denied the right to stand for election to one of the houses of parliament or the presidency. This was based on the fact that the petitioners were not members of one of the 'constituent peoples' of Bosnia-Herzegovina reconciled in the Dayton Agreement but of the Roma and Jewish population respectively. The absence of an equal right to stand for election constituted a violation of the ECHR provisions on non-discrimination.[66] On 27 April 2010 the Court ruled in the case of Tănase and Chirtoacă v. Moldova,[67] a country where a large number of nationals also have Romanian (as in the case of the petitioners) or Russian nationality. In 2008 persons with multiple nationality ('bipatrides') were banned from sitting in parliament. This was a departure from the customary attitude in Europe to dual nationals and it was also not adequately justified. One of the points that the Court took into consideration was that "very few member States of the Council of Europe prohibit dual nationals becoming MPs (...). Of the three countries other than Moldova in which a clear prohibition exists, two do not allow their nationals to hold dual nationality."[68] Both these rulings show that the voice of the majority in a democracy does not entitle it to deprive the minority of a voice. Equality between nationals is one of the essential

---

[65] See 1933 Professional Civil Service Restoration Act (*Gesetz zur Wiederherstellung des Berufsbeamtentums*), proclaimed on 7 April 1933, only ten weeks after Hitler came to power, laid down. "Beamte, die nicht arischer Abstammung sind, sind in den Ruhestand zu versetzen (...)." [Civil servants not of Arian extraction shall be retired (...).]

[66] *Sejdic and Finci v Bosnia and Herzegovina* App no 27996/06 and 34836/06 (ECtHR, 22 December 2009). The Court ruled that there had been a contravention of Article 14 in conjunction with Article 3 of Protocol no 1 as regards the parliamentary election and Article 1 of Protocol no 12 as regards the presidential election.

[67] *Tănase and Chirtoacă v Moldova* App no 7/08 (ECtHR Grand Chamber, 18 November 2008). Here too the Court concluded that there had been a contravention of the ban on discrimination in Article 14 (1) of the ECHR.

[68] Ibid. para. 171.

features of a democracy,[69] and specific criteria to decide whether people comply with identity requirements are a violation of human rights.

The development of international relations in Europe since the Second World War has made wars and civil wars caused by nationalism the exception in this part of the world. Minorities such as the German-speaking Tyroleans in Italy have been accommodated – following a fairly brief period of politically motivated violence – with the recognition of full bilingual status in the autonomous region of Trentino-Alto Adige/ Südtirol.[70] The heated debate on the relationship between the Dutch-speaking and French-speaking Belgians, which has dragged on for decades, is being conducted with peaceful political means. Although the nationality of those who belong to these national minorities or language groups is undisputed, the political struggle is also about the range of their rights, in particular the opportunities to use their own languages and teach in them, either under national guarantees or in institutional structures set up for this purpose. The OSCE, the Council of Europe and the EU have passed standards for the protection of national minorities and their languages and cultures.[71] A host of constitutions also include specific provisions on the subject.

The specter of violent nationalism[72] raised its head with great vehemence, however, after the break-up of the Federal Republic of Yugoslavia. The Yugoslavian civil wars saw an estimated 140,000 deaths, and the trials of crimes against humanity committed there are still ongoing. As a result of these and other civil wars and violent conflicts between ethnic groups in places such as Sri Lanka, Somalia and Iraq, from 1990 relatively large numbers of people started coming to Western Europe.[73] They joined the labor migration from Mediterranean countries, in particular Morocco and Turkey, that had already been under way for several decades,

---

[69] Andrew Fagan, *Human Rights. Confronting Myths and Misunderstanding* (Edward Elgar 2009) 106.

[70] Ernst M.H. Hirsch Ballin, 'The Italian Republic' in Lucas Prakke and Constantijn Kortmann (eds.), *Constitutional Law of 15 EU Member States* (Kluwer 2004) 501–502.

[71] See the European Charter for Regional or Minority Languages [1992] CETS 148; Framework Convention for the Protection of National Minorities [1995] CETS 157; EU Council Directive 2000/43/EC of 29 June 2000 implementing the principle of equal treatment between persons irrespective of racial or ethnic origin [2000] OJ L180/22.

[72] Robert D. Kaplan, *Balkan Ghosts. A Journey Through History* (first published 1993, Picador at St. Martin's Press 2005).

[73] Cf. for the Netherlands R.P.W. Jennissen (ed.), *De Nederlandse migratiekaart. Achtergronden en ontwikkelingen van verschillende internationale migratietypen* [The Dutch migration monitor. Backgrounds and developments of different types of international migration] (Boom juridische uitgevers/CBS/WODC 2011).

and post-colonial migration, mainly from former colonies in the Caribbean and Africa, to the United Kingdom, Belgium, France and the Netherlands. All these movements have been followed by the 'chain migration' of family members and spouses.[74] This resulted in the formation in various European countries of population groups also referred to as 'minorities', who often used the language that was theirs since childhood, especially in informal intercourse. Unlike those of the established minorities, however, their languages and cultures have not enjoyed special international or constitutional protection; as immigrants they have been expected to assimilate gradually with the majority culture. Their legal status is formed in terms of residence permits and – after a certain number of years and completion of the integration process – obtaining the nationality of the country of permanent residence.

This ongoing migration to Western Europe – developments in North America are comparable in many respects – was and is due to various causes, but it is in line with the global historical tendency mentioned in Chapter 1 towards urbanization, the movement of individuals and groups to the cities, and increasing diversity there. The degree to which the emergencies that result in migration – in particular war, genocidal violence, environmental disasters and lack of economic prospects – can be distinguished is more significant legally than in people's actual experience. Only those proved to have been personally victimized within the meaning of the Geneva Convention on Refugees or who, if deported, would be exposed to inhuman or degrading treatment within the meaning of Article 3 of the ECHR or would face a real risk of suffering serious harm[75] in the sense of the EU Qualification Directive[76] enjoy absolute protection against being returned, but they too in effect form part of the broader mixed migration flows to countries and cities that offer greater safety and better chances of tolerable living conditions. While the fact that people

---

[74] Ian Goldin, Geoffrey Cameron and Meera Balarajan, *Exceptional People. How Migration Shaped Our World and Will Define Our Future* (Princeton UP 2011) 141: "Family migration is the largest single category for permanent entry into developed countries, and it is dominated by women".

[75] I.e. death penalty or execution; torture or inhuman or degrading treatment or punishment of an applicant in the country of origin; serious and individual threat to a civilian's life or person by reason of indiscriminate violence in situations of international or internal armed conflict.

[76] Council Directive 2004/83/EC of 29 April 2004 on minimum standards for the qualification and status of third country nationals or stateless persons as refugees or as persons who otherwise need international protection and the content of the protection granted [2004] OJ L304/12.

have moved to the cities (not only in Europe and North America but also in Africa, Asia and Latin America) is in line with the expectations regarding globalization since the 1990s, it has nevertheless added to the discontents of globalization.

Against this background the cultural dimension has played an ever greater role in the politics of the developed countries to which relatively large numbers of migrants have come. Although many people understand perfectly at a personal level why immigrants resist forced return, incomprehension of rapid social change and the tensions caused by some extremist or criminal elements have long elicited concerned and negative reactions, most of all among those who feel they are the losers due to the societal changes around them. While immigrants are not to blame for this, they give a face to negative experiences, and malicious political leaders are thus able to make immigrants the scapegoat. In the political discourse this means that differences are heightened along a 'cultural' axis.[77] This is implemented legally in the form of a group-based categorization of immigrants even if they are socially and economically integrated. The term used particularly in the Netherlands is 'allochtoon' (non-indigenous), which is defined primarily for statistical purposes but is used in government policy and the political arena as a means of demarcation between 'population groups'.[78]

The division of the population into 'indigenous', 'Western non-indigenous' and 'non-Western non-indigenous' is based on the idea that these reflect cultural differences that are relevant to policy, but in effect it is a classification by origin and ethnicity. The Dutch Equal Treatment Commission has ruled on several occasions that discrimination on the basis of origin should be regarded as 'racial discrimination' within the meaning of the Equal Treatment Act (*Algemene wet gelijke behandeling*). Classification as non-indigenous has in recent years taken on lamentable negative connotations in the Dutch political discourse. This detracts from

---

[77] Hanspeter Kriesi, Edgar Grande, Romain Lachat, Martin Dolezal, Simon Bronchia and Timotheos Frey, *West European Politics in the Age of Globalization* (CUP 2008).

[78] See Raad voor Maatschappelijke Ontwikkeling [Council for Social Development], *Tussen afkomst en toekomst, Etnische Categorisering door de overheid* [Between Origins and Future. Ethnic Categorization by the Government] (Raad voor Maatschappelijke Ontwikkeling 2012). This advisory body for the Government of the Netherlands recommended in May 2012 to get rid of this categorization of the population because of its stigmatizing effects. This view had also been taken by the then Minister of Justice in February 2008 and was followed by the city of Amsterdam five years later.

the focus of Dutch citizenship on the future, as Lammert de Jong points out clearly and sharply in his book *Being Dutch, More or Less*.[79]

Thus political differences along the cultural axis have given a fresh boost – fifty years after European politics renounced nationalism – to the inclination to attribute identity features to citizenship. The concept of a 'multicultural society' would seem to provide a counterbalance.[80] It makes sense to interpret this as a society that is actually characterized by cultural diversity. The multiculturalism of societies such as those of the Netherlands, Britain, Germany, Belgium and France is a fact, but this observation gives no indication of the extent to which this has positive or negative consequences. Multiculturalism can be defined as the pursuit or appreciation of the peaceful coexistence of people with different cultural orientations. Charles Taylor provided a political philosophy foundation for multiculturalism against the background of Canadian experience in 1992. His treatise is also important in the case of other countries, now that – as Taylor notes – "more and more societies today are turning out to be multicultural, in the sense of including more than one cultural community that wants to survive."[81] Such societies "are becoming increasingly multicultural, while at the same time becoming more porous", i.e. "they are more open to multinational migration; more of their members live the life of diaspora, whose center is elsewhere."[82]

Taylor contrasts "the politics of dignity", which focuses on everyone's personal autonomy, with the appreciation of cultural and religious individuality in the "politics of difference", which however involves the risk of freedoms being lost.[83] The shared base[84] is "the politics of equal respect", which in conjunction with "equal citizenship" can meet the "demands of multiculturalism"[85] as defined by him. There is room here for difference, but not at any price. The "demands" involve the presumption that any culture that has proved its sustainability historically can have a

---

[79] Lammert de Jong, *Being Dutch, More or Less. In a Comparative Perspective of USA and Caribbean Practices* (2nd edn, Rozenberg Publishers 2011).

[80] For the significance for the law, see W. van der Burg, C.J.M. Schuyt and J.H. Nieuwenhuis, *Multiculturaliteit en Recht* [Multiculturalism and Law] (Kluwer 2008) Handelingen Nederlandse Juristen-Vereniging 138-1.

[81] Charles Taylor, 'The Politics of Recognition' in Amy Gutmann (ed.), *Multiculturalism. Examining the Politics of Recognition* (Princeton UP 1994) 61.

[82] Ibid. 63.

[83] Ibid. 37–41.

[84] Ibid. 43.

[85] Ibid. 68.

place in a free, multicultural society – subject to the proviso of "a comparative cultural study".[86] What this proviso could lead to Taylor does not say, though he does warn against ethnocentrism. The prospect he outlines – albeit a distant one – is a gradual fusing of cultural horizons.[87] The constitution will, in the end, be their common horizon.

Multiculturalism based on mutual respect and – better still – mutual interest would provide scope for gradual integration. The acquisition of citizens' rights in the Netherlands was organized accordingly in the last quarter of the twentieth century. After five years of legal residence, an alien is eligible for a permanent residence permit and may also apply for Dutch citizenship. The development of a multicultural society was not regarded as problematic during this period, rather the contrary was true. After all, the Netherlands had always been a country of minorities who were able to coexist in a tolerant intellectual climate thanks to the 'pillarized' structure of society and the political system. The 'new minorities' – by which was meant Muslims and Hindus in particular – were also fitted into this system of religious and ideological pluralism. Organizations that identified themselves on the basis of their culture of origin were given tied grant aid as representatives of particular sections of the population.

This embedding in a pattern of mutual demarcation based on the pillarization model restricted the dynamics of the Dutch 'multicultural society'. The depth of intercultural study required by Taylor as part of multiculturalism was confined to isolated, sometimes elitist meeting points, thus placing multiculturalism in a radically different perspective: instead of providing a feeding ground for interaction and gradual fusion it became a justification for demarcation. The circles inhabited by immigrants in effectively separate neighborhoods maintained language handicaps in particular for too long, while at the same time the mandatory frameworks laid down by Dutch socio-economic legislation presented a barrier to small-scale entrepreneurship.[88] Isolation moreover helped to preserve customs taken from the rural areas of origin, to the detriment of the urban integration that is characteristic of immigration.[89]

---

[86] Ibid. 73.

[87] Ibid. 67, 73.

[88] Doug Saunders, *Arrival City. How the Largest Migration in History is Reshaping our World* (William Heinemann 2010) 289–292.

[89] Cf. Saunders about Kreuzberg (n. 88) 243 and about Slotervaart (n. 88) 290.

Uncritical accommodation of groups permitted to retain their own value systems and "differentiated group rights" – to quote Ayelet Shachar as early as in 2000 – takes place at the expense of individuals in minority cultures, for example women. "Multicultural accommodation presents a problem (...) when pro-identity group policies aimed at leveling the playing-field between minority cultures and the larger society systematically allow the maltreatment of individuals *within* the religious or cultural group – an impact which is in certain cases so severe that it nullifies these individuals' status as citizens."[90] The same year saw the publication in the Netherlands of a much discussed opinion piece by Paul Scheffer on "The Multicultural Tragedy", in which he criticizes the "lazy multiculturalism" that "fails to put into words what keeps our society together".[91] Here Scheffer is referring to policies that – uncritically following the pillarization model – ignore language handicaps, illiberal attitudes within Islam and the significance of Dutch history. In spite of the nuances in Scheffer's argument, it has been seized upon above all to use the supposed superiority of the 'own' Dutch culture as a basis for policy. Kochenov makes a critical assessment of the culture and language testing of immigrants in EU Member States like the Netherlands and the underlying premises of 'repressive liberalism'.[92] An extensive research project about citizenship tests in three EU countries, conducted by Ricky van Oers, confirmed Kochenov's critical approach. None of these countries has succeeded in developing a test that "can be justified under liberal, republican or communitarian models" of citizenship.[93]

The underlying problem with these and other policies of cultural 'integration' may be that they view immigrants as the object of 'integrating' activities, whereas real 'integration' can only be a mutual process.

---

[90] Ayelet Shachar, 'Should Church and State be Joined at the Altar? Women's Rights and the Multicultural Dilemma' in Will Kymlicka and Wayne Norman (eds.), *Citizenship in Diverse Societies* (OUP 2000) 199. In that article she develops a "joint-governance model" of family law with the aim of dynamically linking various family law traditions with women's rights.

[91] Paul Scheffer, 'Het multiculturele drama' [The Multicultural Tragedy] *NRC Handelsblad* (Rotterdam, 29 January 2000) <http://retro.nrc.nl/W2/Lab/Multicultureel/scheffer.html> accessed 10 January 2011.

[92] Dimitry Kochenov, 'Mevrouw De Jong gaat eten. EU Citizenship and the culture of Prejudice' (2011) European University Institute Working Papers RSCAS 2011/06 <http://ssrn.com/abstract=1765983> accessed 30 July 2013.

[93] Ricky van Oers, *Deserving Citizenship. Citizenship Tests in Germany, the Netherlands and the United Kingdom* (Wolf Legal Publishers 2013) 249.

Instead of subjugating immigrants to assimilation, integration should be understood as a process aimed at reciprocity, social cohesion and shared citizenship.[94] Obviously, such a process requires efforts from both sides: as far as immigrants are concerned, the willingness to learn the language and to understand the symbolic interactions in the country that they join, and as far as the country of arrival is concerned, the appreciation that no living society can be mummified. In his recent book, Paul Scheffer – who continues to be sharply aware of the problems involved in protracted immigration – rightly emphasizes that freedom and responsibility should frame the relationship in a "land of arrival": "A new 'us' is required. Urban residents old and new do not yet seem to have recognized this clearly enough, or at any rate do not behave as if they have. We need to be more aware of our mutual dependence."[95]

Instead of norm-free multiculturalism on the one hand and a desire to assimilate immigrants on the other, however, there is another option: to link the multicultural reality of immigrant nations with citizenship. For multiculturalism to have a positive effect on society as a whole, more is needed than just living side by side: it must take the form of what Guido van Heeswijck calls "active pluralism".[96] This means that multiculturalism cannot be separated from a normative constitutional setting in which fundamental rights are guaranteed to every citizen. This was acknowledged in essence by Will Kymlicka in 1995, when he linked multiculturalism and active participation in the concept of "multicultural citizenship".[97] Common citizenship is "not just a legal status, defined by a set of rights and responsibilities, but also an identity, an expression of one's membership in a political community."[98] As examples, Kymlicka refers to the "qualities and attitudes" of citizens in a modern democracy, "their sense of identity, and how they view potentially competing forms of national, regional, ethnic, or religious identities; their ability to tolerate and work together with others who are different from themselves; their desire to

---

[94] Cf. Ernst M.H. Hirsch Ballin, 'Voorwoord' [Foreword] in Laura Coello, Jaco Dagevos, Chris Huinder, Joanne van der Leun and Arend Odé (eds.), *Het minderhedenbeleid voorbij. Motieven en gevolgen* [Beyond the Minoritypolicies. Motives and Consequences] (Amsterdam UP 2013) 7–9.

[95] Paul Scheffer, *Immigrant Nations* (Polity Press 2011) 297.

[96] Guido van Heeswijck, *Tolerantie en actief pluralisme. De afgewezen erfenis van Erasmus, More en Gillis* [Tolerance and Active Pluralism. The Rejected Heritage of Erasmus, More and Gillis] (Pelckmans 2008).

[97] Will Kymlicka, *Multicultural Citizenship. A Liberal Theory of Minority Rights* (Clarendon Press 1995).

[98] Ibid. 192.

participate in the political process in order to promote the public good and hold political authorities accountable; their willingness to show self-restraint and exercise personal responsibility in their economic demands, and in personal choices which affect their health and the environment; and their sense of justice and commitment to a fair distribution of resources."[99] These aspects of citizenship in a multicultural society reflect the constitutional identity of a democratic constitutional state: each one of them can be related to specific fundamental rights. A characteristic of citizenship in a multicultural society, then, is that it is *not* equated with a particular culture but *is* based on shared values. Citizenship in a multicultural society requires more than just a knowledge of language and procedures. No-one needs to sacrifice their own cultural or religious identity to it, but it is necessary to respect the equality of others. Achieving citizenship is thus part of an ongoing process of integration but not assimilation.

The importance of these theses on multicultural citizenship is paradoxically illustrated by the criticism that has been elicited by Kymlicka's plea – originated from the Canadian context – for group representation.[100] In his criticism of this part of Kymlicka's theory, Jean-Christophe Merle claims that taking special status for these minorities too far not only affects fundamental rights at a personal level,[101] it also presents an obstacle to the dynamic inherent in cultures – to which indigenous cultures are no exception.[102] In a recent report, Kymlicka emphasizes on his account: "No Western democracy has exempted immigrant groups from constitutional norms of human rights in order to maintain practices such as forced marriage, criminalization of apostasy, or clitoridectomy."[103] Multiculturalism is therefore only then a positive force in the social dynamic if it is linked with citizenship based on mutual recognition. Here Trincia makes a connection with the Christian natural justice and existentialist theory of *'Bedürfnis nach den anderen'* (the need for others), from which "follows that – as Kymlicka rightly emphasizes – multiculturalism is

---

[99] Ibid. 175.

[100] Ibid. 144–9.

[101] Jean-Christophe Merle, 'Kulturelle Minderheitenrechte im liberalen Staat' [Cultural Minority Rights in the Liberal State] in Matthias Kaufmann (ed.), *Integration oder Toleranz? Minderheiten als philosophisches Problem* [Integration or Tolerance? Minorities as a Philosophical Problem] (Verlag Karl Alber 2001) 178.

[102] Ibid. 176.

[103] Will Kymlicka, *Multiculturalism. Success, Failure, and the Future* (Migration Policy Institute 2012) 9.

not an alternative to citizenship but its completion."[104] In an article about the (perceived) rise and fall of multiculturalism, Kymlicka points out that "we need to accept that the path to immigrant multiculturalism in many countries will not be smooth or linear. Moreover, we need to focus on how to manage the risks involved", while upholding the goal of "citizenization" in the context of human rights guarantees.[105]

Acceptance and appreciation of cultural diversity, then, are committed to active, open citizenship. A legal relationship with the state is not confined to those in possession of a particular 'indigenous' identity or who have assimilated to it, and citizenship of this kind is therefore compatible with a society characterized by immigration and urbanization. In contrast to what critics of multiculturalism suggest, normative identification with the state – the political-ethical valuation that determines the significance and substance of constitutional law[106] – is not affected by this; on the contrary, it is what makes it possible. Even more than Kymlicka, Merle is aware of the dynamic inherent in this: "Acts, values, principles and concepts of what is good for individuals and the protection and freedom that liberalism has decisively advocated are in turn what influences cultural development – and that of the cultural horizon."[107] Citizens' rights and human rights are themselves included in this cultural development and thus operate in a context defined by time and place.

This cultural development is at the same time a development of personal freedom and of the progressive realization of human rights. The political discourse on multicultural society in the Netherlands and

---

[104] Francesco Saverio Trincia, 'Individuelles "Bedürfnis nach den Anderen", Universalität des Rechts und open citizenship' [The Individual 'Need for Other People', Universality of the Law and Open Citizenship] in Matthias Kaufmann (ed.), *Integration oder Toleranz? Minderheiten als philosophisches Problem* [Integration or Tolerance? Minorities as a Philosophical Problem] (Verlag Karl Alber 2001) 82. German original text: "ergibt sich die Tatsache, daß – wie Kymlicka richtig beobachtet – der Multikulturalismus keine Alternative zur Staatsbürgerschaft ist, sondern ihre Vervollständigung."

[105] Will Kymlicka, 'The rise and fall of multiculturalism? New debates on inclusion and accommodation in diverse societies' in Steven Vertovec and Susanne Wessendorf (eds.), *The Multiculturalism Backlash. European discourses, policies and practices* (Routledge 2010) 47.

[106] The significance of this for the interpretation of constitutional norms has been noted by Johannes van der Hoeven in *De plaats van de grondwet in het constitutionele recht* [The Place of the Constitution in Constitutional Law] (first published 1958, 2nd edn with supplement, W.E.J. Tjeenk Willink 1988).

[107] Original text in German: "Handlungen, Werte, Grundsätze und Konzeptionen des Guten der Individuen, für deren Schutz und Freiheit sich der Liberalismus wesentlich stark gemacht hat, sind wiederum das, was die kulturelle Entwicklung – auch die des kulturellen Horizonts – mitbestimmt." See Merle (n. 101) 176.

Germany, for example, is severely clouded by the abandonment of the relationship with human rights, apart from religious freedom as a questionable argument for not encroaching upon certain religiously motivated cultural practices, e.g. regarding the personal freedoms of women. A one-sided appeal to religious freedom, not linked to other aspects of citizenship related to human rights, is counterproductive. Although freedom of religion requires religious expressions and practices to be respected and no-one to be discriminated against on the basis of his or her religion, the protection of that freedom must not result in the formation of cultural reservations. Referring to a report by the United Nations Human Rights Committee, McGoldrick points out that "the right of members of minority groups to enjoy their own culture under Article 27 [ICCPR] cannot be used as a justification for violating the rights of others."[108]

Religious freedom is designed to protect not rules but people; not the religiously motivated authority of one person over another – let alone dependence – but the personal freedom of believers. In a more considered discussion of multiculturalism, freedom of religion, like other fundamental rights, should be related to the "qualities and attitudes" of citizenship in a modern democracy as described by Kymlicka. The interconnectedness of our lives and how that transcends the boundaries of culture, language, and state determines the significance of legal relations in the twenty-first century. This requires us to consider how generalized assessments affect the personal situation of an individual.[109] Against the background of a human rights ethos, citizenship is a personal entitlement to the progressive realization of fundamental rights.

Migration contributes to social, economic and cultural changes that no-one has ever assumed to be without problems. Scheffer expressed on several occasions the view that such problems have been underestimated too often and for too long, and that this explains the rise of populist parties in various Western European democracies.[110] According to Scheffer many present-day cosmopolitans even "claim to be greatly interested in other cultures and regard the rejection or brushing aside of their own culture as

---

[108] Dominic McGoldrick, 'Multiculturalism and its Discontents' (2005) 5 *Human Rights Law Review* 27, 53.

[109] Ernst M.H. Hirsch Ballin, *Law, Justice, and the Individual* (Thomas More Lecture, Brill 2011).

[110] Scheffer (n. 95) 103. See also the empirical analysis in Ruud Koopmans, 'Trade-offs between equality and difference. Immigrant integration, multiculturalism and the welfare state in cross-national perspective' (2010) 36 *Journal of Ethnic and Migration Studies* 1.

a gesture that underlines that interest."[111] Clearly, denying one's 'own' cultural identity in this way – Scheffer does not provide any data on the extent of this denial – does not contribute to the intended interaction with multicultural citizenship. This is also true of the endeavors of some immigrants, for example, to impose a closed, orthodox Salafist community model on the new country of settlement, but research shows that only a minimal proportion of immigrants seek this.[112]

It makes more sense to focus attention on what Paul Scheffer – notwithstanding his xenosceptic perspective – advocates, namely shared citizenship, for which "reciprocity is key. Anyone wanting to challenge discrimination against migrants and their children must be prepared to oppose other forms of discrimination too – against unbelievers or homosexuals, for example. We can't demand equal treatment for some but not for all."[113] Similarly, Goodhart justifiably criticizes "separatist" variants of multiculturalism which in the 1980s "allowed parallel lives to grow up in some places and made it harder for ordinary Britons to think of some minorities, and especially Muslims, as part of the same imagined community with common experiences and interests."[114] Since however integration "must engage the attention, consent and sympathy of the majority",[115] multiculturalism can succeed only when it supports shared "strong citizenship".[116]

The reality of a multicultural society needs to commit – based on reciprocity – to *citizenship across cultural and religious dividing lines*. This insight also underpins the search for practical answers to tensions that manifest themselves in a multicultural society.

2.2 *Diversity, Reciprocity and Integration*

When migration is seen in the perspective of acquiring full citizenship, it involves rights and duties. The reciprocity that is desirable within a

---

[111] Scheffer (n. 95) 211.

[112] See *Kamerstukken* [Parliamentary Papers] *II* 2010/2011 29 754 no 194 and attached report of Ineke Roex, Sjef van Stiphout and Jean Tillie, 'Salafisme in Nederland. Aard, omvang en dreiging' [Salafism in the Netherlands. Nature, Scale and Threat] (Instituut voor Migratie- en Etnische Studies, Universiteit van Amsterdam 2010).

[113] Scheffer (n. 95) 314.

[114] David Goodhart, *The British Dream. Successes and Failures of Post-war Immigration* (Kindle edn, Atlantic Books 2013) 157.

[115] Ibid. 3870.

[116] Ibid. 3889.

broadened cultural horizon demands elementary skills such as a common language. The law amending the Act on Netherlands citizenship of 17 June 2010[117] has put an end to the possibility of acquiring Dutch nationality in the Caribbean countries of the Kingdom of the Netherlands without knowing the Dutch language. Integration requires genuine participation in social and economic life, and additional educational requirements are therefore a legitimate criterion in immigration policy, provided they are not applied in a discriminatory fashion.

Even this requirement – at first sight just a demand directed towards immigrants – should be situated in a reciprocal understanding of citizenship. State authorities should use language that the citizen can understand. The then German Minister of Justice, Brigitte Zypries, has raised the question whether "Juristendeutsch" (Lawyers' German) is just a tool or an instrument of control.[118] Her question is part of a wider investigation into the extent to which – in Gerd Antos' words – "comprehensibility" should be seen as a "citizens' right", in the sense of a requirement of good administration. The reason he and his co-authors raised this question is the ideal of "communication free from obstacles".[119] Raising this question is definitely not a far-fetched idea for a publication by one of Germany's leading reference books publishers. The Charter of Fundamental Rights includes the "Right to good administration" as Article 41 in the Title on "Citizens' rights". One of its elements is every person's right to "write to the institutions of the Union in one of the languages of the Treaties" and to "have an answer in the same language."

More far-reaching integration requirements, however, are two-faced: they are advocated as a way of achieving better-quality integration but at the same time they are designed to limit the amount (quantity) of immigration. A difficult question to answer is what the learning goals of integration courses should be. A good answer, based on the quest for citizenship guided by reciprocity, can only be given within the constitutional context of human rights. Immigrants can be expected to be willing – and are required – to accept both the individual freedoms and obligations of

---

[117] Rijkswet van 17 juni 2010, houdende wijziging van de Rijkswet op het Nederlanderschap met betrekking tot meervoudige nationaliteit en andere nationaliteitsrechtelijke kwesties (*Stb* 2010, 242) with respect to this amendment entered into force on 1 January 2011.

[118] Brigitte Zypries, 'Juristendeutsch. Handwerkszeug oder Herrschaftsmittel?' in Karin M. Eichhoff-Cyrus and Gerd Antos (eds.), *Verständlichkeit als Bürgerrecht? Die Rechts- und Verwaltungssprache in der öffentlichen Diskussion* (Dudenverlag 2008).

[119] Gerd Antos, '"Verständlichkeit" als Bürgerrecht? Positionen, Alternativen und das Modell der "barrierefreien Kommunikation"' in Eichhoff-Cyrus and Antos (n. 118) 9–20.

the democratic constitutional state, but integration is not cultural brainwashing.

In 2011, the Dutch government at that time presented to the House of Representatives an Integration Memorandum, which strongly emphasized integration in the sense of partial cultural assimilation.[120] The ideal of integration is here that the integrated immigrant fits in with "a fundamental continuity of values, attitudes, institutions and customs that form the leading culture in Dutch society and are a factor in its distinctiveness."[121] Such policies, sometimes designed to discourage immigration, take on the nature of an identity policy. This goes hand in hand with a rejection of the multicultural society, which is said to have failed (*'gescheitert'*, to use the German Federal Chancellor Angela Merkel's term in a political speech on 16 October 2010).[122] Citing the 'Judaeo-Christian tradition', other cultures are viewed in a more or less negative light (the "Clash of Civilizations"), forgetting just how the Judaeo-Christian tradition took shape in a setting where different languages and cultures came together. The Pentecost story is all about the Spirit of the new religious movement that was proclaimed in Jerusalem in many languages: "Look, aren't all these who are speaking Galileans? How is it that each of us can hear in our own native language? Parthians, Medes, Elamites; those who live in Mesopotamia, in Judea and Cappadocia, Pontus and Asia, Phrygia and Pamphylia, Egypt and the parts of Libya near Cyrene; visitors from Rome, both Jews and proselytes, Cretans and Arabs – we hear them speaking the magnificent acts of God

---

[120] 'Integratie, binding, burgerschap' [Integration, Loyalty, Citizenship], appendix to the letter from the Minister of the Interior and Kingdom Relations J.P.H. Donner of 16 June 2011 32824 no 1, 8.

[121] See also 7–8: "The keynotes of social life in the Netherlands have developed historically and provide points of recognition that many Dutch people share and that cannot be relinquished. This is true not only of the achievements and core values that lie at [the] base of the Dutch constitutional state but also of more historical or cultural points of recognition such as the Dutch language, historic buildings or architectural features, or unwritten manners and codes of conduct that have developed down the centuries and that come to the fore depending on the situation. Integration is about integration in Dutch society."

[122] Two days later, she explained (and mitigated) her statement in an authorized interview as follows: "Man muss vielleicht erklären, was Multikulti in Deutschland bedeutet. Das ist ein Modell, bei dem die Zuwanderer und die, die schon immer hier sind, nebeneinanderher leben. Für mich ist Integration etwas anderes als nur dieses Nebeneinanderherleben. Integration bedeutet, dass man die Gesetze des Landes achtet, dass man seine Sprache spricht, damit sich die Bildungschancen verbessern, und ich glaube, wir sind hier auf einem guten Weg." See "'Deutschland wünscht einen fairen Wettbewerb'. Interview mit Angela Merkel in France 2' (*Bundeskanzlerin.de* 18 October 2010) <www.bundeskanzlerin.de/Content/DE/Interview/2010/10/2010-10-18-merkel -france-2.html> accessed 4 May 2013.

in our own languages."[123] St. Paul's letters, likewise, tell of his encounters with people of various ethnicities in those towns and cities around the Mediterranean where Jews had settled among Greeks, Phoenicians and Romans.

The Pentecost story can only be placed in the urban context of Jerusalem as a multicultural city, where people learned to understand one another. The criticism of multiculturalism only has a basis insofar as it is in fact taken to mean the converse, a kind of plural monoculturalism.[124] It is for this reason that Amartya Sen warns against the British "state policy of actively promoting new 'faith schools', freshly devised for Muslim, Hindu, and Sikh children (in addition to preexisting Christian ones)".[125] Not only is this approach problematic educationally, says Sen, it also contributes to a fragmented idea of what it means to live in a country without segregation. His comments are also relevant to the Netherlands, where freedom to set up publicly funded schools on different religious and ideological foundations is enshrined in the Constitution and statute law. Since 1988 this freedom has been used to set up Muslim schools, mostly in primary education. Ostensibly this development merely parallels the many Catholic and Protestant schools, but whereas over the years these have become increasingly pluralist internally, certainly in urban areas, and have many pupils from other religious backgrounds (including children from Muslim families), the newly founded Muslim schools are highly homogeneous. The formation of cultural reservations can be the downside of the Dutch law that makes it possible for schools based on any religion or belief system to be accredited and funded. The vast majority of religiously or ideologically based schools have a very open cultural climate that respects those of different persuasions. If such schools are of an intolerant and closed nature, however, they are an obstacle to participation and integration. Overstretching the freedom of establishment, enshrined in Article 23 of the Dutch Constitution, tends to be harmful rather than conducive to achieving an integrated multicultural society.

---

[123] *Holman Christian Standard Bible* (digital text edn, Holman Bible Publishers 2010) Acts. 2:7–11.

[124] I.e. something very different from sensible multiculturalism, as Sen (*Identity and Violence* (n. 49) 162) points out: "The priorities of multiculturalism can differ a great deal from those of a plural monocultural society."

[125] Sen (n. 49) 160. A diametrically opposed solution has been adopted by an association set up by Dutch residents of Turkish origin, which advocates high-quality education at neutral ('privately-run general') schools for children from various backgrounds as a means of integration and ambitious world citizenship, see <www.cosmicus.nl/onder wijs/basisschool-cosmicus> accessed 28 May 2012.

The legal recognition of citizenship at the end of the eighteenth century, as described in the first chapter, is the achievement of the cultural and political development of the European towns and cities, character-ized by increasing cultural, social and economic diversity. What is still undecided today, however, is the intrinsic link between citizenship and the equal respect for everyone's personal dignity that underlies human rights. Recognition of citizenship, after all, does not remove the tension arising from a tendency – explained by some in terms of tribal instincts and by others in terms of social psychology – to stand up for the group that you identify in one way or another as your 'own'. This is in fact to designate an identity that sets someone apart from other groups or peoples as a condition of citizenship. We have seen how the Romanticism of nineteenth-century nationalism was reflected in the national condi-tioning of citizenship (nationality). For a long time this was linked implic-itly or explicitly to racial characteristics, but these have been so badly discredited by the Holocaust and other genocides that they only play a role surreptitiously. This was taken into account in the broad definition used in the International Convention on the elimination of all forms of racial discrimination of 21 December 1965. Article 1, para. 1 lays down that "the term 'racial discrimination' shall mean any distinction, exclusion, restriction or preference based on race, color, descent, or national or ethnic origin which has the purpose or effect of nullifying or impairing the recognition, enjoyment or exercise, on an equal footing, of human rights and fundamental freedoms in the political, economic, social, cultural or any other field of public life." When acting against discrimination the Dutch Equal Treatment Commission (now the Netherlands Institute for Human Rights) follows the interpretation that 'race' includes a person's "skin color, origin or national or ethnic extraction".[126]

The worldwide migration that is taking place to the towns and cities is the litmus test for citizenship as a legal form of integration. Where migrants are left outside the reciprocity of urban life, as a result of a defensive attitude on the part of the receiving community (as with the European Jews since the Middle Ages) and/or self-imposed segregation, there is room for groupthink and associated claims of superiority – a phe-nomenon that can occur in disappointed and scared majorities as well as radicalized minorities. It was pointed out back in the 1990s that a

---

[126] See CGB [Equal Treatment Commission] 15 March 2012, 2012-50/2011-0719, concerning the admission policy of the 'De Kazerne' bar in Rotterdam, with reference to the judgment of the Dutch Supreme Court: HR 15 June 1976, *NJ* 1976 551, annotated by Th.W. van Veen.

dangerous mix can develop from a perception of a low birth rate, large-scale migration and the presence of a fundamentalist minority that, albeit comprising only "a very small number", feeds fear of Muslims.[127] Concern that politics of identity would take the lead in these "troubled waters" was intensified by the fact that differences were being heightened on two sides: "Some in the press or in power", noted Teitelbaum and Winter in 1998, "cultivate such fears: after the Cold War, another evil empire is just the thing they are looking for. The problem remains, though, that some Muslims do not want to integrate into Western society. They want to live in the West among the infidels but not join them."[128] Samuel Huntington wrote an article in a journal in 1993 on "The Clash of Civilizations?" with a question mark, ending with the sentence: "For the relevant future, there will be no universal civilization, but instead a world of different civilizations, each of which will have to learn to coexist with the others."[129] In 1996, he published a book of the same title, this time without the question mark, "The Clash of Civilizations and the Remaking of World Order",[130] which made a host of people believe that such a clash was inevitable and that the divisions were of a religious and ideological nature.[131] The book became a bestseller and the words in the title grew wings. In fact, Huntington had himself borrowed these words from a 1990 article by Bernard Lewis, an author who – however concerned he may have been – in any event did not give way to a fatalistic, generalized aversion to Middle Eastern Islam: "The movement nowadays called fundamentalism is not the only Islamic tradition. There are others, more tolerant, more open, that helped to inspire the great achievements of Islamic civilization in the past, and we may hope that these other traditions will in time prevail."[132]

In 1998, the same year that "A Question of Numbers" was published, Bassam Tibi introduced the concept of a European *Leitkultur* (defining

---

[127] Michael S. Teitelbaum and Jay Winter, *A Question of Numbers. High Migration, Low Fertility, and the Politics of National Identity* (Hill & Wang 1998) 242.

[128] Ibid. 243.

[129] Samuel Huntington, 'The Clash of Civilizations?' (1993) 72 *Foreign Affairs* 22.

[130] Samuel Huntington, *The Clash of Civilizations and the Remaking of World Order* (Touchstone 1997).

[131] Stefan Halper and Jonathan Clarke, *The Silence of the Rational Center. Why American Foreign Policy is Failing* (Basic Books 2007) 117.

[132] Bernard Lewis, 'The Roots of Muslim Rage: Why so many Muslims deeply resent the West, and why their bitterness will not easily be mollified' *Atlantic Magazine* (Washington, 1 September 1990) <www.theatlantic.com/magazine/archive/1990/09/the-roots-of-muslim-rage/4643/6/> accessed 1 August 2011.

culture, core culture).[133] Tibi, given restrictive immigration and integration policies – the reality in the Netherlands and Germany, notwithstanding the image portrayed in the media –, consistently advocates integrating Muslims as citizens ("Muslime als Bürger zu integrieren").[134] He considers that it is legitimate to integrate Muslim migrants in Europe only as individuals, not as a circumscribed group.[135]

The personal nature of citizenship, then, is crucial here. Regarding immigrants as citizens (or prospective citizens) also means treating the citizenship of the existing population personally, not as a product of an identity that marks them off or privileges them. The concept of a common *Leitkultur*, introduced by Tibi and used by Theo Sommer,[136] has been remolded in the political debate into the keyword for movements that want to keep diverse citizenship at bay. This is the case in the arguments for designating a more or less settled, indigenous majority culture as the 'leading culture', based on a reframing of the concept by the German politician Friedrich Merz in October 2000.[137]

The Integration Memorandum, cited earlier, of the short-lived right-wing Dutch government coalition that collapsed in 2012, attempted to link up with the idea that *Leitkultur* is an oppositional rather than a connecting concept: "The keynotes of social life in the Netherlands have developed historically and provide points of recognition that many Dutch people share and that cannot be relinquished. This is true not only of the achievements and core values that lie at [the] base of the Dutch constitutional state but also of more historical or cultural points of recognition such as the Dutch language, historic buildings or architectural features, or unwritten manners and codes of conduct that have developed down the centuries and that come to the fore depending on the situation.

---

[133] Bassam Tibi, *Europa ohne Identität? Leitkultur oder Wertebeliebigkeit* [Europe without identity? *Leitkultur* or arbitrary values] (Siedler 2000).

[134] Bassam Tibi, *Fundamentalismus im Islam. Eine Gefahr für den Weltfrieden?* [Fundamentalism in Islam: a danger to world peace?] (Wissenschaftliche Buchgesellschaft 2000) 146.

[135] Ibid. 158 ("daß die muslimischen Migranten in Europa nur als Individuen, nicht als abgegrenztes Kollektiv integriert werden dürfen").

[136] As he says himself, following in the footsteps of Amitai Etzioni. See Theo Sommer, 'Einwanderung ja, Ghettos nein: Warum Friedrich Merz sich zu Unrecht auf mich beruft' [Immigration yes, ghettos no: why Friedrich Merz wrongly cites me] *Die Zeit* (Hamburg 2000) <www.zeit.de/2000/47/200047_leitkultur.xml> accessed 28 May 2012.

[137] Friedrich Merz places this in perspective in his article 'Einwanderung und Identität' *Die Welt* (Berlin 25 October 2000) <www.welt.de/print-welt/article540438/Einwanderung-und-Identitaet.html> accessed 28 May 2012.

Integration is about integration in Dutch society."[138] The crux of this passage is the reference to "points of recognition [...] that cannot be relinquished", but it is unclear whether 'cannot' is meant in the descriptive or normative sense here.

The requirement of sufficient knowledge of language and society is not a bone of contention; indeed, it features regularly in the arguments put forward by Etzioni, Sommer and Tibi. This is however not the case with linking integration to the abandonment of distinguishing dimensions of one's 'own' identity and adaptation to a kind of Dutch individuality, the so-called 'points of recognition'. The precise meaning of a policy approach of this kind remains unclear: should building a minaret, for example, be regarded as a deviation from 'architectural features' or as a new application of the core value of tolerance? Here we are seeing a new manifestation of the ambivalence towards the multicultural society that has taken root in areas of Dutch politics – especially since the dramatic events of 2001–2004. In a paper on "the dubious premises of 'repressive liberalism' underlying the policy of cultural 'integration'", Dimitry Kochenov describes how elements have crept into the integration tests that are generally compulsory for immigrants from outside the EU which have nothing to do with a common reciprocal commitment to the democratic constitutional state – the value system whose acceptance can legitimately be demanded on the basis of reciprocity – but merely with the assimilation of personal patterns of behavior.[139]

Sergio Carrera notes that, in spite of national acceptance of the Stockholm Programme, integration has increasingly evolved from support offered to third-country nationals (citizens of non-EU-states) to a binding condition for access to rights, security and inclusiveness.[140] This could be seen as an accentuation of the reciprocity inherent in integration, but Carrera observes "a progressive tendency to expand and increase the burdens" on third-country nationals, in particular in the areas of lifestyle, values and language. Third-country nationals are expected "to relinquish their differences and identity(ies) in favor of the perceived mainstream".[141] He sees this as an implementation of European policy in the service of a more conservative, national – or even nationalist – policy to ward off

---

[138] See (n. 120) 7–8.
[139] Kochenov (n. 92).
[140] Sergio Carrera, *In Search of the Perfect Citizen? The Intersection between Integration, Immigration and Nationality in the EU* (Martinus Nijhoff Publishers 2009) 75–82.
[141] Ibid. 430.

immigrants that opposes heterogeneity and diversity.[142] This has a knock-on effect when it comes to the acquisition of nationality. In the past, a high level of integration was a requirement for immigrants wishing to acquire the nationality of the country of residence, but as part of this hardening such requirements are laid down with a different goal in mind, i.e. in order to place curbs on third-country nationals.[143] The use of integration requirements as an instrument for immigration has also become an element of European policy-making. "The use of integration as a condition for naturalization", according to Carrera, "is a strategy of transforming otherness into the perfect citizenry on the basis of the continuance of the nation-state as it is supposed to be."[144] The negative orientation of such a strategy mistakes integration for assimilation: an implicit image of the "perfect citizen" is set up before immigrants if they wish to pass these restrictions. Moreover, in the context of a neo-liberal shift in policy orientations throughout the European Union severing "the link between social justice and social cohesion",[145] the requirements concerning successful integration have increasingly burdened immigrants with an individual responsibility to seize opportunities and contribute.

Laying down requirements of this kind, which are effectively exclusional, impedes rather than fosters the acquisition of citizenship by immigrants. What is not at issue, however, is that disorderly large-scale immigration cannot result in shared citizenship. In this sense, the success of migration depends both on the extent of the needs and on laying down well thought-out norms, i.e. policies to regulate migration: the one is related to the other. The social and legal exclusion of immigrants with the aim of discouraging immigration, on the other hand, is counterproductive, and criminalization is even worse. "Crimmigration law", as Juliet P. Stumpf dubs these implacable criminal sanctions under migration law, on the other hand makes a noncitizen who breaks the law an outlaw forever.[146] "Crimmigration law picks out one of those moments in the history of the relationship between the individual and the State, and invests it with the power to determine the entire value of the noncitizen's physical, social,

---

[142] Ibid. 431.

[143] Ibid. 441.

[144] Ibid. 442–3.

[145] Yasemin Nuhoğlu Soysal, 'Citizenship, immigration, and the European social project. Rights and obligations of individuality' (2012) 63 *British Journal of Sociology* 1, 12.

[146] Juliet P. Stumpf, 'Doing Time. Crimmigration Law and the Perils of Haste' (2011) 58 *UCLA Law Review* 1705.

economic, and cultural presence in the United States."[147] Making illegal residence a criminal offense – once more proposed in the Netherlands after the formation of the second Rutte government in 2012 – and linking the commission of criminal offenses to loss of residence rights without further consideration means that the migration regulations take on the nature of a special law that disadvantages immigrants. After all, as a matter of principle, the legal system of a liberal democracy offers the possibility of a second chance for other contraventions of the law: law enforcement is not supposed to be relentless.

The objections to proposals such as these should not be used as an excuse for a laissez-faire, laissez-passer attitude to international migration. While urbanization and migration are inescapable socio-economic trends, and necessary from a global perspective, it is the duty of states to order and regulate them, and this involves weighing up pros and cons and making choices. Doing justice to people takes time, so there must be openness to the possibility of a person's situation and attitude to life changing – a viewpoint that colours and fleshes out the relationship with everyone's personal dignity that underlies the protection of human rights. Any significant immigration results – at least to some extent – in de facto integration, even without immediate legal recognition. If this is ignored for too long, it becomes necessary to grant residence rights to whole groups ('regularization' or 'amnesty'), thus in effect correcting a policy that has become divorced from reality. Misuse of the fundamental right of the freedom of family life in order to obtain residence rights, for example, should however be dealt with; willingness to participate and integrate, on the other hand, should play a positive role in immigration policy and promote reciprocity in the acquisition of citizenship. For the German author Seyran Ateş, the importance of not regarding this undercurrent as a shortfall in the enforcement of migration regulations but as a trend that must be linked to the value system intrinsic in a democratic state in the European context, justifies seeing transcultural coexistence as part of a common European *Leitkultur*.[148] The importance of this proposition is that it indemnifies citizenship against ethnic or narrow national demarcations. The form of multiculturalism advocated by Ateş is in line with citizenship

---

[147] Ibid. 1748.
[148] Seyran Ateş, *Der Multikulti-Irrtum: wie wir in Deutschland besser zusammenleben können* [The multiculturalism mistake. How we can live together better in Germany] (Ullstein 2008) 19, 249ff.

in a twenty-first-century democratic state and is referred to by Dominic McGoldrick as 'transculturalism'.[149]

A fresh look at the relationship between citizenship and identity, as advocated in this section, involves going deeper into the relationship with human rights. In "Beyond Multiculturalism", McGoldrick urges the development of "better models for achieving social equality and justice."[150] Human rights demand respect for the personal dignity of everyone just as they are, i.e. with the many facets of their identity. A one-sided aversion to and rejection of the multicultural society, on the other hand, gives rise to the impression that a monocultural society is possible and even desirable – which is out of the question as long as the Netherlands remains a democratic state and will therefore only feed tensions and frustrations. That is the tragedy of the false illusion of a monocultural society.

Linking citizens' rights to ordered migration and urbanization so as to strengthen the binding power of democracy is indisputably a delicate pursuit, as the narrative of the 'failure' of the multicultural society lies in wait. Antillean and Moroccan-Dutch young males are seriously overrepresented in criminal statistics. Corrected with respect to socio-economic background, the number of suspects is still 2–3 times higher than among males without an immigrant background.[151] Of all discriminatory and deprecating utterances in the Netherlands about population groups, about 50% are targeted at Muslims or Islam.[152] A report commissioned by the German Federal Ministry of the Interior shows that many well-integrated young German Muslims feel offended by negative generalizations and that integration, participation and German citizenship have a positive statistical correlation.[153] However, after the publication of Sarrazin's widely debated xenophobic book,[154] the hearts of some young Muslim citizens in Germany sank into their boots.[155] Wherever people fail to observe mutual respect there is the risk of a negative spiral. The only sensible conclusion from this

---

[149] McGoldrick (n. 108) 32, 39.

[150] Ibid. 56.

[151] Centraal Bureau voor de Statistiek (CBS), *Jaarrapport integratie 2012* [2012 Report on Integration] (CBS 2012) 183.

[152] Ineke van der Valk, *Islamophobia in the Netherlands* (Amsterdam UP 2012) 11.

[153] E.g. W. Frindte and others, *Lebenswelten junger Muslime in Deutschland.* (Bundesinnenministerium 2012) 194.

[154] Thilo Sarrazin, *Deutschland schafft sich ab* [Germany abolishes itself] (Deutsche Verlags-Anstalt 2010): a book that notwithstanding official disapproval became a bestseller in Germany.

[155] Frindte and others (n. 153) 542.

description of tensions associated with disrespectful behavior is that action needs to be taken to combat it – not only preventively but also in the form of punishment or other forms of visible disapproval. While crudely identifying the constitutional state with law enforcement is misplaced, the rule of law also demands that the law rules.

The achievement of citizenship has lent a new dimension to constitutional thinking. The constitution of the modern state can no longer be interpreted in categories of authority and ties; instead it is characterized by citizens' say in decision-making, their rights and the substantive qualification of institutions, which are thus dependent on a permanent process of legitimization: "voice, rights and expertise", the phrase by which Halberstam describes constitutional qualities that can be found not only in states but also in the European Union and other institutions.[156]

Citizenship is a legal category carried by values of mutual solidarity, related to a polity such as the πόλις of yesteryear and the modern state. The relationship between citizenship and the twenty-first-century democratic political system guided by the rule of law means that the content and significance of citizenship are colored by human rights. Any citizenship circumscribed by ethnic or religious identity conflicts with this. The requirement of equal treatment irrespective of personal characteristics (e.g. sex, race, religion, beliefs, sexual orientation)[157] is not something that goes alongside citizenship of a democratic constitutional state, it characterizes that very citizenship.

The only sensible – and at the same time indispensable – requirement that can be laid down for citizenship in a democratic state is ability to accept, on the basis of reciprocity, the citizenship of others who have ties with that same society: the identity of democratic citizenship. Knowledge of the common language and the main features of the constitutional system can be established as learning objectives in education and as qualifications for naturalization. A constitution guided by human rights cannot test people's inner disposition, but commitment to the democratic constitutional state based on reciprocity can legitimately be demanded: this,

---

[156] See Halberstam (n. 53) 171: "The constitutional idea of limited collective self-governance can be broken down into three primary values – call them 'voice', 'rights' and 'expertise'."

[157] E.g. the Grondwet [Dutch Constitution] art. 1; International Covenant on Civil and Political Rights (adopted 16 December 1966, entered into force 23 March 1976) 999 UNTS 171 (ICCPR) art. 26; Charter of Fundamental Rights of the European Union [2000] OJ C364/1, arts. 20 and 21.

after all, in the words of Herman Tjeenk Willink, is the most elementary office in a state.[158]

Nor is there anything against promulgating reciprocal and equal citizenship, also by persons in public office. In many states, including the Netherlands, this is part of the mission of the head of state, especially when the monarchy or presidency is not linked with political power.[159] Politicians too who are aware of the significance of their oath of loyalty to the Constitution, opinion leaders, academics and spiritual leaders – especially if they recognize the value of the separation of Church and State – are well advised to promulgate this shared responsibility for respectful social cohesion. This is precisely the democratic identity, excluding no-one a priori, that is intrinsic in citizenship.

2.3 A World on the Move

Much suffering has been visited upon people by making their citizenship dependent on belonging to a particular ethnic group. In some cases as a result of international agreements, whole sections of the population were deprived of their nationality or had one forced upon them, especially after the First World War, when politicians – poorly informed about the social realities, and often manipulated by political power play – thought they could bring about nationally homogeneous states by drawing lines on a map.[160] In Central and Southeast Europe in particular – the region of the 'Vielvölkerstaaten' of the Austro-Hungarian and Ottoman Empire – every town or city of any significance was multiethnic and this political map-making led to lengthy disputes and immense personal suffering. A horrific consequence was the forced deportation of Muslims living in Greece and Greek Orthodox living in Turkey under the Convention Concerning the Exchange of Greek and Turkish Populations signed on 30 January 1923 in Lausanne. About 2 million persons were no longer treated as nationals but as aliens in the country where they and their forebears had their homes, and then felt like aliens in the country where they were resettled, where

---

[158] H.D. Tjeenk Willink in Raad van State, *Jaarverslag 2006* [Annual report 2006 of the Council of State] (Raad van State 2007) 28.

[159] On this subject see Ernst M.H. Hirsch Ballin, *De Koning. Continuïteit en perspectief van het Nederlandse koningschap* [The King. Continuity and perspective in the Dutch monarchy] (2nd edn, Boom Juridische uitgevers 2013) 71–73.

[160] Margaret MacMillan, *Peacemakers. The Paris Conference of 1919 and Its Attempt to End War* (John Murray 2001).

they were granted nationality whether they wanted it or not.[161] Their personal freedom was totally subjugated to the one dimension of their identity that was deemed critical – religion – at the expense of all other fundamental freedoms and human rights. The consequences are among the long series of politically organized atrocities of the twentieth century. Even now – we shall consider relative and absolute statelessness in § 3.4 – there are many places in the world where people are still deprived of the rights associated with citizenship because they are not deemed to belong to the (ruling) nation.

There is every reason to turn in the opposite direction. We have to examine how the rights associated with citizenship could indeed play a worthwhile and stronger role in the social cohesion of a democratic society. A realistic view of the social context of the twenty-first century needs to be taken into account here, as this will determine how citizens' rights work in a democracy like that of the Netherlands, embedded as it is in the European Union and a web of international economic, cultural and social links.

The urbanization that began in Europe in the Middle Ages, and elsewhere at different moments in history, has now spread worldwide; it is not over by a long chalk.[162] In the Netherlands, it is continuing particularly in the western conurbation (the 'Randstad') and Brabant, and worldwide it is a trend whose political, social, economic and cultural consequences have still not sufficiently penetrated our awareness. It is visible and tangible in the physical and social maps of towns and cities, and no-one can ever seriously have assumed that it is unproblematic. Migration to urban areas is taking place on every continent: in Turkey e.g. to Istanbul, which has grown from a population of 7,6 million people in 1990 to 13,8 million in 2012; in Africa e.g. to Cairo, Lagos and Kinshasa, which have developed into conurbations with populations of between 9 and 16 million. China has at present 14 cities with a population larger than 5 million inhabitants and 160 cities of over one million.[163] The misery of nineteenth-century

---

[161] The forced 'exchange' of sections of the population between Greece and Turkey resulted in people being turned into aliens in their country of origin and then feeling like aliens in the country to which they were deported. See Bruce Clark, *Twice a Stranger. The Mass Expulsions that Forged Modern Greece and Turkey* (Harvard UP 2006).

[162] "A third of the world's population is on the move this century", according to Saunders (n. 88) 21. This requires "a global migration agenda", see Goldin, Cameron and Balarajan (n. 74) ch. 8.

[163] See <http://en.wikipedia.org/wiki/List_of_cities_in_the_People%27s_Republic_of_China_by_population> accessed on 2 June 2013.

industrial urbanization gave birth to social ethics in relation to philosophy and a new stage in the development of public law;[164] in our era, the sometimes offensive and criminal manifestations of city street culture have resulted in new approaches to crime-busting, where basically the most effective response to socially undesirable behavior is to promote social cohesion.[165]

Migration inevitably results in transforming political community-building – i.e. the social basis for a public law organization such as the state or a municipality. It is often taken for granted that the ideal migrant should turn his back on his country of origin for ever. The aforementioned Dutch Integration Memorandum (2011) was unable to break away from the idea that the new Promised Land lies behind the dykes: "People leaving their own country to go and live in another one expect to find things that they missed in their country of origin to such an extent that they take the fundamental step of building a new life elsewhere."[166] This manifestly fails to recognize that everyone's identity has various layers and dimensions. The development of citizenship in a city such as Amsterdam is a good example.[167] What is characteristic of the migration patterns of our times is precisely *not* that foreigners leave their house and home for good, never to return, forgetting their families. On the contrary, migration to urban areas – whether in the same country or further afield – takes place for the sake of the development of the family, the family that the migrant is leaving behind and wishes to support financially, but also that will eventually join him.[168] Migrants mostly do not lose the desire to visit their place of origin, and some of them are keen to cooperate with circular migration.

Sound migration policies set criteria for this while not ignoring the worldwide need for migration. The counterproductive effects of restrictive migration policies as part of a policy of identity were discussed in the

---

[164] Auke van der Woud, *Koninkrijk vol sloppen. Achterbuurten en vuil in de negentiende eeuw* [A kingdom full of slums. Back streets and dirt in the nineteenth century] (Bert Bakker 2010).

[165] See Bas van Stokkom and Jan Terpstra, 'Neighbourhood, Youth, and Safety. A dissertation on social cohesion and active citizenship' in Ellen van den Berg and others (eds.), *Justice = Social Cohesion* (Ministry of Justice 2010); Stavros Zouridis and Ernst M.H. Hirsch Ballin, 'A Legal and Justice Strategy towards Strengthening Social Cohesion' in Sam Muller and Stavros Zouridis (eds.), *Law and justice. A strategy perspective* (TOAEP 2012) 105–115.

[166] See n. 120. For the role of similar notions in American politics, see Halper and Clarke (n. 131) e.g. 24.

[167] See Jean Tillie and Boris Slijper, 'Immigrant political integration and ethnic civic communities in Amsterdam' in Seyla Benhabib, Ian Shapiro and Danilo Petranović, *Identities, Affiliations, and Allegiances* (CUP 2007) ch. 9.

[168] Saunders (n. 88) 20.

previous section. Good policies are selective where problems need to be addressed, offer protection where there is no alternative, and encourage people who have found a place in a new environment to find ways of working for it as soon as possible.[169] The relationship between Puerto Rico and the United States described a long time ago has become a worldwide reality, a *vaivén*[170] that brings people separated by long distances closer together. The idea that obstacles should be placed in the way of people wishing to marry someone from another country is not only a restriction on human rights, it also ignores the reality of contacts across large distances. What really has to be dealt with is the misuse of forced marriages and marriages of convenience to circumvent immigration regulations.[171] Recent efforts of the short-lived first Rutte government to introduce a strict requirement of single nationality (see § 3.5) were also based on the idea that anyone integrating in a new society can and should turn his back on his society of origin, even if part of his family is left behind there.

What we are seeing now is the repeated migration of people to urban areas, often as families. This movement arises from a growing group of people, many of whom in their own way set themselves apart from those around them – *Exceptional People* is the title that Goldin, Cameron and Balarajan gave to their book on the subject, already cited –, people who are able to make a difference by not eternally perpetuating the traditional rural lifestyle. Not all of them succeed; some try to make it using criminal methods, or lapse into crime after repeated failures. Others experience the problems of conflicting expectations. It is up to the law, however, to provide incentives and opportunities for those who accept an offer of integration and citizenship, so it should not impose requirements that serve no useful purpose. Fundamental rights protect people's identity precisely when it does not conform with supposed standards.

In his book *Arrival City*, Doug Saunders describes the extent and complexity of this worldwide urbanization. By the middle of this century, the urban areas will have gained 3.1 billion inhabitants, owing partly to population growth and partly to depopulation of the rural areas.[172] This will

---

[169] These in a nutshell were the aims of the Act of 20 May 2010 amending the Aliens Act 2000 (*Stb* 2010, 175) in the context of revision of the asylum procedure and the Modern Migration Policy Act of 7 July 2010 (*Stb* 2010, 290).

[170] Jorge Duany, *The Puerto Rican Nation on the Move. Identities on the Island and in the United States* (University of North Carolina Press 2002).

[171] This is nothing new, however: see the letter from the then Minister for Housing, Residential Areas & Integration, the Minister of Justice and the Deputy Minister of Justice, *Kamerstukken II* 32 175 no 1 (9 October 2009).

[172] Saunders (n. 88) 22.

avert the long-feared global overpopulation, as everywhere the urban way
of life results in declining birth rates, but in those parts of the world where
there is a danger of population shrinkage – e.g. Western Europe – immigration could help to cushion the consequences.[173] As Goldin, Cameron and
Balarajan argue, migration is a necessary phenomenon, and beneficial on
the whole,[174] albeit it just as inevitably involves tensions and problems,
individually and collectively.[175]

No-one can ignore the aforementioned over-representation of badly
integrated young males in the crime figures in the Netherlands and elsewhere.[176] If we adjust the comparison with other population groups to
take education, employment and other social conditions into account,
however, we see that the difference evaporates to a large extent, and we
would do better to focus our attention on those conditions rather than
bashing population groups.[177] It is both wrong and pointless, then, to
respond to migration by throttling citizens' rights. Crude policies designed
to put obstacles in the way of immigrants maintaining their family connections are counterproductive,[178] with consequences such as dependency on criminal networks. A sensible policy aims to control, qualitatively
and quantitatively, the need to migrate and focuses on migrating workers,
businessmen, researchers and students. This is the goal of recently stream-
lined immigration procedures like that of the Dutch Modern Migration
Policy Act of 2010.

At the same time we need to note another point. While researchers and
policy-makers have acknowledged that "increasing ethnic diversity tests
the adaptive capacity of receiving countries and localities",[179] not enough
serious study has gone into how to avoid marginalization processes at
the receiving end. Recent German research shows that political rhetoric

---

[173] Jan H. van de Beek, *Kennis, Macht en Moraal. De productie van wetenschappelijke
kennis over de economische effecten van migratie naar Nederland, 1960–2005* [Knowledge,
power and morality. The production of scientific knowledge on the economic effects
of migration to the Netherlands, 1960–2005] (Vossiuspers 2010) 102ff; cf. Fareed Zakaria,
The Post-American World (W.W. Norton & Company 2008) 196–9, on the political limitations that in this context affect Europe far more than the United States.

[174] Goldin, Cameron and Balarajan (n. 74).

[175] Saunders (n. 88) 85.

[176] Cf. Frank Bovenkerk, *Etniciteit, criminaliteit en het strafrecht* [Ethnicity, criminality
and the criminal law] (Valedictory lecture, University of Utrecht, Boom 2009).

[177] Cf. Lucassen and Lucassen (n. 8) 48.

[178] Cf. Dennis Broeders and Godfried Engbersen, 'The Fight against Illegal Migration.
Identification Policies and Immigrants' Counterstrategies' (2007) 50 *American Behavioral
Scientist* 1592.

[179] Goldin, Cameron and Balarajan (n. 74) 176.

targeting migration, such as that of Thilo Sarrazin, only makes integration processes more difficult.[180] We must not ignore the social position of those residents of the receiving countries who have nothing to gain from the dynamics of globalization and migration, however. While researchers and policy-makers have acknowledged that increasing ethnic diversity at the *receiving* end tests people's ability to adapt,[181] there has not been enough serious study into how to avoid marginalization processes at the receiving end and set positive dynamics in motion there. Researchers such as Paul Scheffer have pointed out that people at that end experience the arrival of migrants in their neighborhood as confirmation that they themselves are merely losers.[182] It is not a lack of efforts to encourage participation by the migrants that is the problem, but a lack of care for those already living in deprived and depopulating areas. Policies that target vulnerable residential areas, then, are not only more useful than target group policies, they also prevent the government from reinforcing segregation by its policies instead of reducing it. This is another reason why integration should include an active citizenship dimension,[183] which makes towns and cities, despite problems – in some cases, for example in Britain, serious ones[184] – into "cultural as well as economic engines."[185] These places have fomented – and are still fomenting – people's desire for recognition, not just as members of a tribal or ethnical organism but in *person*, as *citizens*.[186]

A strategy targeting personal and social conditions – both by tackling problems and by offering prospects – will get the best out of the trend towards equal citizenship. In this context, Goldin and his co-authors have made important comments on the risks of exclusional groupthink: encounters between people with different viewpoints encourage "divergent thinking", whereas "Groups composed of similar people are more likely to engage in 'convergent thinking', which reinforces the status quo." This is also true of how policies are developed and implemented. Encounters with different viewpoints contribute to "more effective and

---

[180] Frindte (n. 153) 574–592.
[181] Goldin, Cameron and Balarajan (n. 74) 176.
[182] Scheffer (n. 95) 20–27.
[183] Saskia Sassen, *Globalization and Its Discontents* (The New Press 1998) 8.
[184] For the 2011 riots, see David Lammy, *Out of the Ashes?* (Guardian Books 2011).
[185] Roberts (n. 1) 136.
[186] Cf. Blockmans (n. 6) 81: "These citizens were legally free, i.e. released from any limitations associated with the status of a serf on a manor. No chores, payments in money or kind, no restrictions on freedom of movement or choice of marriage partner."

creative decision-making than consultation among similar people,"[187] though I would add that this requires a quality of public leadership that is in short supply.[188]

Migration from the rural to the urban areas, as we have seen, is a basic pattern in the history of humanity; the cultivation of pre-urban lifestyles is merely a transitional phenomenon. As a result of urbanization, closed communities defined by their origins – organized on tribal and hierarchical lines – in Europe have increasingly made way, since the Middle Ages, for a situation where people who are ethnically, culturally and religiously different live alongside and with one another but share life as citizens with one another in one city. And not only in one particular city, but also in networks of cities trading with one another with patterns of shuttle migration continuing between them.

2.4 Citizenship and Democracy

Living together as citizens in a single polity means that there are relationships between the citizens and the institutions of the polity, and these relationships are ordered by the constitution: to this extent constitutional law determines the meaning of citizenship. Democracy has always been defined as that polity in which ultimate decision-making power rests with citizens of the state. As we have already seen, however, this is not the whole story by any means: a polity in which the majority has the final say, with no constitutional limitations and safeguards for minorities, goes at the expense – as Andrew Fagan argues – of human rights.[189]

Citizens' rights are therefore a defining element in the constitution of a constitutional state or other polity that accepts the principles of democracy and the rule of law. This is also true of the European Union: while it was superimposed on the European Communities under the Maastricht Treaty (1992) as an institutional corroboration, its further development around the turn of the century was shaped particularly by the point of view of the European citizenry.[190] The Charter of Fundamental Rights of

---

[187] Goldin, Cameron and Balarajan (n. 74) 177.

[188] Cf. Jan Prij, 'Theedrinken als kern van het politieke' [Tea-drinking as the core of politics] (2010) 32 *Filosofie & Praktijk* 19.

[189] Fagan (n. 69) 100–1.

[190] For the 'migration' of constitutional ideas and for their influence on the constitutional idea and the development of the EU, see Neil Walker, 'The migration of constitutional ideas and the migration of the constitutional idea: the case of the EU' in Sujit Choudry (ed.), *The Migration of Constitutional Ideas* (CUP 2006).

the European Union (2000) and both the aborted Constitution for Europe and its replacement, the Lisbon Treaty, were written from the point of view of a 'Europe of the citizens', whose fundamental rights and democratic control needed to be strengthened.[191]

In the transition from the nineteenth to the twentieth century, a kind of ideal constitutional pattern for modern Western constitutions seemed to take shape, with democracy as the watchword, characterized by a *trias politica*, fundamental rights and regular elections.[192] The underlying normative concept that state powers should be legitimized and limited by a constitution has been framed as "constitutionalism". Rosenfeld and Sajó identify the recent "proliferation of transitions from authoritarianism and colonial rule to constitutional democracy in virtually every corner of the world" as the "spread and consolidation of liberal constitutionalism."[193] Paradoxically, the fact that repressive regimes were also keen to parade as democracies only confirmed the ideals that they trod underfoot.

With the diversification of forms of political organization at the end of the twentieth century – including the advent of manifold new international structures – constitutionalism too has taken on diverse manifestations. Constitutionalism as a normative concept may also be applied to polities other than the state. Legitimation and limitation of powers vested in parastatal, supranational and international legal bodies are equally important with respect to the requirements of democracy, the rule of law and good governance. For this reason, recent research deals with postnational or transnational constitutionalism[194]

---

[191] This resulted inter alia in the Council Decision 2007/340/EC of 19 April 2007 establishing for the period 2007–2013 the specific programme 'Fundamental Rights and Citizenship' as part of the general programme 'Fundamental Rights and Justice' [2007] OJ L110/33. During the period of the program, however, this subject was increasingly sidelined by acute concerns and tensions due to the financial and economic situation.

[192] Giuseppe Volpe, *Il constituzionalismo del Novecento* (Editori Laterza 2000) 173: "Democrazia è la parola d'ordine che, nei secoli XIX e XX, domina quasi universalmente gli spiriti" [Democracy is the slogan that dominated minds almost universally in the 19th and 20th centuries], but – as Volpe adds – like so many slogans it soon lost its power of differentiation.

[193] Michel Rosenfeld and András Sajó, 'Spreading liberal constitutionalism. An inquiry into the fate of free speech rights in new democracies' in Sujit Choudhry, *The Migration of Constitutional Ideas* (CUP 2006) 142.

[194] Cf. Gunther Teubner, 'Societal Constitutionalism: Alternatives to State-Centred Constitutional Theory?' in Christian Joerges, Inger-Johanne Sand and Gunther Teubner (eds.), *Transnational Governance and Constitutionalism* (Hart 2004); Nicholas Tsagourias, *Transnational Constitutionalism. International and European Perspectives* (CUP 2006); Nico Krisch, *Beyond Constitutionalism. The Pluralist Structure of Postnational Law* (OUP 2010) 23; Gunther Teubner, *Verfassungsfragmente. Gesellschaftlicher Konstitutionalismus in der Globalisierung* (Suhrkamp 2012); Gráinne de Búrca, 'The ECJ and the international legal

and transconstitutionalism,[195] a subject to which we will return in relation to transnational citizenship.

Through their citizenship, people exercise the democratic right to co-decide on the rules that will govern the relations among them and the organization of their state and society. Their citizenship protects them at the same time against exclusion from society, be it in the guise of a denial or a limitation of their legal entitlements, or through expulsion. It is the status on which "the right to have rights" depends: with these words, Hannah Arendt in the aftermath of the Second World War described exactly that which is unjustly denied to stateless persons.[196] Since then, efforts have been made to mitigate the legal disenfranchisement of stateless persons. The situation, however, of aliens permanently living under the jurisdiction of a state that is not theirs is often similar.

Daniel Halberstam refers to the "foundational principles of legitimacy" in constitutions as being "voice, rights and expertise".[197] These dimensions of constitutionalism are closely linked with our theme of citizenship. 'Expertise' refers to the ability of the polity to perform public functions that are necessary to ensure that people can live in freedom and dignity. A democratic polity, after all, is a way of organizing mutual solidarity in a developed society that meets the needs of citizens, having taken over from earlier tribal units. Citizens have a say in decision-making: they are not 'subjects' subordinated to the state but enjoy rights, including their fundamental rights. Equal treatment of citizens as regards their social and economic rights too is thus a fundamental prerequisite for a democratic constitutional state; favoring or disadvantaging a group on the basis of ethnicity, conversely, is a serious violation of this,[198] and taken to extremes – e.g. causing starvation in the deprived group – it is a crime against humanity.[199]

Constitutional law, then, is about people, their dignity and their freedom. The state is important here – more important than present-day

---

order: a re-evaluation' in de Búrca and Weiler (n. 53) 129. See also the nuanced analysis in Dieter Grimm, *Die Zukunft der Verfassung II. Auswirkungen von Europäisierung und Globalisierung* (Suhrkamp 2012) 342.

[195] Marcelo Neves, *Transconstitutionalism* (Hart 2013).

[196] Hannah Arendt, *The Origins of Totalitarianism* (first published 1948, Harcourt 1973) 296.

[197] Halberstam (n. 53).

[198] Sen, *Identity and Violence* (n. 49) 142–144.

[199] UNGA, Rome Statute of the International Criminal Court (adopted 17 July 1998, entered into force 1 July 2002) 2187 UNTS 90/37 ILM 1002 (1998)/[2002] ATS 15, art. 8 para. 2 (xxv).

worshippers of the Golden Calf have been willing to admit in recent decades.[200] The principles of law and norms derived from them determine what exercise of power is permissible. The powers of the state include not only the use of physical coercion but also control over the monetary system and a specific type of symbolic interaction: the official modes of communication typical of the state.[201] Even apparently all-powerful banks, oil companies and media need the state for their continued existence.[202] Sooner or later the legitimacy of every exercise of power must be judged, in terms of principles based on the intrinsic dignity of every person.

The question posed by Colin Crouch about the extent to which a democratic state can withstand massively funded lobbying,[203] indubitably has consequences for the effectiveness of the exercise of political rights, hence for the meaning of citizenship in twenty-first-century democracy. Conversely, the enshrining of citizens' rights in the constitutional system is significant as regards the extent to which the institutions can resist the power of lobbying. Arguments put forward by some politicians in favour of curbing judicial powers to protect entitlements as fundamental rights[204] are consistent with their positions in favour of neoliberal models of socio-economic organization. The safeguarding of fundamental rights by an independent judiciary is however particularly important as a counterbalance to the possibility of majorities being mobilized to represent group interests at the expense of outvoted minorities – the risk against which, as already noted, Andrew Fagan has warned.

2.5 Citizenship and Constitutional Legitimacy

There is thus a close two-way relationship between citizens' rights and democracy, in particular as regards the political decision-making process. The political nature of democratic decision-making by and on behalf

---

[200] Nicholas Dunbar, *The Devil's Derivatives. The Untold Story of the Slick Traders and Hapless Regulators Who Almost Blew Up Wall Street… and Are Ready to Do It Again* (Harvard Business Review Press 2012).

[201] Prakke referred to this as 'officiality' in *Pluralisme en staatsrecht* [Pluralism and constitutional law] (inaugural address, University of Amsterdam, Kluwer 1974).

[202] Colin Crouch, *The Strange Non-Death of Neoliberalism* (Polity Press 2011) ch. 4.

[203] Ibid. ch. 6.

[204] See David Cameron, 'Speech on the European Court of Human Rights' (Parliamentary Assembly of the Council of Europe, Strasbourg, 25 January 2012) <www.gov.uk/government/speeches/speech-on-the-european-court-of-human-rights> accessed 20 June 2012. In the same spirit, a Dutch conservative-liberal Member of Parliament in September 2012 presented a private bill aiming at the suspension of the constitutional primacy of treaties

of the citizens creates legitimacy, but only within the framework of
the constitution that safeguards the citizens' rights. It is important,
therefore, to ascertain more precisely how constitutional requirements
such as citizens' rights relate to the specifically political nature of this
decision-making.

Politics thus needs to be seen in the constitutional context, albeit that
context is constantly colored by the valuations that emerge in the political
discourse. 'Politics' is not all the same, irrespective of philosophy or ideology; rather is it characterized by a distinctive view of the public interest
that, in competition with different views of the public interest, aims to
have control over the state functions of legislation and government policy.
The democratic constitutional state cannot command legitimacy; it
must derive it from the moral orientation of society, where citizens –
thanks to processes of education and social motivation – are involved
in self-determination. This is the meaning of the so-called 'Böckenförde
dictum': "The liberal, secularized state depends on premises that it cannot
itself guarantee. This is the great risk that it takes on for the sake of freedom. On the one hand it can only exist as a liberal state if the freedom it
grants its citizens is regulated from within, based on the moral substance
of the individual and the homogeneity of society. On the other hand it
cannot try to guarantee these inner regulating forces itself, i.e. by means
of legal coercion and authoritative regulation, without relinquishing its
liberal nature and – at secularized level – falling back on the claim of totality from which it proceeded in the religious civil wars."[205]

Böckenförde's observation is crucial to our subject. Democracies can be
eroded by the neglect of the foundational principles of their legitimacy.
These principles require a continuous confrontation with changing societal and economic conditions; without that, democratic procedures are at
risk of becoming the vehicle for decisions that are detrimental to human
rights, freedom and the rule of law, sometimes with an ideological justification. Such justifications come not only from the twentieth-century
ideologies of nazism or marxism-leninism, but also from various religious
fundamentalisms, from free market fundamentalism, or from totalitarian

---

like the ECHR. Voorstel van rijkswet van het lid Taverne houdende verklaring dat er grond
bestaat een voorstel in overweging te nemen tot verandering in de Grondwet, strekkende
tot aanpassing van de procedure voor vaststelling van rechtstreekse werking van een ieder
verbindende bepalingen van verdragen en van besluiten van volkenrechtelijke organisat-
ies, *Kamerstukken II* 33 359 (R 1986).

[205] Translation of the text in Ernst-Wolfgang Böckenförde, *Recht, Staat, Freiheit*
(2nd edn, Suhrkamp Verlag 2006) 112.

understandings of public safety.[206] The need to understand constitutional concepts in the light of foundational principles of legitimacy, especially the "ethos of human rights",[207] is the more important since purely historical interpretations lose sight of the real questions of doing justice. The theory of 'originalism' defended by some people in the United States is based on the idea that the constitution has an unchanging, historically determined significance that is resistant to developments in the ethical and political pattern of valuations.

Somewhat similar historicizing methods of constitutional interpretation have had the upper hand in the Netherlands too,[208] albeit not as outspoken as some originalist views in the United States. Over and against this is the method of interpreting the constitution applied by J. van der Hoeven in his still important Amsterdam dissertation, which accepts the possibility that an unchanged text can undergo transformations within a developing ethical and political frame of reference.[209] The Dutch form of government, for example, is often described as a 'constitutional monarchy' as opposed to the absolute monarchies of the *Ancien Régime*. This characterization is not incorrect, but it does not tell us very much, as it could just as easily have been applied to the form of government in 1814. In the nineteenth and twentieth centuries, the Netherlands and other European states that were socially and culturally similar to the Netherlands developed into democracies, i.e. states whose power derived their legitimacy not from the sovereignty of the monarch but from the involvement of and pronouncements by the citizenry (δῆμος, 'people', is the Ancient Greek word for the totality of free citizens[210]).

Meanwhile subtler versions of originalism have emerged,[211] but the opposite view of the 'living constitution'[212] is more productive for the

---

[206] See Conor Gearty, *Liberty and Security* (Polity 2013) 110–11; Joseph Stiglitz, *The Price of Inequality* (W.W. Norton 2012) 262, 391.

[207] Franz Böckle, *Ja zum Menschen. Bausteine einer Konkreten Moral* (Kösel 1995) 102.

[208] Cf. A.M. Donner, 'Grondwetsstudie in Nederland 1848–1948' [Constitutional studies in the Netherlands 1848–1948] in *Tussen het echte en het gemaakte. Uit de geschriften van Prof. mr. A.M. Donner* [Between the real and the artificial: from the writings of Prof. A.M. Donner] (W.E.J. Tjeenk Willink 1986) 25–60.

[209] See van der Hoeven (n. 106). See also Johannes van der Hoeven, 'De waarde van de Grondwet' [The value of the Constitution] in *Staatsrecht en bestuursrecht, Opstellen van Mr. J. van der Hoeven* [Constitutional law and administrative law, essays by J. van der Hoeven] (W.E.J. Tjeenk Willink 1984) 39–73, which is a preliminary report to the Vereniging voor de Wijsbegeerte des Rechts (Philosophy of Law Association).

[210] Meier (n. 11) 161.

[211] Jack M. Balkin, *Living Originalism* (The Belknap Press of Harvard UP 2011).

[212] David A. Strauss, *The Living Constitution* (OUP 2010).

understanding of 'constitutional transformations'.[213] Long-term constitutional transformation processes have placed citizenship and citizens' rights at the heart of democratic constitutionalism. Originally, citizenship had developed in contrast to the medieval rule of sovereigns over their 'subjects',[214] forged into a people. The 'unity of destiny' organizational principle of a people of citizens – the archetype of solidarity – was thus established as the starting point of modern statehood. It was not until the civil revolutions of the eighteenth and nineteenth centuries that a situation developed where the citizenry themselves were the authors of that organization and the focus shifted from a predetermined unity of destiny to a solidarity deliberately laid down by law. The concept of the *contrat social* symbolized the self-evident, silent agreement between people who share a common social and political destiny.[215]

While the social dimension of the democratic constitutional state may have become a central theme later than liberal freedoms, the recognition of social rights is the inescapable consequence of citizens taking the organization of their interrelationships into their own hands. Nevertheless, solidarity of everyone with everyone is under permanent pressure. Tribal, ethnic or religious patterns of inclusion and exclusion can be exploited politically. One manifestation of this is the conservative political theory associated with the name of Carl Schmitt, whose friend/foe distinction is well known, and its consequences notorious.[216] This was based on the idea that everything aimed at the acquisition of power with the intensity of a band of like-minded people as 'friends' against 'foes' is 'political'. Religion, morality, economics and ethnicity(!) too, in Schmitt's view, could become political, depending on the intensity of the fight with those who think differently.[217] Thomas Bedorf has noted that according to Schmitt's reasoning all conflicts are 'politicizable' insofar as they are polarized into 'antagonism'.[218] In an antagonistic concept of democracy, citizens' rights

---

[213] Bruno de Witte, 'The European Union as an international legal experiment' in de Búrca and Weiler (n. 53) 28.

[214] Often an amalgam of tribes (e.g. in Britain next to the Celts the Angles, Saxons, Jutes and Normans).

[215] This interpretation of the idea of a social contract is the basic concept in my Liberation Day Lecture *Een verbond van vrijheid* (Nationaal Comité 4 en 5 mei/Stichting Collectieve Propaganda van het Nederlandse Boek 2013). With annotations <www.4en5mei .nl/4_en_5_mei/nationale_viering_van_de_bevrijding/5_mei__lezing/5_mei_lezingen/ verdiepende_informatie_lezing_ernst_hirsch_ballin> accessed 16 July 2013; English translation <www.4en5mei.nl/english/celebrating> accessed 8 September 2013.

[216] Schmitt (n 64).

[217] Ibid. 35.

[218] Thomas Bedorf, 'Das Politische und die Politik. Konturen einer Differenz' in Thomas Bedorf and Kurt Röttgers (eds.), *Das Politische und die Politik* (Suhrkamp 2010) 21.

such as the right to vote should be exercised in the context of collectivities fighting for power with other collectivities regarded as political enemies. And this is how it worked out in practice: political parties organized themselves as *Kampfverbände* (fighting associations): both the NSDAP, which Carl Schmitt supported in the decisive years since 1933, and communist movements conformed with this profile. They did not tolerate individual dissidents, either in their internal organization or – once they came to power – in public life.

Backed up by public opinion as a result of the gruesome experiences of this kind of politics – the Second World War, the Holocaust, the Gulag archipelago, Prague 1968 – a radically different type of political theory became influential in Western democracies in the second half of the twentieth century: democracy as a process of joint decision-making based on free expression of political opinion. This view was based on the idea of a *contrat social* and the European idea of freedom,[219] but added dynamics to these concepts. During the lengthy period of economic growth following the Second World War centrifugal forces were able to be neutralized as almost everyone experienced increasing prosperity. A common external foe – the power block led by the Soviet Union – did the rest. Individual citizens' rights, in conjunction with political freedoms, became the yardstick. In a line of thinking to which the present author too owes a debt, Jürgen Habermas has in a long sequence of publications over half a century[220] given shape to the idea of "deliberative politics": comparing a "liberal" and a "republican" view of politics,[221] Habermas has argued that a discourse theory allows one to take the strengths of both into account. "In agreement with republicanism, it gives centre stage to the process of

---

[219] Bernard Lakebrink, *Die Europäische Idee der Freiheit. 1. Teil: Hegels Logik und die Tradition der Selbstbestimmung* (Brill 1968).
[220] Including Jürgen Habermas, *The Structural Transformation of the Public Sphere. An Inquiry into a Category of Bourgeois Society* (Thomas Burger and Frederick Lawrence trans., MIT Press 1991), translated from the German original *Strukturwandel der Öffentlichkeit. Untersuchungen zu einer Kategorie der bürgerlichen Gesellschaft* (Luchterhand Verlag 1974).
[221] Habermas distinguishes here between "the republican understanding of the state as an ethical community" and "the liberal conception of the state as the guardian of a market society". His treatment of the subject focuses on "the democratic opinion- and will-formation that issue in popular election and parliamentary decrees", an approach that is closely connected with citizens' rights. In the republican view, "democratic will-formation is supposed to take the form of an ethical discourse of self-understanding and of justice". In the liberal view, "the democratic process takes place exclusively in the form of compromises between competing interests." See Jürgen Habermas, *Die Einbeziehung des Anderen. Studien zur politischen Theorie* (Suhrkamp 1996) 285 or *The Inclusion of the Other. Studies in Political Theory* (Ciaran P. Cronin and Pablo de Greiff trans., MIT Press 1998) 246.

political opinion- and will-formation, but without understanding the constitution" [German original: *die rechtsstaatliche Verfassung*] "as something secondary; on the contrary, it conceives the basic principles of the constitutional state" [*Grundrechte und Prinzipien des Rechtsstaates*] "as a consistent answer to the question of how the demanding communicative presuppositions of a democratic opinion- and will-formation can be institutionalized".[222]

In recent years several authors have built on these insights in their publications.[223] Amartya Sen emphasized the "intimate connection between justice and democracy", since "the demands of justice can be assessed only with the help of public reasoning", which "is constitutively related to the idea of democracy".[224] "The role of democracy", in its turn, "in preventing community-based violence depends on the ability of inclusive and interactive political processes to subdue the poisonous fanaticism of divisive communal thinking."[225] The importance of equal access to citizens' rights surfaces here as well. In a similar vein, Seyla Benhabib carries "the universalistic norms of discourse ethics beyond the confines of the nation-state".[226] She argues that a "discursive approach should place *significant limitations* on what can account as *morally permissible* practices of inclusion and exclusion within sovereign politics."[227] "The 'right to have rights,' in Arendt's memorable formulation, prohibits states from denaturalizing individuals by denying them citizenship rights and state protection."[228]

In another recent work, Axel Honneth too views "the political sphere of public deliberation and decision-making", characterized by a comprehensive 'we', as the essence of achieving freedom.[229] A common struggle for freedom is essential for democratic politics – a view that ties in most naturally with the constitutional idea and an 'ethos of human rights'. The intrinsic property of every human being – personal dignity – has precedence over that which distinguishes people from one another. After the endorsement of political participation rights since 1968 in Western Europe,

---

[222] Ibid. 287/248.

[223] Building on, but also going beyond the work of Hannah Arendt, is Alison Kesby's recently published discussion of various placeholders for the subject of "the right to have rights". See Alison Kesby, *The Right to Have Rights. Citizenship, Humanity, and International Law* (OUP 2012).

[224] Amartya Sen, *The Idea of Justice* (The Belknap Press of Harvard UP 2009) 326.

[225] Ibid. 352.

[226] Benhabib, *Another Cosmopolitanism* (n. 29) 18.

[227] Ibid. 19.

[228] Ibid. 25.

[229] Axel Honneth, *Das Recht der Freiheit. Grundriß einer demokratischen Sittlichkeit* [The right to freedom. Outline of a democratic morality] (Suhrkamp 2011) 470–471, cf. 509.

gradually spilling over to Eastern Europe – ending up with the collapse of the communist political systems in 1989 – a line could finally be drawn under the post-war remnants of collectivism. Democratic citizenship – in a fortunate concurrence of liberation from authoritarian structures and ways of thinking – seemed to be an achievement. In neoliberalism – which claimed the dissolution of the communist power block ascribed to Ronald Reagan and Margaret Thatcher as its achievement – the liberation from ideology took on a radical form: not only were authoritarian ideologies pushed aside, so were democratic social and emancipatory movements. As a result, political citizens' rights were more and more separated from the broader context of fundamental rights, which after all includes social fundamental rights and the 'third generation' of collective fundamental rights such as the right to development. The unprecedented economic growth in the last two decades of the twentieth century and the first few years of the twenty-first in fact made it possible to dismantle many structures based on public solidarity, now that more and more people could meet their needs themselves. The neoliberal philosophy of the Chicago School has turned this policy shift into a political ideology.[230]

In various Western European states, even Christian Democrat and Social Democrat parties (or parts of them) had at that time aligned themselves with the new economic approach, which also prompted a momentous change of direction in the development of the European Union.[231] In the last decade of the twentieth century, the assimilation required for the common market and economic and monetary union was no longer sought primarily – as in the original community conception – through rules and standards applicable to the whole of the Union but by abolishing government interference in certain areas. The banking system, public utilities and other public services were gradually surrendered to market forces, and the common currency was exposed to the financial markets without a common budgetary policy being introduced.

In terms of formal properties, democratic citizenship and the rights associated with it did withstand the vicissitudes of the political climate, but the demise of the basis of interpersonal solidarity was not without consequences. Two different developments, both affecting the understanding of citizenship, were key factors here.

---

[230] Crouch, *The Strange Non-Death of Neoliberalism* (n. 202) 15–23.
[231] Ernst M.H. Hirsch Ballin, *Christianity and the Future of Christian Democracy* (2013 Annual Lecture Christianity and Society, Tilburg University School of Catholic Theology 2013).

First, the security of this kind of society – apparently unassailable once the military threat from the Soviet block disappeared – was brought into question in a highly visible manner by the terrorist attacks by Al Qaeda. This movement, which arose partly from the aversion of spiritual leaders such as Sayyid Qutb to the ostentatiously liberal, non-solidarity-based American lifestyle, selected for their extremely violent attack a symbolic target par excellence in the World Trade Center and the people who were working there. After the collapse of the Soviet power block, the common enemy was no longer an external foe but a cultural enemy "within our gates", part of the so-called "Clash of Civilizations".[232] The prejudicial characterization of many immigrants as cultural aliens placed the essence of democratic citizenship under pressure. Partly as a result of this development, a basic feature of liberal political culture, namely individual freedom of thought and action, was shown to be fundamentally fragile. After the 9/11 attacks and other similarly motivated terrorist activities (e.g. the attack on the Atocha railway station in Madrid and the murder of the Dutch film director Theo van Gogh), immigrants in Western Europe – especially those from Muslim countries – were increasingly branded as a fifth column whose aim is to bring down the Western liberal political system. This opinion was disseminated particularly in parts of the mass media and by populist parties, but occasionally by people from the liberal 'elite' too. They justifiably dismissed taboos about violent and intolerant instances of islamic presence in immigrant communities[233] – in reality only small minorities – but overlooked how they themselves fell prey to endorsing the extremists' view of "the true Islam" as their concept of the enemy.[234] During the first decade of the twenty-first century, and particularly from the beginning of the second decade, in Western Europe we have seen a pattern described in a longitudinal sociological study by the University of Bielefeld as "group-targeted misanthropy",[235] often based on fears about "demographic Islamization, threat of terrorism, political Islam, fanaticism, cultural difference".[236] These fears, combined with the demise

---

[232] Huntington (n. 130).

[233] See Hanspeter Kriesi and Timotheos Frey, 'The Netherlands. A challenge that was slow in coming' in Kriese and others (n. 77) 162–163.

[234] Anne Norton, *On the Muslim Question* (Princeton UP 2013).

[235] Wilhelm Heitmeyer (ed.), *Deutsche Zustände. Folge 10* [German conditions. No 10] (Suhrkamp 2012).

[236] Anna Klein and Wilhelm Heitmeyer, 'Demokratie auf dem rechten Weg? Entwicklungen rechtspopulistischer Orientierungen und politischen Verhaltens in den letzten zehn Jahren' [Democracy on the right track? Developments in right-wing populist movements and political behavior in the last ten years] in Heitmeyer (n. 235) 91.

of economic growth and rising unemployment, are resulting in 'precariza-tion' – an increasing feeling of being in a precarious situation – that is only fueling these social phobias.[237] They are reflected politically and legally in renewed attempts to segregate and exclude aliens and other discredited groups (e.g. benefit recipients and artists living on an 'infusion from the state'). This development is significant to our topic in that it represents an attack on the reciprocity without distinction that underlies the notion of democratic citizenship.[238]

Secondly, the protection of the socio-economic autonomy of citizens came under pressure. The post-war endorsement of the social market economy throughout Western Europe[239] came under pressure from the 1990s, with such things as the deregulation of protective legislation and the restriction of social security entitlements. The movement in economic theory which had originated in the Anglo-Saxon world from the "Chicago School" triggered a curtailment of public law solidarity under the political leadership of Ronald Reagan in the United States and Margaret Thatcher in the United Kingdom. This pattern of changes spread in the last decades of the twentieth century to the continent of Europe. In several countries, social security rights were restricted. Other aspects of the deregulation were the aforementioned abolition of restrictions on banks and audi-tors,[240] whereas relatively broad sections of the population – politically more or less in return – were allowed to reap the benefits of economic growth, partly – through public borrowing and private mortgages – as an

---

[237] Jürgen Mansel, Oliver Christ and Wilhelm Heitmeyer, 'Der Effekt von Prekarisierung auf fremdenfeindliche Einstellungen. Ergebnisse aus einem Drei-Wellen-Panel and zehn jährlichen Surveys' [The effect of precarization on xenophobic attitudes. Results from a three-wave panel and ten annual surveys] in Heitmeyer (n. 235) 105–28.

[238] At first sight it is curious to see politicians with a neoliberal economic agenda – in the United States, Israel and the Netherlands and elsewhere – entering into alliances with xenophobic populist movements. The need for a large, flexible workforce plays an impor-tant role in the neoliberal program, so support is readily obtained from this area for policy that withholds protection for immigrants who lose their jobs, even though they are helping to meet this need; cf. the agreements on the removal of immigrants who lose their income in the VVD-PVV-CDA parliamentary support agreement (concluded in October 2010 and renounced by the PVV in April 2012), and the criticism of European and international rules that provide social security for people from third countries.

[239] This was not a system "of unrestrained market, but of *Ordoliberalismus* – an economic liberalism, whose competitive order would be guaranteed by law", see Crouch, *The Strange Non-Death of Neoliberalism* (n. 202).

[240] Ibid. 16–17; cf. Crouch, *The Strange Non-Death of Neoliberalism* (n. 202) 95: "The deregulation agenda that led to the irresponsible development of financial markets during the 1990s was itself the result of impressive lobbying in the US Congress and administra-tion by banking interests."

advance on future economic growth.[241] The abandonment of the state's redistribution function was thus rendered acceptable by a vast expansion of private credit. This was in fact a partial retreat by the state from its core function of providing solidarity based on public law. According to Colin Crouch, the "ideological triumph of neoliberalism has led to too much reliance been placed on the bundles of quasi-market and corporate forces that constitute the economy."[242]

The implications for the legal and the constitutional order were – and still are – far-reaching. The idea that firms "are the sole sources of wealth creation" effectively de-centered citizenship and democratic processes of law-making about e.g. education, research, and the systems of civil and criminal justice."[243] Although this view proved no longer tenable after the 2008 banking crisis and the monetary crisis in the euro zone that followed two years later, neoliberalism mostly survived. The fact that the state had no option but to save the situation by taking on the debts of the banking system and cutting its own expenditure, consolidates to a large extent the preceding curtailment of the functions of the state. Where human rights are cited to protect e.g. the social security of artists or migrating workers, leading politicians of the liberal party in the Netherlands have even argued in favor of restricting the judicial function of protecting human rights.[244]

Nevertheless, some signs of a change of direction surface. On the one hand "even some neoliberals now concede a need for some regulation",[245] on the other hand "forces generally known as civil society (...) generate a genuine pluralism. Civil society will be stronger, the more the state and the giant firm are challenged – by churches, voluntary organizations, professions and other participants in the fragmented world of values – and required to participate in a pluralist dialogue that escapes their control."[246] The democratic rights based on citizenship basically reinforce the significance of being an active citizen in the wider sense of citizenship, i.e. being an active member of society.

In the previous section I described the democratic polity as a way of organizing mutual solidarity. This role has not been played out; indeed it

[241] Crouch, *The Strange Non-Death of Neoliberalism* (n. 202) 115 calls this "privatized Keynesianism".
[242] Ibid. 166.
[243] Ibid. 1567.
[244] Stef Blok, Klaas Dijkhoff and Joost Taverne, 'Verdragen mogen niet langer rechtstreeks werken' [Treaties should no longer be directly applicable] *NRC Handelsblad* (Rotterdam, 23 February 2012).
[245] Crouch, *The Strange Non-Death of Neoliberalism* (n. 202) 170.
[246] Ibid. 175.

has regained significance because of the destabilizing effects of free market fundamentalism and 'group-targeted misanthropy'. Upholding good democratic customs, however valuable they may be, is meanwhile not enough, to reassure people experiencing the loss of certainties previously associated with the post-war twentieth-century political and social system. The crisis of confidence that at the beginning of the twenty-first century undermined liberal democracy – that had only recently been eulogized – was not only due to a negative turn in the economic trend, but also to the fact that the state has paid no heed to the losers of globalization.[247] In his book "Post-Democracy", Crouch emphasizes that the victims of irresponsible profit-directed economic behaviour are being told that globalization, personified in "the immigrants", is the root-source of their decline.[248]

2.6 Democratic Citizenship

Reinforcement of the idea of citizenship has a role to play here. It must be energetic, and it must not be confined to those who are 'insiders' in some way or other. If they are to fulfill their purpose, citizens' rights will at least have to bridge the gap between the realities of society and the democratic political system once more, which means combating exclusion mechanisms and promoting greater cohesion. This – as Seyla Benhabib points out – requires constitutional law to develop so as to cut across the segregating, restrictive effects of nationality,[249] internally in the relationship between immigrants and the established population, externally when citizens themselves migrate. In another context she refers to this as "transformations of citizenship".[250] As soon as and insofar as we acknowledge this, we have to draw on ideological sources of dedication to shared freedom and mutual respect in the politics of the early twenty-first century. The remainder of this book will continue on these lines. This will be essential if we are to keep the idea of the democratic constitutional state alive. I shall not seek the answer in the idealistic but unrealistic espousal

---

[247] See also Hanspeter Kriesi and others, 'Globalization and its impact on national spaces of competition' in Kriesi and others (n. 77) 8.

[248] Crouch, *Post-Democracy* (Polity 2004) 119.

[249] Benhabib, *Another Cosmopolitanism* (n. 29) 47–9: in "democratic iterations" that result in "jurisgenerative processes".

[250] Seyla Benhabib, 'Transformations of Citizenship. The Case of Contemporary Europe' in Richard Bellamy and Antonino Palumbo (eds.), *Citizenship* (Ashgate 2010) 414.

of an all-embracing, cosmopolitan citizenship in the legal sense, nor shall I seek it in citizenship related to a single state in mutual exclusivity. The democratic, open citizenship that I subsequently outline also provides a building block for the foundation and fine-tuning of theoretical concepts of the state. In Seyla Benhabib's definition – a fundamental one – the principle of democracy means that "the people are not only the object but also the authors of the law to which they are subject".[251]

While citizenship is legally grounded in ties with a state, as political power remains predominantly organized at that level,[252] the effects of twenty-first-century citizenship are just as transnational as life itself.[253] As the political vicissitudes discussed in this section show, a constitutional system is built on quicksand if it ignores real social and economic differences. This is what happens when the utilitarian lines of reasoning customary in neoliberal arguments take the free will of 'everyone' as their starting point, "neglectful of the claims of those who are too subdued or broken to have the courage to desire much."[254] In reality, as Amartya Sen showed back in 1990, it is the absence of an individual's "basic capabilities" due to personal and social deprivation that is the cause of poverty and "lack of substantive freedom."[255] In his *Identity and Violence*, Sen has pointed out how inequality, combined with differences in imputed 'identity', results in structural injustice and violence.[256]

Here we need to consider whether, as Bedorf says, a politics of shared freedom is still feasible in the current historical and media situation.[257] Has the dominating role of mass media triggered a drying out of the public sphere?[258] Political theory based on equal democratic citizenship seems to be almost too good to be true, and not everyone will still have the confidence to answer Bedorf's question in the affirmative. Nevertheless, the broad meaning of a polis[259] is also apparent in our twenty-first-century urbanized world. Citizenship therefore shows itself to be meaningful in a combination of roles that are all related to it: as participants in the political process, even though this has become subject to the influence of

---

[251] Benhabib, *Another Cosmopolitanism* (n. 29) 47–48.
[252] Crouch, *Post-Democracy* (n. 248) 173.
[253] Crouch, *Post-Democracy* (n. 248) 178.
[254] Amartya Sen, *Inequality Reexamined* (Russell Sage Foundation/Clarendon Press 1992) 149.
[255] Ibid. 151.
[256] Sen, *Identity and Violence* (n. 49) 1–4, 145–146.
[257] Bedorf (n. 218) 36–37.
[258] Honneth (n. 229) 556.
[259] Crouch, *Post-Democracy* (n. 248) 152.

economic superpowers; through active participation, making use of and where necessary invoking human rights as a whole; and as it were at the crossroads of political and social participation in civil society that – in Crouch's view – is the only hope of countering the major corporations that determine our socio-economic reality. The answer to Bedorf's urgent question is therefore not cynical resignation. We ought to explore the force of citizenship that has the courage to stand up for itself, encouraged by a practical necessity – in the disquieting context of a world that seems to have become the plaything of processes beyond democratic control.

From this springs the dynamism of the constitutional concept of citizenship at this juncture. Democratic citizenship is a feature of the constitutional order if it is based on the human rights ethos of the "sacredness of the person":[260] solidarity among equals, within a state but also transnationally. It is always tied to a polity, but not necessarily and exclusively to one particular polity, which is why I intend to examine the possibility of transnational citizenship in the ensuing part of this book. The realities of the twenty-first century include the fact that centuries of migration – stepped up in our present era – have brought together in the towns and cities people of different origins, to whom a variety of ethnic, cultural and religious identities can be imputed. Polarization along such dividing lines of identity hampers the state's attempts to organize the mutual solidarity that is needed. It is *in* the state and other constitutional relationships that democratic citizenship will need to unite them, without ignoring differences and tensions. My analysis of the relationship between citizenship and human rights in the next chapter will therefore have to take into account the intrinsic interrelationship between the various facets of human rights, including social, economic and cultural rights.

---

[260] Hans Joas, *The Sacredness of the Person* (n. 36).

CHAPTER THREE

REDEFINING CITIZENSHIP

3.1 *What Makes a Person a Citizen?*

The previous chapter explored the social and political context in which citizenship takes on its current constitutional significance.[261] Linking citizenship to a supposed specific ethnic or religious identity – even if that appeared to be "natural" in closed societies of the past – is unjustifiable in a modern society. On the contrary, in a world on the move, a fundamental openness is needed to what people contribute to the communities in which they live and work. Citizenship or nationality of a state – for reasons that will be explained further on, I will not attribute a substantive difference in meaning to these terms – has thus become the basis for equal protection, solidarity and a democratic voice in the norms by which citizens feel bound. With this in mind let us now consider what legally makes a person a citizen or national of a state, and in particular which rights accompany citizenship.

Nationality is the status that entitles a person to citizens' rights, the status that is fleshed out in the legal relationships between the state and the citizen.[262] Whether nationality is regulated by the constitution differs from one state to another, but there can be no doubt that its demarcation is one of the constitutional characteristics of a state ("the boundaries of the constitution").[263] In traditional European theory the state is paramount. Klaus Stern, for instance, in his definition of *Staatsangehörigkeit* (literally 'belonging to a state'), considers that it is from its sovereignty that

---

[261] On the definition of citizenship and the counter-concept of alienage, see Linda Bosniak, *The Citizen and the Alien. Dilemmas of Contemporary Membership* (Princeton UP 2006).

[262] Klaus Stern discusses whether *Staatsangehörigkeit* is a legal relationship or a status under German constitutional law in *Das Staatsrecht der Bundesrepublik Deutschland, bd 1* [The constitutional law of the Federal Republic of Germany, vol 1] (2nd edn, C.H. Beck 1984). He regards the International Court of Justice's Nottebohm judgment as containing a synthesis [*vermittelnde Theorie*], which he himself summarizes as an *Inbegriff von Rechten und Pflichten* [quintessence of rights and obligations].

[263] Kim Rubenstein and Niamh Lenagh-Maguire, 'Citizenship and the Boundaries of the Constitution' in Tom Ginsburg and Rosalind Dixon (eds.), *Comparative Constitutional Law* (Edward Elgar 2011) 143.

the state derives its right to regulate the conditions for belonging to that state. *Staatsangehörigkeit* is part of the state's "internal affairs", and Stern interprets it as forming part of a collective, the *Staatsvolk* (nation).[264]

Dutch textbooks do not generally expatiate on theories of Dutch nationality; they simply describe as a matter of fact how it is acquired, what rights and obligations it entails, and how it is regulated. Article 2 (1) of the Dutch Constitution merely issues a superfluous instruction to the legislature, laying down no substantive norms: "It shall be laid down by law who is a Dutch national." More significant in normative terms are the ensuing provisions, which guarantee equal appointability to public office (Article 3) and equal rights to vote and to stand for election (Article 4) to all Dutch nationals.

Ways of acquiring nationality recognized in international law are the nationality of one or both parents (*ius sanguinis*, literally 'right of blood') and the place of birth (*ius soli*, 'right of the soil') and certain subsequent life events, namely adoption, recognition and voluntary acts like marriage, the acquisition of permanent domicile (legal place of residence), and entering the service of the state.[265] Based on the customary international yardsticks, an international group of scholars has surveyed the rules on the acquisition and loss of nationality that are applied in fifteen EU member states.[266] A study by Rubenstein and Lenagh-Maguire focusing on a number of common-law countries shows that the extent to which and the way in which nationality is regulated constitutionally differs from one country to another and one period to another. Inherent in any system of constitutional law, however, is that nationality helps to determine the scope – the boundaries – of a constitution and is manifested in the constitutional and other rights that citizens derive from this status.[267]

The fact that traditional international law has little to say about individual persons is understandable, given the principle upon which it is

---

[264] Stern (n. 262) 156: "Aus der Souveränität des Staates folgt sein Recht, die Bedingungen der Angehörigkeit zu ihm zu regeln. Staatsangehörigkeit ist ein Bestandteil der inneren Angelegenheiten eines Staates; durch sie wird das Staatsvolk konstituiert und der Träger der Souveränität formiert" [From the sovereignty of the state follows its right to regulate the conditions for its nationality. Nationality is part of the internal affairs of a state; through it the nation is constituted and the carriers of sovereignty are formed].

[265] Cf. Olivier Vonk, *Dual Nationality in the European Union. A Study on Changing Norms in Public and Private International Law and in the Municipal Laws of Four EU Member States* (Martinus Nijhoff Publishers 2012) 37 note 135; James Crawford, *Brownlie's Principles of Public International Law* (8th edn, OUP 2012) 512.

[266] Rainer Bauböck and others (eds.), *Acquisition and Loss of Nationality. Policies and Trends in 15 European States. Vol. I: Comparative Analyses* (Amsterdam UP 2006).

[267] Rubenstein and Lenagh-Maguire (n. 263).

based, namely the sovereignty of individual states.[268] The nationality of persons plays a particularly important role in the demarcation of jurisdiction: deciding which persons to regard as its nationals is a *domaine réservé* of the state.[269] The fact that each state is able to enforce its own nationality legislation, however, raises the question of whether that legislative freedom is limited by international law. The standard ruling on this subject by the International Court of Justice, in the Nottebohm case on 6 April 1955, confirmed that this is the case. Friedrich Nottebohm, born 1881 in Germany, had lived and worked mainly in Guatemala from 1905. In 1943, when Guatemala had joined Germany's opponents in the Second World War, he unsuccessfully claimed Liechtenstein nationality, which he had acquired in 1939. The International Court of Justice rejected Liechtenstein's petition against this, based on the following fundamental considerations, cited in many treatises:

> It is for Liechtenstein, as it is for every sovereign State, to settle by its own legislation the rules relating to the acquisition of its nationality, and to confer that nationality by naturalization granted by its own organs in accordance with that legislation. It is not necessary to determine whether international law imposes any limitations on its freedom of decision in this domain. Furthermore, nationality has its most immediate, its most far-reaching and, for most people, its only effects within the legal system of the State conferring it. Nationality serves above all to determine that the person upon whom it is conferred enjoys the rights and is bound by the obligations which the law of the State in question grants to or imposes on its nationals. This is implied in the wider concept that nationality is within the domestic jurisdiction of the State.[270]

> Nationality is a legal bond having as its basis a social fact of attachment, a genuine connection of existence, interests and sentiments, together with the existence of reciprocal rights and duties. It may be said to constitute the juridical expression of the fact that the individual upon whom it is conferred, either directly by the law or as the result of an act of the authorities, is in fact more closely connected with the population of the State conferring nationality than with that of any other State. Conferred by a State, it only entitles that State to exercise protection vis-à-vis another State, if it

---

[268] Cf. Ernst M.H. Hirsch Ballin, *Wereldburgers. Personen in het internationale recht* [World Citizens. Persons in International Law] (inaugural lecture Tilburg University, W.E.J. Tjeenk Willink 1995).

[269] See Anne Peters, 'Extraterritorial Naturalizations. Between the Human Right to Nationality. State Sovereignty and Fair Principles of Jurisdiction' (2010) 53 *German Yearbook of International Law* 623, 629 referring to PCIJ 17 February 1923 Series B no. 4, 24.

[270] *Liechtenstein v Guatemala (Nottebohm case)* [1955] ICJ (1955) 4 ICJ Reports 20.

constitutes a translation into juridical terms of the individual's connection with the State which has made him its national.[271]

The international law doctrine and the arguments put forward in this judgment contain the nucleus of the answer to whether nationality should be regarded primarily as something inherent in a person – owing to something over which he or she has no control (descent or place of birth, the result of a "Birthright Lottery", to quote the title of Ayelet Shachar's book[272]) – or something determined by his or her personal life story.[273] In the former case, the role of the national government is that of an authority that decides unilaterally, based on statutory rules, whereas in the latter citizens may have a share in the possession of nationality. In principle, states are free to formulate and apply their nationality legislation, but without a "genuine link" and an "effective link" such legislation is legally meaningless in relation to other states.[274]

Also questionable in international law is the unsolicited granting of nationality to populations resident outside the state's own territory.[275] An amendment to the Hungarian Nationality Act that came into force on 1 January 2011 allows Hungarian-speaking descendants of former Hungarian nationals to apply for Hungarian nationality even if they do not live in Hungary. This would enable the Hungarian population of 10 million to be swelled by some two million expats. In this case, the 'link' could be the previous extension of Hungarian nationality, but this cannot be equated with the retention of a link with the former fatherland on emigration. Although strictly speaking this is not a collective naturalization of nationals of other states, the neighboring countries concerned regarded it as such[276] in breach of the June 1920 Treaty of Trianon. In that treaty, Hungary, placed under extreme international pressure, had not only relinquished

---

[271] Ibid. 23.

[272] Ayelet Shachar, *The Birthright Lottery. Citizenship and Global Inequality* (Harvard UP 2009).

[273] Rubenstein and Lenagh-Maguire (n. 263).

[274] Ian Brownlie, *Principles of International Public Law* (OUP 2008) 398–99.

[275] See Anne Peters, 'Les Changements Collectifs De Nationalité' [Collective Change of Nationality] (2011) in The Société Française pour le Droit International, *Droit International et Nationalité* (Editions A. Pedone 2012) <http://ssrn.com/abstract=1971860> accessed 31 July 2012; For the effects of granting or taking away nationality in contravention of international law cf. Gerard-René de Groot and Nicole Doeswijk, 'Nationaliteitsrecht en het internationale recht' [Nationality law and international law] in F.J.H. van der Velden, G.-R. de Groot and N. Doeswijk, *De nationaliteit in internationaal en Europees perspectief. Mededelingen van de Nederlandse Vereniging voor Internationaal Recht no. 129* (TMC Asser Presss, 2004) 94–96.

[276] Peters, 'Les Changement Collectifs De Nationalité' (n. 275) 169.

large areas to neighboring countries[277] but had also accepted a nationality system imposed upon it.[278] At that time, states controlled the nationality of their subjects. Nowadays, this can no longer be regarded as decisive, nor can it be collectively undone in a top-down manner. Individual confirmation of the continued existence of a bond with Hungary by the persons concerned would therefore have to be the deciding factor.

There is one aspect of the Nottebohm case that has only been considered by a few commentators,[279] namely why Nottebohm – who had left Germany 34 years previously – was trying to obtain a different nationality (that of the country where his brother was living): now that he was an internationally active resident of Guatemala, he had good reasons for not wanting to be treated as a national of a 'belligerent nation'. The judges at the International Court of Justice differed regarding the extent to which, as Guatemala contended, Nottebohm or the Principality of Liechtenstein could be accused of fraudulent behavior. But was it reasonable for Guatemala and the United States (whence Nottebohm, regarded by the latter as a German, was deported, his property having been confiscated) to disenfranchise someone who for his part had done everything so as not to be identified with his country of birth as an enemy subject? In the First World War, *The Sunday Times* had described the morality of this line of conduct in clear terms: "It seems false sentiment or foolish generosity not to treat the citizens of those countries in exactly the way that our fellow-countrymen are treated in the German empire."[280] This rule was still uncontroversial at the time of the Second World War. The United Kingdom too, for example, initially interned even Jewish refugees who had fled from Germany as 'enemy aliens', heedless of the fact that the Nazi regime had revoked their German citizenship. This approach reduces people to subjects of their states, the relationship between those states being the deciding factor in the treatment they receive in the other state. However long Nottebohm had lived and worked in Guatemala legally, what befell him was the antithesis of protection as a citizen, enabling his physical freedom

---

[277] MacMillan (n. 160) 265–78.
[278] Article 61 of the Treaty of Trianon reads: "Toute personne ayant l'indigénat (pertinenza) sur un territoire faisant anterieurement partie des territoires de l'ancienne monarchie austro-hongroise acquerra de plein droit, et à l'exclusion de la nationalité hongroise, la nationalité de l'État exerçant la souveraineté sur ledit territoire." (Any person indigenous to a territory formerly forming part of the territories of the former Austro-Hungarian monarchy shall acquire by full right, and to the exclusion of Hungarian nationality, the nationality of the State exercising sovereignty over the said territory.)
[279] Brownlie (n. 274) 407–18.
[280] 'Enemy Subjects - shall all be interned?' *Sunday Times* (Perth, 23 May 1915) front page.

and property rights – rights that are part of everyone's human rights – to be affected. Since then, the notion has developed that the treatment of non-combatants in war should comply with the principle of proportionality. As Betsy Parebo describes it, "enemy subjects should be treated in accordance with three criteria, which I will refer to as 'conduct', 'status', and 'guilt'".[281] This should apply even more to the treatment of residents as enemy subjects.

In 2005, the Inter-American Court of Human Rights pithily defined nationality as "a juridical expression of a social fact that connects an individual to a State".[282] In the terminological observations at the beginning of his book on *Dual Nationality in the European Union*, Olivier Vonk explains why he eschews the term 'citizenship', instead using 'nationality', with reference to continental European traditions.[283] By this he means "a formal legal bond between an individual and a State"; he regards 'citizenship' as a non-legal term referring to "political membership of a State". Later on, Vonk concurs with G.R. de Groot's view that 'nationality' is an "empty notion": what rights are associated with it is determined by particular legislative decisions.[284] Conversely, the major work on comparative constitutional law edited by Ginsburg and Dixon uses the term 'citizenship' with no further discussion, sometimes alternating with 'nationality' as a synonym.[285]

The Dutch legal scholar H.U. Jessurun d'Oliveira notes that "nationality represents a formal, privileged relationship between a person and a particular state, to which as a rule certain fixed rights and obligations are linked, the aggregate of which is referred to for short as 'citizenship'".[286] Given the view that states in principle have the sovereign right to decide who their subjects are, John Dugard regards the term 'nationality' as more appropriate in international law, where it "denotes that there is a legal connection between the individual and the state for external purposes".[287] The rights of the persons concerned only come into the picture when he

[281] Betsy Perabo, 'The Proportionate Treatment of Enemy Subjects. A Reformulation of the Principle of Discrimination' (2008) 7 *Journal of Military Ethics* 136, 138.

[282] *Yean and Bosico v Dominican Republic* [2005] Inter-American Court of Human Rights Series C No. 130 (8 September 2005).

[283] Vonk (n. 265) 1 note 1, 19.

[284] Ibid. 32–34.

[285] Rubenstein and Lenagh-Maguire (n. 263) 143ff.

[286] Hans Ulrich Jessurun D'Oliveira, 'Europees burgerschap: dubbele nationaliteit?' [European citizenship: dual nationality?] in *Europees burgerschap* (Asser Instituut Colloquium Europees recht, 33ste zitting – 2003, T.M.C. Asser Press 2004) 92.

[287] John Dugard, *International Law. A South African Perspective* (Juta & Co. 2000) 208.

examines this subject from the point of view of states' own legal systems: "Citizenship, on the other hand, is a term of constitutional law and is best used to describe the status of individuals internally, particularly the aggregate of civil and political rights to which they are entitled."[288]

It goes without saying that different terms can be used depending on the context, but this only makes sense if they can be used with different meanings. International law cannot lend significance to nationality if domestic law fails to do so; conversely, once a state adopts a wider (or for that matter more limited) application to nationality than international law permits, this causes problems for its own nationals. Whatever the underlying problem may have been, this was precisely the significance of the Nottebohm judgment.

Legal terms are not terminological keys that open every door; they are connected with social realities in an ongoing historical process of creation, interpretation and development of the law – the 'iterations' referred to in § 3.2.[289] Attempts to distinguish between nationality and citizenship (of a state) in a legal sense[290] – the sociological aspects are a different story – are fairly pointless,[291] unless national law (like the British Nationality Act 1981) distinguishes between "citizenship" and "nationality". In their comparative law study cited earlier, Rubenstein and Lenagh-Maguire prefer the term 'citizenship', but other legal scholars like to use 'nationality' to denote a legal status. Although 'citizenship' and 'nationality' are used synonymously in this book, we should not ignore the terminological connotations. 'Nationality' particularly evokes associations with a national state that decides on this status by virtue of its 'sovereignty', where a person is a subject of the state, formerly of the sovereign. 'Citizenship', on the other hand, expresses the fact that it is the legal status of a citizen of a polity, and this term should therefore be preferred, especially in view of the iterations of this concept and its relationship with human rights. This is also true of the French, Italian and Spanish terms *citoyenneté*, *cittadinanza*, *ciudadanía* and the German and Dutch terms *Staatsbürgerschaft* (which avoids the connotations of *Staatsangehörigkeit*) and *staatsburgerschap*.

---

[288] Ibid. 209.

[289] This is also the case e.g. with the legal concept of marriage and the Dutch constitutional concept of 'the Monarch'. For the development of this latter concept in Dutch constitutional law, see Hirsch Ballin, *De Koning* (n. 159).

[290] E.g. Pieter Boeles and others, *European Migration Law* (Intersentia 2009) 19.

[291] Cf. Flora Goudappel, *The Effects of EU Citizenship. Economic, Social and Political Rights in a Time of Constitutional Change* (T.M.C Asser Press 2010) 25.

It may be pointed out that not all citizens of a state enjoy 'full citizenship rights', for example because they are minors or non-residents, just as resident aliens can sometimes exercise limited citizens' rights, such as voting in local elections, but it is not particularly helpful for legal purposes to invent a separate status ('citizenship without nationality'?),[292] as the rights assigned to this status will also differ from one case to another. It is more transparent conceptually to consider that in principle – only a conviction in court for serious crimes could under certain conditions[293] present an obstacle to this – citizens fully enjoy citizenship rights and most of these are reserved for the nationals of that country. What legal consequences determine the precise nature of e.g. nationality/citizenship at a particular place and time is not an unchanging fact of nature but the subject of legal study and interpretation. The idea that 'nationality' is an empty notion ignores the fact that *every* legal term is subject to continual reinterpretation.

'Nationality' and 'citizenship' denotes – as explained in § 1.2 – a specific legal bond between a state (or other public entity) and a person, entailing rights and obligations. However, 'citizenship' – unlike 'nationality' – does not have exclusive connotations in relation to a national state; in the case of 'citizenship', what the person is a citizen *of* in the legal sense always needs to be specified. It could be a town or municipality (although this is of little significance legally in most twenty-first-century societies), a state (here 'citizenship' can be used synonymously with 'nationality'), and in principle of a political entity comprising more than one state. Because the definition of 'citizenship' can thus be related to various polities, this notion should be preferred to 'nationality', even though this latter term can be used as a synonym. 'Citizenship' is also the term used in the Constitution of the United States of America. Paragraph 1 of the 14th amendment (Citizenship Rights) reads as follows: "All persons born or naturalized in the United States, and subject to the jurisdiction thereof, are citizens of the United States and of the State wherein they reside. No State shall make or enforce any law which shall abridge the privileges or immunities of citizens of the United States; nor shall any State deprive any person of life, liberty, or property, without due process of law; nor deny to any person within its jurisdiction the equal protection of the laws."

---

[292] There is good reason, however, to ensure that lack of nationality does not operate as a criterion that rules out rights, cf. T. Alexander Aleinikoff, *Semblances of Sovereignty. The Constitution, the State, and American Citizenship* (Harvard UP 2002) 1, 77–81.

[293] *Hirst v United Kingdom* (No. 2) [2005] ECHR 681 (2006) 42 EHHR 41.

There is another substantial argument for referring to 'citizenship' rather than 'nationality', however. As explained in Chapter 1, citizenship can be traced back historically to the emancipation of citizens, based on political and legal values, initially in the towns and cities, and etymologically to the Latin word *civitas* (city), whereas nationality refers to *natio*, the fact of being born (*natus*) in a relationship of descent. It would seem more appropriate intrinsically, then, to use the term 'citizenship' rather than 'nationality', even if current thinking is that the latter can be acquired not only by birth but also by means of a legal decision. Citizenship is a concept that is determined by social ethics values and capable of being specified, and its current and possible future meaning is examined in legal studies such as the present one.[294]

In the Dutch Constitution and Dutch law, both facets of this phenomenon are summed up neatly terminologically in the name given to this status: 'Nederlanderschap' (literally "Netherlandership"; see Article 3 (1c) of the Charter for the Kingdom of the Netherlands, Article 2 (1) of the Constitution of the Kingdom of the Netherlands, and the Dutch Nationality Act) is the common nationality of the entire Kingdom, i.e. including its Caribbean countries.

The former second-class nationality of 'Dutch subject' disappeared from the legislation with the transfer of sovereignty over Western New Guinea: the people concerned were collectively given a different nationality.[295] Under the British Nationality Act 1981, being a "British subject" is one of the six different classes of British nationality. The Dutch Aliens Act 2000 (Section 1 (m)) defines 'alien' as "any person who does not hold Dutch nationality and is not required under a statutory provision to be treated as a Dutch national".[296] In migration law, also in other legal systems, 'nationality' or 'citizenship' is the one central concept and 'national' and 'citizen' are synonyms, in contradistinction to the other central concept, i.e. that of 'alien'.[297]

---

[294] This is what jurisprudence does and what differentiates it from the study of 'law' (i.e. the law in force); cf. Ernst M.H. Hirsch Ballin, 'Object en methode van de wetenschap van het staatsrecht en het bestuursrecht' [The object and method of the study of constitutional law and administrative law] in *Rechtsstaat & beleid. Een keuze uit het werk van mr. E.M.H. Hirsch Ballin* (W.E.J. Tjeenk Willink 1992) 95.

[295] Cf. Gerard-René de Groot, *Nationaliteit en rechtszekerheid* [Nationality and security under the law] (inaugural lecture University of Aruba, Boom 2008) 15. Other states too have made distinctions of this kind between citizens and non-citizen nationals, e.g. the United States and Italy. See Brownlie (n. 274) 397.

[296] This latter clause relates to the Act of 9 September 1976 containing rules on the position of Moluccans resident in the Netherlands who do not hold Dutch nationality (Wet betreffende de positie van Molukkers).

[297] Boeles and others (n. 290) 20.

3.2 Citizens' Rights

Citizenship can therefore best be regarded as the status that entitles a person to citizens' rights. What fundamental rights have the nature of citizenship rights can be seen from the documents in question, including the *Déclaration des droits de l'homme et du citoyen*, conventions and a host of constitutions. The connection is the human right to have citizens' rights, the right to nationality.[298] The best way of specifying what citizenship is, then, is to determine what rights are fundamental but not human rights, in other words those that depend – or at least can depend – on a specific, differentiating relationship to the state. Participation and reciprocal involvement in common responsibilities are essential parts of the experience and ideas from which citizenship has developed. These citizens' rights encompass and shape active citizenship,[299] which is why their protection is closely linked to that of human rights (not confined to citizens) such as free speech and freedom of (political) assembly and association. This explains why – as Butenschøn confirms in his article, cited earlier[300] – the recognition of civil rights, i.e. rights that make it possible to participate in civil society, historically preceded that of political rights and social rights (in relation to the authorities); it is also why participation skills are paramount both in the education of every growing young citizen and in the acquisition of citizenship. Jürgen Habermas too notes a recent tendency to regard *Staatsbürgerschaft, citoyenneté,* citizenship not only as "political membership" but also "in terms of civil rights".[301]

The fundamental rights associated with citizenship, citizens' rights, can be divided into three categories:

I. The political rights of a citizen are an extension of the rights enshrined since the *Déclaration des droits de l'homme et du citoyen* in a host of constitutions and – in particular as regards the right to vote – in conventions and, for European Union citizens, in the Charter of Fundamental Rights of

---

[298] Cf. International Covenant on Civil and Political Rights (n. 157) art. 24 (3). As part of the 1983 general revision of the Constitution, the instruction to statutorily regulate Dutch nationality was moved to the chapter on fundamental rights. "This instruction to the legislature as such offers a safeguard to citizens", as the explanatory notes put it in a nutshell, *Kamerstukken II* 1976–1977 14 200 no 3, 6.

[299] 'Aktivbürgerschaft', 'status activus'; cf. Habermas (n. 221) and Friedrich Koja, *Allgemeine Staatslehre* [General Theory of the State] (Manz Verlag 1993) 15–17.

[300] Butenschøn (n. 30) 562.

[301] Jürgen Habermas, 'Citizenship and National Identity: Some Reflections on the Future of Europe' (1992) 12 *Praxis International* 1; included in Richard Bellamy and Antonino Palumbo, *Citizenship* (Ashgate Publishing 2010) 341–59.

the European Union. These are the right to participate in the discussion of public affairs, to vote and stand for election,[302] the right to hold public office,[303] and the right to submit petitions.[304] Article 25 of the ICCPR defines some of the most important citizens' rights:

> Every citizen shall have the right and the opportunity, without any of the distinctions mentioned in article 2 and without unreasonable restrictions:
>
> (a) To take part in the conduct of public affairs, directly or through freely chosen representatives;
> (b) To vote and to be elected at genuine periodic elections which shall be by universal and equal suffrage and shall be held by secret ballot, guaranteeing the free expression of the will of the electors;
> (c) To have access, on general terms of equality, to public service in his country.

II. A citizen's entitlements to protection by his state arise from the idea expressed in old theories of the state, such as Thomas Hobbes', that the sovereign has the duty to protect his subjects, and therefore a citizen, for his part, has a duty of obedience and is required to assist with the defense of the country and other duties in the public interest, such as sitting on a jury and – in Belgium, for example – voting in elections. Rights to protection, in the context of states that subject themselves to the rule of law, are among the fundamental rights associated with citizenship. Some of these have been recognized internationally for a long time: diplomatic and consular protection by states of their 'subjects' living or trading in other states is one of the classic areas of foreign relations. Article 3 of the Vienna Convention on Diplomatic Relations classifies the protection of nationals as a responsibility of diplomatic missions; Article 5 of the Vienna Convention on Consular Relations defines consular functions as including providing assistance and protection in the state of accreditation to nationals of the sending state resident there and their businesses. Article 46 of the EU Charter of Fundamental Rights sets out a corresponding subjective right of European Union citizens: "Every citizen of the Union shall, in the territory of a third country in which the Member State of which he or she

---

[302] E.g. International Covenant on Civil and Political Rights (n. 157) art. 5 and the Grondwet (n. 157) art. 4.
[303] E.g. Grondwet (n. 157) art. 3.
[304] Ibid. art. 5.

is a national is not represented, be entitled to protection by the diplomatic or consular authorities of any Member State, on the same conditions as the nationals of that Member State." Even more elementary is every citizen's right of access to the territory of his or her state, as set out inter alia in Article 3 of the Fourth Protocol to the ECHR and expressed in the case of European Union citizens inter alia in Article 45 of the EU Charter of Fundamental Rights. This right too, assuming the existence of a constitutional state, is a fundamental right of every citizen to protection within his or her state and its legal system. Abolishing the punishment of exile was regarded as a strengthening of citizens' fundamental rights, but this could still happen when a person is deprived of his or her citizenship as a punishment. Everyone however also has the right to leave the country, acknowledged as a human right.[305] Many states ban the extradition of their own nationals; where this has been qualified in order to combat international crime it is combined (for example under Dutch law) with the entitlement to serve any sentence imposed abroad in one's own country.[306] The relaxation of the restrictions on extradition between European Union member states is based on the idea that together they now form an "area of freedom, security and justice"[307] that provides adequate safeguards. How real this assumption is, however, is something we undoubtedly need to keep under continual monitoring.

III. Citizens' rights are at the same time connected with social and economic life, and far more than is acknowledged in the contemporary political view. The French Revolution was also an economic revolution, which put an end to the feudal system and gave free citizens opportunities and rights – in principle – to engage in economic activities on an equal footing. The punishment of total confiscation of property was declared unconstitutional in the Netherlands in 1815. Both of these were reminiscent of the former punishment of civil death. The struggle by the descendants of former slaves to gain their civil rights in America was partly a struggle to end social and economic discrimination. As we know, economic freedom played a key role in the development of European citizenship. The emancipation of women certainly required the ending of restrictions on social

---

[305] E.g. Protocol no. 4 to the Convention for the Protection of Human Rights and Fundamental Freedoms (as amended by Protocol no. 11) art. 2(2) and International Covenant on Civil and Political Rights (n. 157) art. 12 (2).

[306] Uitleveringswet [Extradition Act] art. 4.

[307] Treaty on European Union (Maastricht Treaty), preamble and Treaty on the Functioning of the European Union, part 3 title V.

and economic life, such as the legal incapacity of married women, which was not abolished in the Netherlands until 1956, and the achievement of equal pay, which was imposed by European Union legislation. Citizens' rights thus include the right to act on an equal footing as a legally capable subject. In contrast, limitations on the residence rights of non-nationals restrict their social and economic freedom.

Taken together, these three groups of citizens' rights amount to a framework of freedom protected on a reciprocal basis – hence freedom in a highly meaningful sense, encompassing not only the absence of official compulsion but also protection against want, dependency and humiliation.[308] The individual rights are also protected in many ways by conventions. Certain citizens' rights can form part of the stages leading up to nationality, for example the legal status of aliens with permanent residence permits.[309] Living in another country may mean not being able to exercise all citizens' rights: there are often limitations on voting rights, for instance, and if the person holds the nationality of the state where he or she lives, this may involve limitations on the right to claim protection under a different nationality (see § 3.5).

3.3 Loss and Acquisition of Citizenship

The 1948 Universal Declaration of Human Rights classifies the right to nationality and the right to acquire, retain or change nationality as human rights. Article 15 is clear on the subject:

(1) Everyone has the right to a nationality.
(2) No one shall be arbitrarily deprived of his nationality nor denied the right to change his nationality.[310]

A similar provision can be found in the American Convention on Human Rights:[311]

---

[308] Cf. Sen, *The Idea of Justice* (n. 224) 366–70.

[309] Thomas Faist, 'The Fixed and Porous Boundaries of Dual Citizenship' in Thomas Faist (ed.), *Dual Citizenship in Europe. From Nationhood to Societal Integration* (Ashgate 2007) 37.

[310] Mirna Adjami and Julia Harrington, 'The Scope and Content of Article 15 of the Universal Declaration of Human Rights' (2008) 27 *Refugee Survey Quarterly* 93; cf. the Venice Commission (European Commission for Democracy through Law) of the Council of Europe, cited by Peters, 'Extraterritorial Naturalizations' (n. 269) 660.

[311] Cf. Peters, 'Extraterritorial Naturalizations' (n. 269) 659–61.

Article 20 – Right to Nationality
1. Every person has the right to a nationality.
2. Every person has the right to the nationality of the state in whose territory he was born if he does not have the right to any other nationality.
3. No one shall be arbitrarily deprived of his nationality or of the right to change it.

In a judgment of 8 September 2005, the American Court of Human Rights made some fundamental observations on this provision [136–143], confirming what it had stated in a previous recommendation in 1984:

It is generally accepted today that nationality is an inherent right of all human beings. Not only is nationality the basic requirement for the exercise of political rights, it also has an important bearing on the individual's legal capacity. Thus, despite the fact that it is traditionally accepted that the conferral and regulation of nationality are matters for each state to decide, contemporary developments indicate that international law does impose certain limits on the broad powers enjoyed by the states in that area, and that the manners in which states regulate matters bearing on nationality cannot today be deemed within their sole jurisdiction; those powers of the state are also circumscribed by their obligations to ensure the full protection of human rights. [...] The classic doctrinal position, which viewed nationality as an attribute granted by the State to its subjects, has gradually evolved to a conception of nationality which, in addition to being the competence of the State, is a human right.[312]

The Council of Europe's European Convention on Nationality of 6 November 1997 stipulates norms about nationality, albeit the fact that these are qualified as principles leaves it open how the contracting states are to ensure that it is enforced:

Article 4 – Principles
The rules on nationality of each State Party shall be based on the following principles:
a everyone has the right to a nationality;
b statelessness shall be avoided;
c no one shall be arbitrarily deprived of his or her nationality;
d neither marriage nor the dissolution of a marriage between a national of a State Party and an alien, nor the change of nationality by one of the spouses during marriage, shall automatically affect the nationality of the other spouse.

---

[312] *Yean and Bosico v Dominican Republic* (n. 282) para. 138.

The right to have a nationality is also recognized by the International Convention on the Elimination of All Forms of Racial Discrimination (Article 5 (d) (iii)), but it is not included in the 1966 International Covenant on Civil and Political Rights (ICCPR), which was intended to give legal effect to the Universal Declaration.[313] As a result the Human Rights Committee does not effectively supervise this right. Article 24 (3) of the ICCPR merely lays down that "every child has the right to acquire a nationality", just like Article 7 (1) of the International Convention on the Rights of the Child. A similar provision is part of the International Convention on the protection of the rights of all migrant workers and members of their families, from which so far Europe – apart from a few south-eastern states – has remained aloof. Article 29 reads: "Each child of a migrant worker shall have the right to a name, to registration of birth and to a nationality."

As we have seen from the previous section, however much it may be one of the sovereign powers of a state to decide on nationality, a state may not give it and take it away arbitrarily. This is precisely where we find the connection between the two domains of citizens' rights and human rights. The fact that full enjoyment of citizens' rights is built upon nationality is in line with the original, active meaning of citizenship, *citoyenneté*. But this is also precisely where – apart from its non-binding legal status – Article 15 of the Universal Declaration falls short, as nothing in it prevents states from denying nationality to a person who qualifies for it on the basis of *de facto* integration and long-term residence. The right to a nationality (note the indefinite article!) set out in Article 15 (1) does not have the required normative significance, leaving it open what state is responsible to comply with that right. As a result it is also inadequate when it comes to providing the right to an *effective* nationality for the person concerned, i.e. to protect against *de facto* statelessness (see the next section).[314]

In practice, a situation has come about where many states regard it as their responsibility to recognize people who form permanent members of their society, e.g. *de facto* integrated aliens, as citizens, i.e. to grant applications for naturalization under a fair procedure. In an opposite way, as a result of opposition to migration, denial of nationality – and in some

---

[313] The reason why this right has been omitted was the "complexity of the problem" with respect to statelessness. See Marc J. Bossuyt, *Guide to the "Travaux Préparatoires" of the International Covenant on Civil and Political Rights* (Martinus Nijhoff 1987) 463, 466–467.
[314] Cf. Adjami and Harrington (n. 310) 104.

schemes even deprivation of nationality[315] – is used as part of a policy that aims to raise barriers to migration. The fact that such policies are counter-productive does not always prevent politicians from adopting them. In a penetrating comparison of arrival cities in Europe and elsewhere, Doug Saunders shows that where isolation and denial of nationality have been put into practice, the arrival cities and neighborhoods fail to perform their 'gateway' function, and conversely that acknowledging immigrants in their new social position as citizens makes it successful, to everyone's advantage.[316]

As an example of a failing policy, he describes the effects of denying German nationality to the vast majority of immigrants from Turkey: only 42% of them have become Germans, half the proportion of comparable populations in the United Kingdom.[317] Unlike the situation in the Netherlands in 1992–97, in Germany the requirement to renounce the original nationality when acquiring German nationality has presented a continual obstacle to the integration of immigrants. Doug Saunders describes how counterproductive the German policy is.[318] Germany's great reluctance – compared with other countries – to grant nationality results in low involvement in the receiving society. The effective result of this social and cultural isolation is that immigrants perpetuate or return to practices formerly typical of Turkey's rural areas, which have long been out of date by current Turkish standards.[319]

German nationality legislation is based primarily on descent. This was enshrined in Article 116 of the 1949 Constitution, as Kay Hailbronner points out, mainly because of a desire to offer protection to the many ethnic Germans scattered over Central and Eastern Europe who had been driven out after the Second World War.[320] This system of nationality law, however, was totally unsuitable in the last quarter of the twentieth century

---

[315] The short-lived first Rutte Government intended to introduce 'conditional naturalization': "The Government shall come forward with a proposal to deprive of their Dutch nationality persons who within five years of acquiring Dutch nationality are convicted of a crime that carries a sentence of twelve years or more." (*Kamerstukken II* 32 417 no. 15, 26 and 71.)
[316] Saunders (n. 88).
[317] Ibid. 35.
[318] Vonk (n. 265) 63 mentions Spiro's view that "obstacles to naturalization" are highly undesirable; the possibility of multiple nationality "is even demanded by republican, communitarian and liberal conceptions of citizenship".
[319] Saunders (n. 88) 35, 241ff. Ateş (n. 148) 16 describes this lack of reciprocal integration as the development of "Parallelgesellschaften" [parallel societies].
[320] Kay Hailbronner, 'Germany' in Rainer Bauböck and others (eds.), *Acquisition and Loss of Nationality. Policies and Trends in 15 European States. Vol. II. Country Analyses* (Amsterdam UP 2006) 229.

to acknowledge the many immigrants, mainly from Turkey, as fellow citizens. Even after decades of legal residence and active participation they remain *de jure* aliens, as do their children born and raised in Germany. On top of this, their naturalization has been hampered by the fact that German law requires them to renounce their Turkish nationality, which at the time involved significant disadvantages when it came to inheriting real estate in their country of origin. Following a heated political debate, a moderate revision of the Nationality Act (*Staatsbürgerschaftsgesetz*) was carried out in 1999, allowing those born in Germany to opt for German nationality (*ius soli*) and providing for exceptions to the renunciation requirement.[321]

Thus whereas the opportunities for Turkish immigrants and their children to participate fully in society were expanded in Germany, the political tide in the Netherlands turned around the year 2000.[322] Some of the opportunities for acquiring Dutch nationality, which in the 1992–97 period were greater than in Germany, were removed again, on top of which the negative consequences of the segregatory interpretation of multiculturalism discussed in § 2.1 became apparent: "the fact that in cases of far-reaching cultural and ethnic differences pillarisation might equally feed autarchy and segregation", as Ewald Engelen puts it.[323] In a comparison of the Dutch and German labor markets for immigrants, Engelen observes that the Netherlands is lagging behind, owing partly to the severe deprivation of Moroccan immigrants and discrepancies in the economic system.[324] According to reports by the Netherlands Bureau for Economic Policy Analysis, however, Turkish immigrants and their children are in a better position on the Dutch labor market than the German one, especially as regards language skills and level of education.[325] The report on the integration of young Muslims commissioned by the German Ministry of the Interior shows that those who acquire German nationality integrate better than others in Germany. Obstacles to the acquisition of nationality

---

[321] Ibid. 230.

[322] Ewald Engelen, 'Towards an explanation of the performance differences of Turks in the Netherlands and Germany. The case for a comparative political economy of integration' (2006) 97 *Tijdschrift voor Economische en Sociale Geografie* 69.

[323] Ibid. 72.

[324] Ibid. 72–73 and 75.

[325] Rob Euwals and others, 'Immigration, integration and the labour market; Turkish immigrants in Germany and the Netherlands' (2006) CPB Discussion Paper No. 75; Rob Euwals and others, 'The labour market position of Turkish immigrants in Germany and the Netherlands; reason for migration, naturalisation and language proficiency' (2007) CPB Discussion Paper no 79.

adversely affect integration.[326] This empirical material points towards a reciprocal multiplier effect of legal and social and economic integration. It also reminds us that a barrier to the acquisition of the new home country's nationality would be removed if dual nationality were to be accepted.[327] Legally acknowledging people as nationals, then, is only effective if it is combined with reciprocal recognition in the social roles of citizenship, and Saunders gives examples of this too, such as the negative and positive experiences in the Netherlands.[328] Something of the kind applies to other human rights, in fact, what is why the 'classic' fundamental rights (the liberties that made up first-generation human rights) can no longer be separated from the subsequent generations of human rights, in particular social human rights.

Good legislation on the acquisition of nationality is certainly not a panacea for strengthening social cohesion, but its *absence* is an additional impediment. Because of the historical and current relationship between citizenship and the various dimensions of social participation, the entitlement to this legal status, the right to be a citizen, is an indispensable dimension of the full protection of human rights. Although the citizenship dimension has been surprisingly neglected, it is right and proper that the rights of migrant workers have now become an issue in 'third-generation' human rights.[329] The European Union has laid down important rules to protect people from 'third countries',[330] but they do not cover the opportunities for acquiring nationality, which remains the deciding factor as regards the enjoyment of citizens' rights, without which the rights of man (e.g. as a political subject) are incomplete. Rights that stop half-way are not citizens' rights. This is the position of people who are not given the opportunity to become Germans even though they are long-term residents of Berlin or Frankfurt. People who on arrival at the border

---

[326] Frindte and others, *Lebenswelte junger Muslime in Deutschland (Abschlussbericht). Ein sozial- und medienwissenschaftliches System zur Analyse. Bewertung und Prävention islamistischer Radikalisierungsprozesse junger Menschen in Deutschland* [The worlds of young Muslims in Germany (final report). A social and media studies system for the analysis, assessment and prevention of Islamist radicalization processes of young people in Germany] (Bundesinnenministerium 2012) 182, 360, 655.

[327] Ibid. 494, 656.

[328] Saunders (n. 88) 85.

[329] See Theo van Boven, 'Categories of Rights' in Daniel Moeckli, Sangeeta Shah and Sandesh Sivakumaran (eds.), *International Human Rights Law* (OUP 2010) 184.

[330] This has reduced the difference between their legal status and that of EU citizens, cf. Helen Staples, *The Legal Status of Third Country Nationals Resident in the European Union* (Kluwer 1999).

of their home country – and on countless other occasions – are identified as aliens cannot feel they are accepted as fellow citizens of that country.

The yardsticks for giving and taking away nationality and making it a reality therefore need to be revised, based on its significance to human rights in our era. In nationality law, descent (*ius sanguinis*) or country of birth (*ius soli*) has traditionally been accepted as the starting point for the acquisition of nationality, but these criteria – as the Canadian Ayelet Shachar argues – are no longer fit for purpose, as they result in "over- and under-inclusion",[331] i.e. a situation where more – or fewer – people are regarded as nationals than is warranted by their actual involvement. Rubenstein and Lenagh-Maguire insist that "[a]s Peter Spiro has written, 'inclusion waters down the strength of national identity'; under-inclusiveness, however, can also be perceived as socially divisive and unjust".[332] Shachar, referring to the enormous number of aliens without documents in the United States, argues that the application of a new "*jus nexi* principle" – based on the degree of rootedness, the presence of a genuine bond (though there is a grammatical error here: the genitive of *nexus*, a fourth-declension noun, is not *nexi* but *nexus* with a long *u*) – "would offer appropriate access to nationality if other paths to citizenship turn out to be closed off".[333]

Rafael Domingo develops a similar line of thought as part of his global perspective on the development of the law: "the idea that a citizen can remain so strongly and permanently linked to a sovereign state – and so closed to others – by the fact of his or her family's origin (*ius sanguinis*), place of birth (*ius soli*), or any other non-voluntary basis for nationality is making less and less sense. One of the basic human rights is the freedom to determine one's place of residence with a view to personal, family, and professional development."[334] Although this freedom is subject to conditions and limitations in many states, there are many people whose careers or life stories take them to different countries with which they develop ties through education, love and work. Domingo says that it would be unfair to pin them down to the one nationality given to them at birth and hinder them from entering into new citizenshipties.[335] He therefore goes on to argue that the immigration phenomenon should be analyzed "from a

---

[331] Shachar (n. 272) 111–3. See also Ayelet Shachar, 'Earned Citizenship. Property Lessons for Immigration Reform' (2011) 23 *Yale Journal of Law & the Humanities* 110, 115.

[332] Rubenstein and Lenagh-Maguire (n. 263) 150.

[333] Shachar (n. 331) 157; Shachar (n. 272) 164–182.

[334] Rafael Domingo, *The New Global Law* (CUP 2010) 106.

[335] Ibid. 107.

perspective that goes beyond the still sovereignty-tinged Universal Declaration of Human Rights", and I concur. States no longer ought to have unrestrained control over the nationality of their subjects; instead they should take reasonable decisions on citizenship aspirations. The same ought to apply to the renunciation of nationality, as now laid down in Article 7 of the European Convention on Nationality. The only condition that states may (but need not) attach to this, under Article 8 (2), is that the person concerned is no longer resident in the country. The rule laid down in Article 7 "reflects the recent development of recognition of nationality as a human right", as Kay Hailbronner rightly notes.[336] Liberalizing nationality law in this way places the emphasis on the decisions of the person concerned while respecting the reciprocal character of citizenship.

If we compare this approach to citizenship with the one in which states had control over their subjects – even, as we saw in the example of the Treaty of Trianon (there are many other examples), by transferring whole populations – we are forced to conclude, as Seyla Benhabib does, that there are both a "reconfiguration of sovereignty" and "reconstitutions of citizenship" taking place: "We are moving away from citizenship, understood as national membership, increasingly toward a *citizenship of residency*, which strengthens the multiple ties to locality, to the region, and to transnational institutions."[337] What we are discussing here is the legal framework for such a transformation of citizenship. Alongside the physical gateways to another society that have become arrival cities, there need to be legal gateways. We may conclude that the right to nationality, formulated in abstract terms as a human right, needs to be implemented in accessible procedures, with reasonable requirements and legal protection, for the acquisition of nationality by *de facto* integrated aliens, so that they are not deprived of equal citizens' rights and have a voice in public affairs. The requirements should include acceptance of the principles of a democratic constitutional state (which is not the same as believing in it, which is after all not required of anyone else), familiarity with its language and institutions, but not nationalist ideological indoctrination or cultural transmutation.[338]

---

[336] Kay Hailbronner, 'Nationality in public international law and european law' in Rainer Bauböck and others (eds.), *Acquisition and Loss of Nationality. Policies and Trends in 15 European States. Vol. I. Comparative Analyses* (Amsterdam UP 2006) 67.

[337] Seyla Benhabib, *Dignity in Adversity* (Polity Press 2011) 111.

[338] Cf. David Miller, 'Immigrants, Nations, and Citizenship' (2008) 16 *Journal of Political Philosophy* 371; also included in Richard Bellamy and Antonino Palumbo, *Citizenship* (Ashgate Publishing 2010) 294–298.

The realization that integrating migrants has to be a reciprocal process enhances the value of citizenship. What is customarily required is *de facto* integration over a period of many years and sufficient knowledge of the country's language and institutions. United States law requires inter alia, in addition to legal and de facto residence, that the person "be of good moral character during the required residence period and up to the time of admission".[339] The results of applying this criterion are problematic, however, as those who are refused naturalization on these grounds often nevertheless continue to participate in social and economic life as legal holders of permanent residence permits.

Naturalization that does not adversely affect social cohesion requires the ability to build communication bridges, and there can be no doubt that this calls for a common language. As long ago as 1798, under the Batavian Constitution, knowledge of the Dutch language ("Nederduytsche taal") was a sufficient condition, along with the required period of residence, for eligibility to vote. This requirement, however, – in contrast to what is often suggested by politicians – is not an obstacle to multilingualism and passing on that multilingualism to subsequent generations.[340] Requirements in this area must not take on the character of erasure of origin, with its language, beauty and rituals. Given that nationality, especially the political dimensions, includes the capacity to participate in decision-making, a sufficient command of at least one of the country's official languages is a reasonable criterion for the acquisition of nationality. In the case of Dutch nationality, this requirement was not introduced for all parts of the Kingdom of the Netherlands until the amendment of 17 June 2010.[341] Decisions on the granting and denial of nationality, then,

---

[339] The Immigration and Nationality Act, 8 USC para. 1427(a)(3), 1430 (a)(1) (USA).

[340] See Guus Extra, *De omgang met taaldiversiteit in de multiculturele samenleving* [Dealing with language diversity in a multicultural society] (valedictory lecture, Tilburg University, Tilburg 2011) 36: "The Netherlands is increasingly developing into a multicultural society, and multilingualism is an intrinsic characteristic of this, not a 'temporary problem'. There are no examples of multicultural societies that are monolingual. In the Netherlands, however, the multilingualism of minority groups is invariably regarded as a source of deprivation and problems, rarely acknowledged as a source of knowledge and enrichment."

[341] See *Stb* 2010, 242. In his article 'Who is '"One of Us"? The Nexus between Naturalisation, Language, and Minority Protection' (2012) forthcoming in Karin Jóhanna Knudsen, Hjalmar P. Petersen and Káriá Rógvi (eds.), *Four or More Languages for All. Language Policy Challenges of the Future* (Novus 2012) <http://papers.ssrn.com/sol3/papers.cfm?abstract_id=2063800> accessed 31 July 2012, Dimitry Kochenov critically examines this amendment, which in his view makes it too difficult to acquire Dutch nationality in the Caribbean territories of the Kingdom. On the other hand, Dutch is the language of the law there too,

must not form part of a cat-and-mouse game with immigrants; they must
serve the function that citizenship is all about the ability and obligation to
contribute to a shared system of law and social existence.

3.4 *Statelessness*

The problems associated with the long-term deprivation of citizens' rights
are most strongly highlighted when we consider the position of those who
have *no nationality whatsoever*, neither of the country where they live nor
of a country of origin, i.e. 'stateless persons'. Robert Schnepf points out
that the phenomenon of statelessness did not occur before the end of the
eighteenth century: as long as no nationality arrangements had been
made, monarchs treated aliens as temporary subjects alongside their own
subjects. In accordance with the prevailing principle of territoriality, origin was of secondary importance.[342]

Not until during and after the Second World War did statelessness come
into view as an acute problem. All Jewish German citizens staying outside
Germany had their citizenship collectively revoked by the 11th Decree pursuant to the Reich Citizenship Act (*Reichsbürgergesetz*) of 25 December
1941. In addition to this *de jure* statelessness, there were situations resulting from warfare or terror, in both Europe and other parts of the world,
whereby large groups of people had to leave the countries of which they
were nationals, thus becoming *de facto* stateless (the 'displaced persons'
for whom the United Nations High Commissioner for Refugees has been
responsible since 1951). As Schnepf notes: "The catastrophes of the twentieth century are reflected in the concept of *de facto* statelessness."[343] The
1951 Geneva Convention relating to the Status of Refugees is of value to
individual refugees in that it facilitates access to citizenship in the country
of asylum. Article 34 (Naturalization) reads as follows: "The Contracting

---

and naturalized citizens have the right to settle in any part of the Kingdom. The problems
he raises would involve splitting up nationality and changing the language regime in the
Caribbean territories (also e.g. in education). The consequences would amount to a split in
the constitutional arrangements that is at present wanted by only a small minority in the
Caribbean territories.

[342] Robert Schnepf, 'Zum Problem der Staatenlosigkeit' [On the problem of stateless-
ness] in Matthias Kaufmann, *Integration oder Toleranz? Minderheiten als philosophisches
Problem* (Verlag Karl Albert 2001) 63–64. See about current situations of *de facto* statelessness, Peter Rodrigues, '*De facto* staatloosheid of de uitdaging van onuitzetbaren' (2013) 5/6
Asiel- & Migrantenrecht 281.

[343] Schnepf (n. 342) 65.

States shall as far as possible facilitate the assimilation and naturalization of refugees. They shall in particular make every effort to expedite naturalization proceedings and to reduce as far as possible the charges and costs of such proceedings."

Those who are *de jure* or *de facto* stateless are to a large extent without citizens' rights.[344] Conventions to protect the civil and political rights of stateless persons and reduce the situations in which statelessness occurs were signed under the auspices of the United Nations in 1954 and 1961.[345] States are often unwilling to acknowledge the statelessness of people within their territory, as this results in an obligation to integrate them. Hannah Arendt discussed this as long ago as 1949, in the article in which she based human rights on "the right of every person to be a member of a polity",[346] recalling how eager governments were to ignore statelessness ("abolish it once and for all by simply ignoring it") and instead aim at 'repatriation', i.e. returning people to a 'country of origin' that either does not want them at all or is all too keen to prosecute them.[347] While the Geneva Refugee Convention and Article 3 of the ECHR do now provide safeguards against this latter course of action, in situations where states are trying to restrict the influx of asylum seekers – e.g. on the Italian island

---

[344] For the South Moluccans in the Netherlands, who were stateless by international law standards and did not want to take a different nationality because of their strong desire to claim citizenship of an unrecognized republic in exile, special statutory provision was made to equate them with Dutch nationals and thus eliminate the adverse effects of their statelessness in 1976: see (n. 44). Since 1992 (Act of 4 December 1991, *Stb* 672) they have had the option of applying for Dutch passports. From an international law point of view it could perhaps be argued that they thus form a special category of Dutch nationals.

[345] Convention Relating to the Status of Stateless Persons (adopted 28 September 1954, entered into force 6 June 1960) 360 Treaty Series 117; Convention on the Reduction of Statelessness (adopted 30 August 1961, entered into force 13 December 1975) 989 Treaty Series 175. The Council of Europe's important European Convention on Nationality (adopted 6 November 1997, entered into force 1 March 2000) ETS 166 too is designed inter alia to prevent statelessness and therefore combats ex lege loss of nationality. See Gerard-René de Groot and Maarten Vink, *Meervoudige nationaliteit in Europees perspectief. Een landenvergelijkend overzicht* [Multiple nationality in a European perspective: a comparison between countries] (ACVZ 2008) 28.

[346] Hannah Arendt, 'Es gibt nur ein einziges Menschenrecht' [There is only one human right] in Menke and Raimondi (n. 35) 406.

[347] Ibid. 395: "ein für allemal einfach durch ignorieren aus der Welt zu schaffen. Nichtanerkennung der Staatenlosigkeit heißt immer Repatriierung, Rückverweisung in ein 'Heimatland'" (abolish it once and for all by simply ignoring it. Non-recognition of statelessness is always referred to as repatriation, return to a 'homeland'); cf. Arendt (n. 196) and § 2.4.

of Lampedusa off the African coast – the compliance with these safe-guards is coming under severe pressure.[348]

A UN Convention relating to the Status of Stateless Persons was signed in 1954, followed by the UN Convention on the Reduction of Statelessness in 1961 (ratified to only a limited extent outside Europe). The Committee of Ministers of the Council of Europe has repeatedly made recommendations on the subject, most for example on 15 September 1999 concerning the avoidance and reduction of statelessness.[349] A variety of specific human rights conventions also include provisions with the same aim, including the UN Convention on the Rights of the Child, Article 7 (2) of which lays down that states must avoid situations where children grow up stateless. Under Article 7 (3) of the 1997 European Convention on Nationality, a state is not permitted to revoke nationality if this would make the person concerned stateless. From the consistent line adopted in conventions and recommendations, Kay Hailbronner infers that the obligation to avoid statelessness is part of international customary law.[350] The notes to the European Convention on Nationality also proceed from this assumption.[351]

States have the sovereign power to regulate their nationality, but not "in a way that violates fundamental human rights".[352] Both of the general conventions on statelessness and other international efforts have indeed narrowed "the 'rights gap' into which the stateless tumble" but not closed it entirely. Stateless persons still remain deprived of rights "that traditionally belong to the very heart and function of citizenship": residence rights, the right to vote and to stand for election, and entitlement to diplomatic protection.[353] Based on practical experience in Sri Lanka, Laura van Waas describes how the supposedly universal operation of human rights

---

[348] Anna V. Dolidze, 'Lampedusa and Beyond. Recognition, Implementation, and Justiciability of Stateless Persons' Rights under International Law' (2011–2012) 6 *Interdisciplinary Journal of Human Rights Law* 123; (2011) IGL&P Working Paper No. 2011/5, <http://ssrn.com/abstract=1927033> accessed 31 July 2012.

[349] Recommendation no R (99) 18 on the Avoidance and Reduction of Statelessness <https://wcd.coe.int/com.instranet.InstraServlet?command=com.instranet.CmdBlob Get&InstranetImage=538369&SecMode=1&DocId=409946&Usage=2> accessed 19 August 2013.

[350] Hailbronner (n. 336) 65.

[351] Vonk (n. 265) 38–39; Explanatory Report on the European Convention on Nationality <http://conventions.coe.int/Treaty/EN/Reports/Html/166.htm> accessed 20 August 2013, para. 33.

[352] Vonk (n. 265) 45.

[353] Laura van Waas, *Nationality Matters. Statelessness under International Law* (Intersentia 2008) 398.

crumbles whenever people remain deprived of any protection as nationals.[354] Even in the case of persons who are not *de jure* stateless but cannot make use of their nationality, this is a violation of their fundamental rights. It may be that 'their' state is unwilling to grant them protection, or it is so badly disrupted that this is effectively ruled out, as is the situation e.g. in Somalia. Merely the absence of (or refusal to issue) travel documents robs people of their normal freedom of movement, and even issuing a stateless person's or alien's passport provides only partial compensation.

This is where the importance lies of procedures to establish whether a person is indeed stateless. Although the Kingdom of the Netherlands has ratified the conventions on statelessness, the legislation falls short in that there is no procedure to determine whether a person is stateless.[355] The absence of a procedure of this kind, the results of which are binding on all the authorities concerned, is the main deficiency noted by the UNHCR in its report on statelessness in the Netherlands. The principle generally applied after the rejection of an asylum request is that a person is entitled to "return", as everyone is assumed to hold the nationality of his or her country of origin.[356] The limited possibility of granting an asylum permit under the 'no-fault procedure' is with respect to situations of *de jure* or *de facto* statelessness unsatisfactory. In order to combat statelessness, the UNHCR aims to achieve improvements in the identification, prevention and limitation of this phenomenon and the protection of persons who are already stateless. Similar problems exist in other countries. For that reason, the UNHCR issued in 2012 four sets of Guidelines pursuant to its responsibilities to address statelessness mandate.[357]

---

[354] Laura van Waas, 'Nationality and Rights' in Brad K. Blitz and Maureen Lynch, *Statelessness and Citizenship. A Comparative Study on the Benefits of Nationality* (Edward Elgar 2011) 41.

[355] United Nations High Commissioner for Refugees (UNHCR), 'Mapping Statelessness in the Netherlands' (2011) UNHCR <www.refworld.org/docid/4eef65da2.html> accessed 30 July 2013.

[356] Sangita Jaghai and Caia Vlieks, 'Buitenschuldbeleid schiet tekort in bescherming staatlozen' [No-fault policy inadequately protects stateless persons] (2013) 5/6 *Asiel- & Migrantenrecht* 287.

[357] UNHCR, 'Guidelines on Statelessness no 1: The definition of "Stateless Person" in Article 1(1) of the 1954 Convention relating to the Status of Stateless Persons' (2012) HCR/GS/12/01 <www.refworld.org/docid/4f4371b82.html> accessed 19 August 2013]; UNHCR, 'Guidelines on Statelessness no 2: Procedures for Determining whether an Individual is a Stateless Person' (2012) HCR/GS/12/02 <www.refworld.org/docid/4f7dafb52.html> [accessed 19 August 2013]; UNHCR, 'Guidelines on Statelessness no 3: The Status of Stateless Persons at the National Level' (2012) HCR/GS/12/03 <www.refworld.org/docid/5005520f2.html> accessed 19 August 2013; UNHCR, 'Guidelines on Statelessness no 4: Ensuring Every

A number of decisions by international courts indicate that the denial
of nationality constitutes a violation of human rights. In the case of Kurić
and Others v. Slovenia, No. 26828/06, the European Court of Human Rights
(Grand Chamber) ruled on 26 June 2012 on the status of former nationals
of other Yugoslavian states who were long-term residents of Slovenia but
had been denied residence rights in Slovenia after the collapse of the
Yugoslavian Federal Republic. The Court ruled that "[356] (...) the applicants, who, prior to Slovenia's declaration of independence, had been lawfully residing in Slovenia for several years, had, as former SFRY citizens,
enjoyed a wide range of social and political rights. Owing to the 'erasure',
they experienced a number of adverse consequences, such as the destruc-
tion of identity documents, loss of job opportunities, loss of health insur-
ance, the impossibility of renewing identity documents or driving licenses,
and difficulties in regulating pension rights. Indeed, the legal vacuum in
the independence legislation (...) deprived the applicants of their legal status, which had previously given them access to a wide range of rights. [357]
Allegedly, the 'erasure' was a consequence of their failure to seek to obtain
Slovenian citizenship. However, the Court points out that an alien lawfully
residing in a country may wish to continue living in that country without
necessarily acquiring its citizenship."[358] Following on from the fundamental arguments regarding nationality cited earlier, the Inter-American Court
of Human Rights ruled in the case of the Yean and Bosico children v. the
Dominican Republic on 8 September 2005[359] in §142: "Statelessness deprives
an individual of the possibility of enjoying civil and political rights and
places him in a condition of extreme vulnerability." Discrimination in the
registration of nationality and births in the Dominican Republic had
caused descendants of Haitians to be stateless. This discrimination in the
acquisition of nationality contravenes Articles 20 and 24 in conjunction
with Article 19 of the American Convention on Human Rights (§174), and
this is not affected by the "migratory status of a person" (§155–6).

My own conclusion is a development of this: not only must stateless
persons be able to share in accessible procedures for acquiring a suitable
nationality; the precarious situation of people who *de jure* or *de facto* lack

---

Child's Right to Acquire a Nationality through Articles 1–4 of the 1961 Convention on the
Reduction of Statelessness' (2012) HCR/GS/12/04 <www.refworld.org/docid/50d460c72
.html> accessed 19 August 2013.

[358] *Kuric and Others v Slovenia* App no 26828/06 (ECtHR, 26 June 2012). Nationality issues
were also dealt with in the ECtHR judgments in the cases of *Karassev v Finland*, *Konstatinov
v The Netherlands* and *Andrejeva v Latvia*, see <www.unhcr.org/45179cbd4.html>.

[359] *Yean and Bosico v Dominican Republic* (n. 282).

the protection of a state of their own requires that they will be eligible to settle or resettle in a state that will provide them with adequate protection,[360] and hence will be eligible for citizenship. Human rights policy and the United Nations framework for human security converge on this point.[361] The relevance of these findings lies not only in combating statelessness, or reducing its adverse effects; the point is that migrants must be able to acquire a nationality that ensures a connection with the community in which they have settled, *instead of* or – if there are reasons not to break permanently the ties with the country of origin – *in addition to* their original nationality.

Here again we see the impact on the effective protection of human rights. In her study *Making People Illegal*, Catherine Dauvergne teases out how migration law and nationality law in various countries have taken on the nature of a new barrier to international migration: anyone residing illegally in another country is excluded from the acquisition of nationality.[362] The consequences she describes are negative in more than one respect: permanent lack of rights for the illegal immigrants who come in nevertheless,[363] and thus also failure of the attempt to prove national sovereignty.

The absence of citizens' rights that characterizes the position of stateless persons is, as it were, the worst degree of denial of citizenship. Their fate makes it clear why, as I do in this book, we need to place contemporary citizenship issues in the context of migration and the resulting connections between people and the communities they live in. With the British experience in mind, David Miller points out that in such circumstances denial of nationality is a violation of human rights and principles

---

[360] Cf. Kristin Bergtora Sandvik, 'A Legal History. The Emergence of the African Resettlement in International Refugee Management' (2010) 22 *International Journal of Refugee Law* 20.

[361] See Alice Edwards and Carla Ferstman, 'Humanising non-citizens: the convergence of human rights and human security' and Mark Manly and Laura van Waas, 'The value of the human security framework in addressing statelessness', both in Alice Edwards and Carla Ferstman (eds.), *Human Security and Non-Citizens. Law, Policy and International Affairs* (CUP 2010). For the relation of these concepts with "human dignity" see Ralf Bodelier, *Kosmopolitische perspectieven. Reflecties op 'Human Development' en 'Human Security'* (Celsus juridische uitgeverij/Wereldpodium 2012).

[362] Catherine Dauvergne, *Making People Illegal. What Globalization Means for Migration and Law* (CUP 2008) 119–24.

[363] In developing countries, illegal migration may take the form of large-scale – fraudulent but effective – acquisition of 'documentary citizenship' through networks of complicity. See Kamal Sadiq, *Paper Citizens. How Illegal Immigrants Acquire Citizenship in Developing Countries* (OUP 2009).

of fairness.[364] Granting nationality is not a formality, nor is it a favor
that can be arbitrarily bestowed or denied; it must be seen in the context
of "an implicit two-way contract"[365] that complies with the idea underlying citizenship. In this way, citizenship is recognized as a constitutional
institution. This means more than theoretically equal treatment: the law
should provide effective protection and tools for obtaining citizenship
equally.[366]

3.5 Multiple Citizenship

The "increasingly widespread institution of dual citizenship", as David
Miller describes it, is an inevitable consequence of more intensive
international traffic and migration. Ever since the time when a political
and ideological preference for 'national states' coincided with large-scale
transatlantic migration – the second half of the nineteenth century –, multiple nationality has been a controversial subject of policy and legislation.
The fact that some states based nationality on descent (*ius sanguinis*) and
others on place of birth (*ius soli*) resulted in multiple nationality taking on
increasing importance. To this was subsequently added the greater significance of the mother's line of descent next to the father's, with the rise of
equal treatment for men and women. A report for the Migration Policy
Institute describes the situation.[367] Multiple citizenship is a common and
largely accepted phenomenon worldwide at the beginning of the twenty-
first century, which is due to migration and the multiplicity of personal ties
that have resulted from intense international traffic. The fears of disloyalty,
espionage and legal confusion associated with dual citizenship in the nineteenth and a large part of the twentieth century are not borne out by the
facts,[368] even though they may be whipped up by politicians – sometimes
in unexpected places such as the Netherlands. The real question is however not whether dual citizenship should exist. Aleinikoff and Klusmeyer
notice "an emerging international consensus that the goal is no longer to

---

[364] Miller (n. 338) 378/288: "international human rights norms combine with domestic
principles of social justice to exclude the creation of a class of long-term resident
non-citizens".

[365] Ibid. 388/298.

[366] Ibid. 381/291.

[367] Thomas Faist and Jürgen Gerdes, *Dual Citizenship in an Age of Mobility* (Transatlantic
Council on Migration 2008).

[368] Ibid. 3.

reduce plural nationality as an end in itself, but to manage it as an inevitable feature of an increasingly interconnected and mobile world."[369]

The complicated legal history of this subject since the nineteenth century has been described in detail by Olivier Vonk in his book *Dual Nationality in the European Union* (already cited), and the relationship to international law by Alfred Boll.[370] Dutch law until 1892 was based on the *ius soli* principle. As a result of alarm at the acquisition of Dutch nationality by the children of the many German immigrants, who thereby gained dual nationality, the Netherlands switched to the *ius sanguinis* principle in its 1892 legislation. This decision was thought to be appropriate, according to Vonk, "to foster loyal and nationalist feelings".[371] Since then, attempts to combat dual citizenship have had the effect of not only reducing the *de jure* acquisition of nationality by children of immigrants but also requiring the renunciation of the original nationality on naturalization. The 'success' of such measures is always limited. A renunciation requirement cannot reasonably be laid down if the law of the state concerned does not permit this (as is the case with e.g. Morocco). In other cases, this requirement can result in people deciding not to acquire the nationality of the new country of residence (an adverse effect from the point of view of integration but one that does fit in with xenophobic political agendas).

In the first half of the twentieth century, the desire to have perfect symmetry between nationality and national state was translated into a preamble to the Hague Convention concerning Certain Questions relating to the Conflict of Nationality (12 April 1930) with the premise "that every person should have a nationality and should have one nationality only", but this convention actually did "little to bring it about."[372] Nevertheless, this convention included arrangements for situations of multiple citizenship, e.g. in Article 5, requiring third states to treat a person having more than one nationality as if he had only one, "either the nationality of the country in which he is habitually and principally resident, or the nationality of the country with which in the circumstances he appears to be in fact most closely connected." Since the end of the twentieth century, attempts to

---

[369] T. Alexander Aleinikoff and Douglas Klusmeyer, 'Plural Nationality. Facing the Future in a Migratory World' in T. Alexander Aleinikoff and Douglas Klusmeyer, *Citizenship Today. Global Perspectives and Practices* (Carnegie Endowment for International Peace 2001) 87.

[370] Alfred M. Boll, *Multiple Nationality and International Law* (Martinus Nijhoff 2007).

[371] Vonk (n. 265) 209.

[372] Aleinikoff and Klusmeyer identify some (perceived) problems associated with dual nationality, but stress that they do not "represent the major flash points between states" (n. 369) 63, 72, 80.

combat dual citizenship through conventions have more or less come to a standstill.[373] The respective provisions of the Convention on the Reduction of Cases of Multiple Nationality and on Military Obligations in Cases of Multiple Nationality signed in Strasbourg on 6 May 1963 have never been put into effect by the vast majority of the Council of Europe member states or have meanwhile been rescinded. At present, they are in force in only four states (Austria, Denmark, the Netherlands and Norway), and the Danish government that came into office in October 2011 also plans to abrogate the Convention.[374] The 1997 European Convention on Nationality, on the other hand, which twenty states have signed, is neutral on the issue of dual nationality. Its aim is to reduce situations of statelessness, facilitate the acquisition of a new nationality and combat unfair deprivation of nationality. In the Netherlands, about 1.15 million people out of a total population of 16.8 million hold a second nationality in addition to Dutch citizenship.[375]

The Netherlands belongs to the minority of European Union member states that, though with important exceptions, lay down renunciation of the current nationality as a requirement for naturalization. In 2010, renunciation was also required in Denmark (whose government however intends to change this) and several states where the confirmation of national identity is a particularly major issue as a result of recent history, namely the Czech Republic, Estonia, Hungary, Latvia, Lithuania, Poland, Slovenia and Slovakia.[376] Elsewhere within and outside Europe it is recognized that the renunciation requirement, which is not only detrimental to the dimensions of personal identity but also decidedly disadvantages people (cf. the need to apply for visas to visit their families), constitutes a serious limitation of personal freedom. As Jessurun d'Oliveira points out,

---

[373] Many countries have no renunciation requirement or it is not customary there. See Peters, 'Extraterritorial Naturalizations' (n. 269) 631; Rubenstein and Lenagh-Maguire (n. 263) 152. Australia is an exception. In the United States and Canada dual nationals do not encounter any constitutional impediments, apart from the fact that only 'native born US citizens' can be elected as President or Vice-President (which is not the same, however, as having single nationality: 157).

[374] Convention on Reduction of Cases of Multiple Nationality and Military Obligations in Cases of Multiple Nationality (adopted 6 May 1963, entered into force 28 March 1968) ETS 43; Gerard-Réne de Groot, 'Wijzigingsvoorstel Rijkswet op het Nederlanderschap; Terug naar af' [Proposed amendment to the Dutch Nationality Act. Back to where we started] (2012) 4 *Asiel- & Migrantenrecht* 180.

[375] Official CBS statistics for 1 January 2012, see <http://statline.cbs.nl/StatWeb/publication/?VW=T&DM=SLNL&PA=70798NED&D1=a&D2=0&D3=1-5,21,51,116,171,187,l&D4=(l-6)-l&HD=130605-1004&HDR=T,G3&STB=G1,G2> accessed on 17 July 2013; cf. de Groot and Vink (n. 345) 111–3.

[376] Dimitry Kochenov, 'Double Nationality in the EU: An Argument for Tolerance' (2011) 17 *European Law Journal* 323.

it is inconsistent with their principles that in the Netherlands "the liberal party holds, but with no rationale, that being coerced to retain only a single nationality is compatible with liberal principles."[377] Here we see the influence of "populist politics", where – as Thomas Faist notes in the introduction to his comparative studies of European countries – "dual citizenship is linked, for example, either to ethnic or assimilationist elements or to unrelated policy issues such as increased immigration, threats to welfare systems, and criminality".[378] It is in countering such politically symbolic utterances that the manifest importance lies of theoretically and empirically well-founded analyses such as the ones cited here.

Multiple nationality has a variety of causes and occurs in all sorts of combinations, in particular with the nationalities of the countries of origin of migrants and those of neighbor countries.[379] The realities of social interactions in our times will further increase the situations of multiple citizenship; attempts to reverse this trend reflect misconceptions of these realities.[380] The debate is nevertheless not finished in the Netherlands[381] and some other countries. After a brief but well utilized period when the renunciation requirement was effectively set aside (1992–97),[382] ideologically motivated attempts[383] were made between 2004 and 2006 and again

---

[377] Hans Ulrich Jessurun d'Oliveira, 'Multiple Nationality and International Law by Alfred Boll' (2007) 101 *American Journal of International Law* 922.

[378] Faist (n. 309) 38.

[379] For this development and an assessment of it, see the report of the Adviescommissie voor Vreemdelingenzaken (ACVZ), 'Nederlanderschap in een onbegrensde wereld. Advies over het Nederlandse beleid inzake meervoudige nationaliteit' [Dutch nationality in a world without borders: Report on Dutch policy on multiple nationality] (2008) ACVZ.

[380] Cf. Betty de Hart, *Een tweede paspoort. Dubbele nationaliteit in de Verenigde Staten, Duitsland en Nederland* (Amsterdam UP 2012).

[381] On this subject, see Betty de Hart, 'The End of Multiculturalism: The End of Dual Citizenship? Political and Public Debates in The Netherlands (1980–2004)' in Faist (ed.), *Dual Citizenship in Europe* (n. 309) 77–102.

[382] See the official CBS statistics on <www.cbs.nl/en-GB/menu/themas/bevolking/publicaties/artikelen/archief/2012/2012-3578-wm.htm?Languageswitch=on> accessed on 17 July 2013. For the resulting better naturalization rates compared with those in Germany, see Faist and Gerdes (n. 367) 8–9. The immediate cause of this policy change was the passing of a CDA-PvdA motion by the House of Representatives (Soutendijk-Van Appeldoorn/Apostolou motion, *Kamerstukken II* 1991/92 21 971 no 29), the preamble to which noted that renouncing or not renouncing the original nationality should be "an individual choice". Vonk (n. 265) 228 considered that the CDA had adopted this position so as to offer an alternative to the PvdA's plan to grant the right to vote to long-term resident aliens. He was not aware, however, that other Christian Democrats had realized at the time that substantive criteria such as adequate knowledge of the language and society are more important to acquiring Dutch nationality than formal criteria such as renouncing the original nationality.

[383] Vonk (n. 265) 205–6 notes on this subject: "The renunciation requirement, and its underlying objective of forcing immigrants to make an exclusive choice for the Netherlands,

in 2011/2012 to curtail or even abolish the exemptions from the require-ment.[384] This was in spite of the fact that the notes to the amendment to the Dutch Nationality Act, which came into force in 2010, had clearly rejected the prejudice that multiple nationality would represent a lack of loyalty or an obstacle to integration: Dutch nationality encourages participation in society. Multiple nationality need not stand in the way of this. (...) What really matters is involvement in Dutch society and the legal system.[385]

On top of this, conservative liberals and populists have since 2007 called into question the appointability of people with dual nationality to high public office, whereas under the Dutch Constitution, the legitimacy of this is beyond doubt and discrimination would in fact be unconstitutional.[386] Article 17 (1) of the 1997 European Convention on Nationality also expressly lays down that "Nationals of a State Party in possession of another nation-ality shall have, in the territory of that State Party in which they reside, the same rights and duties as other nationals of that State Party."

The US Constitution and United States nationality law do not prevent American-born citizens from retaining their American nationality on acquiring a new nationality. In practice, in spite of the requirement to take an Oath of Renunciation of former allegiances, naturalized American citi-zens are not required to renounce their original nationality either. This is sometimes regarded as lack of enforcement,[387] but arguments in favor of

---

is almost unanimously rejected by the legal doctrine but politicians seem little impressed by the legal arguments or stern facts and statistics that are brought forward."

[384] See bill 30166 (R1795), submitted on 21 June 2005 under the responsibility of Minister Verdonk and withdrawn by the fourth Balkenende government on 12 December 2007 and bill 33201 (R1977), submitted on 14 March 2012 under the responsibility of Minister Spies and withdrawn by the second Rutte government on 18 March 2013: the draft version of which the then Minister, J.P.H. Donner, put out for consultation from 28 March to 22 April 2011. See <www.internetconsultatie.nl/nationaliteitsrecht> accessed on 13 June 2013. In their response, C.A. Groenendijk and A. Kruyt pointed out that the draft bill put out for consultation would have an adverse effect on integration, but neither their comments nor other reactions resulted in any changes, see <www.internetconsultatie.nl/nationaliteitsrecht/reacties> accessed on 13 June 2013. The formation of a new government coalition in September 2012 put an end to these attempts.

[385] See *Kamerstukken II* 2007/2008 30 166 (R1795) no 25. The bill referred to in the pas-sage cited became law on 17 June 2010 (*Stb* 2010, 242).

[386] Grondwet (n. 157) art. 3 reads as follows: "All Dutch nationals shall be appointable to public office on an equal footing." This clause in the Constitution does not permit any dis-tinction based on holding or not holding a second nationality. In the 1998–2002 period, one of the VVD ministers – who subsequently joined the ranks of those campaigning against ministers holding dual nationality – was a citizen of another state, and this had happened previously.

[387] Thus Karin Scherner-Kim, 'The Role of the Oath of Renunciation in Current U.S. Nationality Policy – To Enforce, to Omit, or Maybe to Change' (1999–2000) 88 *Georgetown Law Journal* 329.

enforcement are reflections, at least to some extent, of something different, namely the demand to exercise stricter control over integration in the USA and acceptance of its values. This argument fails to appreciate the realities: shortcomings in integration cannot be remedied by taking an oath, and a person can be guided by different values even after renouncing his or her original nationality, either compulsorily or voluntarily. The other nationality has no legal consequences within the US. There is a trend in US case law away from a disapproving view of dual nationality towards a more well-disposed attitude.[388]

The political fight against the freedom to be a citizen of more than one state essentially involves two contentions, which amount to (a) the demand for the undivided *loyalty* of a citizen to one state and (b) the idea that a person's national *identity* should by nature be single.[389] The paternalistic argument is sometimes added that it is difficult for the person concerned to live with two sets of rights and obligations. This is not really convincing, however; if it were the case, it could be a reason for the person to decide to renounce his or her second nationality. Vonk concludes that there is in fact hardly any evidence of serious practical drawbacks to dual nationality.[390] Individually, however, there could be disadvantages if a state – Turkey is a case in point – imposes compulsory military service on its nationals even if they are not resident there during that period of their lives. Moreover, if a state were to place obstacles in the way of renouncing its nationality, this could cross the boundary of permissibility under international law, as in practice it would amount to a violating of everyone's human right to leave the territory of a state. As I shall explain later on, the voluntary nature of acquiring and rejecting nationality should be included on the international political agenda.

The argument of undivided *loyalty* in effect goes back to a concept of nationality that has not yet been abandoned everywhere in the world, which regards nationals as subjects, as men or women who are expected to follow official instructions. Many legal systems claim extraterritorial jurisdiction over offences committed by their own 'subjects' outside the country, even if no fellow citizens have been victimized by the crime.

---

[388] Keith Duckett, 'The meaning of citizenship: a critical analysis of dual nationality and the oath of renunciation' (2000) 21 *Immigration and Nationality Law Review* 717.

[389] The argument used to explain a Dutch compromise bill in 2008, that restricting multiple nationality would be less complicated legally (the "significance to the legal system" of the principles on which the legislation was based: see *Kamerstukken II* 2008–2009, 31 813 (R1873) no. 3, 1), given the slight practical significance, does not result in any substantive impediment to dual nationality, nor was this the aim of the bill.

[390] Vonk (n. 265) 113.

This active nationality principle is accepted in international law, but many states confine its application to serious offenses or crimes, like treason, which have effects at home.[391] It can be a useful facility in cases where extradition is prevented by statutory or constitutional rules, the state where the offense was committed does not have a properly functioning legal system, or the offense was committed outside the jurisdiction of any state (Antarctica is a commonly-cited example). Meanwhile, however, the extradition of a state's own subjects has become less uncommon – subject to the condition of the sentence being served in the country of the person's nationality – and within the European Union such extradition is even mandatory under a European arrest warrant.[392]

There is another motive for extending jurisdiction to offenses committed by nationals on the territory of other states, however, which reflects the old view of nationality, i.e. that subjects should behave in line with the standards of their country's regime, wherever they are in the world. This view no longer has any obvious legitimacy. The criminal codes of the Netherlands, Germany[393] and many other states restrict the application of the active personality principle as a rule to acts that are also criminal offenses under the law of the country where they were committed. (Jurisdiction based on the universality principle that applies to war crimes and crimes against humanity is a different story.) This condition is essential to acceptability under international law, as Kai Ambos points out,[394] and we could add that it is also indispensable given the fact that people moving around the world need to be able to obey the laws that are compatible with the society of which they temporarily form part. Although the textbooks do not usually have anything to say on the subject, it would seem to be a reasonable interpretation of the human law adage *nullum crimen sine praevia lege poenali* (ECHR Article 7, ICCPR Article 15) to regard the *lex praevia* solely as that of the country where the crime was

---

[391] Crawford (n. 265) 459–460.

[392] EU Council Framework Decision 2002/584/JHA of 13 June 2002 on the European arrest warrant and the surrender procedures between Member States [2002] OJ L190/1.

[393] Albeit with a few exceptions, designed mainly to prevent the deliberate relocation of certain acts: in the Netherlands, these include human trafficking, genital mutilation of girls and child pornography, and in Germany crimes against the democratic constitutional state, related to sexual autonomy and abortion, crimes linked to the exercise of public office and trading in human organs. See Christoph Safferling, *Internationales Strafrecht. Strafanwendungsrecht – Völkerstrafrecht – Europäisches Strafrecht* [International criminal law. Sentencing law – international criminal law – European criminal law] (Springer 2011) 23–24.

[394] Kai Ambos, *Internationales Strafrecht. Strafanwendungsrecht – Völkerstrafrecht – Europäisches Strafrecht* [International criminal law: sentencing law – international criminal law – European criminal law] (C.H. Beck 2006) 37.

committed, or as some other foreseeable or universally applicable norm there. If the 'absolute active personality principle' is applied, on the other hand, people could be subject to the criminal law of the country of their nationality even if the act is lawful under the law of the country where it was perpetrated. Ambos notes that underlying this is an ideological exaggeration of the purely nationality law ties between a state and a citizen: the postulated "duty of loyalty to the home state" reflects an "authoritarian notion of the state" that is incompatible with the international law principle of non-interference. This view, says Ambos, should therefore be rejected under international law.[395]

Nevertheless some countries, such as the United States and Turkey, claim extraterritorial jurisdiction even if (under the passive personality principle) none of their nationals are victims in the case of offenses committed by their subjects that are regarded as an attack on political or legal principles. This dual standard, which may conflict with the legal system of the country where the offense was committed, is wrong and undesirable for the reason stated by Ambos, but it is not confined to dual nationality situations: the same conflict occurs where the extraterritorial offense is committed by a subject with no other nationality. Extraterritorial criminalization sometimes takes on a political slant, for example in the case of content-related offenses detrimental to the national dignity of a state or its officials (e.g. denigration of the Turkish Nation under Article 301 of the Turkish Criminal Code) or economic interests in international competition (e.g. the criminalization under US law of antitrust offenses). This should be limited by the international law doctrine of jurisdiction;[396] nationality law is unsuitable for this purpose.

Citizens' rights exist thanks to the human right to a nationality. In a world where – as we can all see around us – people are in motion, government policies should not aim solely at controlling this; they should also prevent the geographical dividing lines between countries of origin from becoming divisions in society.[397] It is precisely for this reason that, as I concluded in the previous section, nationality must not be denied or

---

[395] Ibid. 36.

[396] See the discussion concerning the passive personality principle, the security principle and the effects doctrine in Crawford (n. 265) 461–464; cf. Vonk (n. 265) 88.

[397] Cf. Rebecca Tuck, 'Asylum and the path to citizenship. A case study of Somalis in the United Kingdom' (2011) UNHCR Research Paper no. 210 2, 13. It all depends, of course, on what is meant by 'multicultural society' and what the alternative is. Insofar as striving for 'social cohesion' amounts to a modification of multiculturalism, the division suggested loses a lot of its force.

taken away arbitrarily. While not everyone may be entitled to, say, *Dutch* nationality, having a nationality that connects a person with the society of which he or she forms part should be regarded as a fundamental right and not a 'favor'. It is also permissible to demand of a state that it should not throw up any impediments to a citizen wishing to relinquish his or her nationality, which at present is not possible under the laws of various states – including Morocco – in spite of the *change of nationality* clause in the Universal Declaration of Human Rights.[398]

My conclusion here is that this freedom should be recognized internationally. As regards the rights and obligations associated with citizenship, states should recognize the right – as a human right – to renounce (change) nationality. This freedom should also be the guiding principle when it comes to the possibility of retaining a nationality. Multiple citizenship is the legal reflection of the social reality that people's involvements in a society and its system of law can be multiple. This will have an increasing influence on nationality and the exercise of citizens' rights in the twenty-first century. It needs to be recognized that multiple nationality, with the associated citizens' rights, can in fact be a positive factor in relations with co-citizens after moving from one life situation to another.

Awkward attempts to combat multiple citizenship do much more harm than good. It makes more sense to lay down priority rules when determining legal consequences, and here – as the Advisory Committee on Migration Affairs (Adviescommissie voor Vreemdelingenzaken, ACVZ) suggests – the permanent place of residence could be the deciding factor. This would enable changes in this depending on the person's life stage and situation to be taken into account. In their laws, states would do well to recognize – building upon the concept of effective nationality – that there can be a primary and a secondary nationality, and that this can change, depending on life stage and situation. In the case of differences in the legal consequences of a particular act depending on nationality, e.g. in personal and family law, the primary nationality could be the deciding factor, hence usually the law of the country where the person is permanently resident.[399]

The other state should recognize the priority of the state of permanent residence and – apart from situations of reprehensible avoidance – refrain

---

[398] Universal Declaration of Human Rights (adopted 10 December 1948 UNGA Res 217 A(III) (UDHR) art. 15 (2): "No one shall be arbitrarily deprived of his nationality nor denied the right to change his nationality." See on the right to renounce one's nationality also Article 6 of the aforementioned Hague Convention concerning Certain Questions relating to the Conflict of Nationality (12 April 1930).
[399] ACVZ (n. 379) 44.

from attempts to burden its dual citizen living abroad with intruding obligations like conscription. However nice it may appear to give voting rights in elections to non-resident citizens, as the Netherlands and many other countries have done, in situations of permanent absence the consequences are objectionable. These voters influence decisions that will not affect them (e.g. on taxation, health care and social security). It makes more sense for them to have voting rights in their country of residence. In the Netherlands, aliens who have been residents for five years have voting rights in municipal elections. The voting rights of European citizens – including an initiative to give them the right to vote for the national parliament in the Member State of residence – will be discussed in the next paragraph.[400]

As all the recent studies[401] and practical experience show, then, acceptance of the possibility of multiple nationality is appropriate and necessary as a legal reflection of the multiplicity of relationships between citizens and society in the twenty-first century. Legal desiderata follow from this conclusion, namely that citizens should also have the freedom to renounce a nationality, and states should apply rules of precedence to compulsory military service, where it still exists, and to the legal status of persons, e.g. the age of majority and certain issues in international family and inheritance law. International private law resolves this latter point by deciding which is the effective nationality.[402] In the Netherlands, statutory criteria for this are laid down in the recent Book 10 of the Civil Code.[403]

The contention persistently put forward in some quarters that a person's loyalty to the system of law and order can be measured by his or her legal status was a prejudice in the days when states had subjects, and in the twenty-first century it is no more than a politicized defamation. Multiple citizenship should not be regarded as split personality but as the

---

[400] Treaty on the Functioning of the European Union, art. 22 (1).
[401] Likewise Peter J. Spiro, 'A New International Law Of Citizenship' (2011) 105 *American Journal of International Law* 694.
[402] Cf. J.C. Schultsz [1979] NJ 1979, 546 (note); Hans Ulrich Jessurun d'Oliveira, [1979] *Ars Aequi* 1979, 268ff (note). See on this subject also Vonk (n. 265) 84, 125.
[403] See inter alia the Vaststellings- en Invoeringswet Boek 10 Internationaal Privaatrecht van het Burgerlijk Wetboek [Act of laying down and introducing Book 10 International Private Law of the Civil Code] (*Stb* 2011, 272) section 11 (1): "Whether a natural person is a minor and to what extent he is capable of performing legal transactions shall be determined by his domestic law. If the person concerned holds the nationality of more than one state and he has his habitual residence in one of those states, his domestic law shall be the law of that state. If he does not have his habitual residence in one of those states, his domestic law shall be the law of the state of his nationality with which he has the closest ties, taking all circumstances into account."

acceptance and recognition of the fact that people do not have single identities.[404] This view is increasingly accepted internationally, as already noted: "The renunciation requirement is increasingly regarded as a denial of factual reality: an application for naturalization is often based on pragmatic reasons and hardly ever means that the applicant no longer feels attached to the country of origin. This is especially true today, where due to modern technology and affordable transport, emigration is no longer by implication a choice for life. Circular migration and remigration are much more frequent phenomena than in the past."[405]

The "sphere of citizenship" should therefore increasingly be brought into the human rights domain,[406] taking the place of the – no longer exclusive or permanent – state-citizen relationship. A human-rights approach to nationality regards as paramount not the authority of the state but the freedom of citizens, and therefore the multi-faceted nature of their personal identities. The full safeguarding of citizens' rights associated with citizenship is a 'completion' of human rights, in such a way that citizens are enabled to fulfill their political and social responsibilities. Permanently excluding people from the rights that nationals of the particular state do enjoy is ultimately a violation of human rights, directly and indirectly. Another approach is needed, therefore, that – once the conditions for reciprocal involvement have been met – provides *access* to nationality. Only in this way statelessness, arbitrary deprivation of nationality and discrimination can be reversed in due course.

3.6 *Transnational Citizenship*

The fact that human rights are based on the principle of human dignity[407] implies that they are unconditional, irrespective of capabilities, views and other personal qualifications.[408] Restricting citizens' rights to nationals is

---

[404] See Sen, *Identity and Violence* (n. 49) and the report of the Scientific Council for Government Policy, *Identificatie met Nederland* [Identifying with the Netherlands] (Amsterdam UP 2007) along with the preliminary studies.

[405] Vonk (n. 265) 54.

[406] James Goldston, 'Epilogue' in Brad K. Blitz and Maureen Lynch, *Statelessness and Citizenship. A Comparative Study on the Benefits of Nationality* (Edward Elgar 2011) 213.

[407] UDHR (n. 398) art. 1; Charter of Fundamental Rights of the European Union (n. 157) art. 1.

[408] Werner Maihofer, *Rechtsstaat und menschliche Würde* [The constitutional state a nd human dignity] (Vittorio Klostermann 1968) 25ff; Wilfried Härle, *Würde. Groß vom Menschen denken* [Dignity. Thinking of mankind magnanimously] (Diederichs Verlag 2010) 49ff.

only compatible with this under the condition that everyone is adequately protected by a state – whichever that may be. Even then, however, in migration situations the problem remains that resident non-nationals do not have the same legal status as nationals, and therefore not the same citizens' rights. This results in a legal mismatch with the political and social environment.

"All persons in the Netherlands shall be treated equally in equal cases" says Article 1 of the Constitution, but as one of the comments on Article 2 notes, Dutch nationals "are clearly one step ahead".[409] In view of the need for the equal protection of fundamental rights, the question has therefore been raised whether citizens' rights could be divested of their national limitations in some way or other. Iris Marion Young exposed the moral shortcomings of a legal mindset that restricts distributional equity – e.g. in social policy – to "co-nationals": "The claim that members of national groups have obligations to justice *only* to fellow nationals (...) appears to be based on contingent psychological and historical circumstances rather than moral principle."[410] Nevertheless, over-stretching solidarity with the unchecked inclusion of large groups of immigrants can put its acceptance at risk[411] because of its negative impact on experienced reciprocity. Solidarity has to be supported and sustained in long-term oriented government policies; anti-immigration rhetorics cannot replace this.

This explains the quest for a sustainable approach to the recognition of citizens' rights. If such rights are granted to those "who step by step become members of our political communities", it is fair to speak of "open citizenship".[412] Given migration and the need to protect migrant workers, Goldin and his co-authors advocate extending the possibility of retaining their social security entitlements ("Transnational Rights" and "portability" of entitlements).[413] Since its creation in 1957, the European Economic Community has understood the importance of the free movement of

---

[409] B.P. Vermeulen, Artikel 2 [Article 2] in A.K. Koekkoek (ed.), *De Grondwet. Een systematisch en artikelgewijs commentaar* [The Constitution. A systematic article-by-article commentary] (W.E.J. Tjeenk Willink 2000) 75.

[410] Young (n. 54) 241.

[411] Goodhart recommends a "sense of 'emotional citizenship'" in the "solidarity versus diversity debate" (n. 114) intro, part 3.

[412] Francesco Saverio Trincia, 'Individuelles "Bedürfnis nach den Anderen", Universalität des Rechts und open citizenship' [The Individual 'Need for Other People', Universality of the Law and Open Citizenship] in Matthias Kaufmann (ed.), *Integration oder Toleranz? Minderheiten als philosophisches Problem* [Integration or Tolerance? Minorities as a Philosophical Problem] (Verlag Karl Alber 2001) 82.

[413] Goldin, Cameron and Balarajan (n. 74) 272–3.

persons for the socio-economic development of the Community. It sets itself the goal of ending obstacles to freedom of movement so that nationals of the member states can work and engage in other economic activities across borders.[414] The resulting case law on the rights of migrant workers constitutes "the embryo of what later became EU citizenship".[415] In this area, the European Union has taken a highly significant step – building upon the free movement of persons – by creating "citizenship of the Union" in 1993 under the Maastricht Treaty.[416]

This transnational citizenship[417] under Article 9 of the Treaty on European Union, unnecessarily repeated in Article 20 (1) of the Treaty on the Functioning of the European Union, operates alongside national citizenship and not in place of it. According to Article 10 (3), "Every citizen shall have the right to participate in the democratic life of the Union. Decisions shall be taken as openly and as closely as possible to the citizen." The specific rights of the citizens are laid down in – mostly overlapping – provisions in the Treaty on the Functioning of the European Union (Articles 20–24) and the Charter of Fundamental Rights of the European Union.[418] These rights include the right to move around freely and reside freely within the territories of the member states, and to vote and stand in municipal elections – whether or not the person holds the nationality of the state in question – and elections to the European Parliament. A new fundamental right of EU citizens to 'good administration' (under Article 41 of the Charter) accentuates the reciprocal relationship with the functioning of EU government. Following in the footsteps of Ulrich Preuß, Catherine Barnard points out that Union citizenship initially boiled down

---

[414] Barnard (n. 58) 224.

[415] Ibid. 294.

[416] Currently regulated by the Treaty on European Union (Maastricht Treaty) art. 9; Treaty on the Functioning of the European Union art. 20–25; Charter of Fundamental Rights of the European Union (n. 157) ch. IV with many parallel clauses.

[417] According to Faist, Fauser and Reisenauer "the term 'transnational citizenship' results in conceptual overstretching. While this criticism may apply to world citizenship, which is not institutionalized in a legal sense, there are forms of citizenship beyond that of nation-states, such as European Union citizenship." See Thomas Faist, Margit Fauser and Eveline Reisenauer, *Transnational Migration* (Polity 2013).

[418] Relevant from the point of view of transnational citizenship is also the recent Citizens' Initiative about voting rights for European citizens in the Member State, not being their "own" state, where they reside, especially when according to national law they are not entitled to vote in their home country: <http://ec.europa.eu/citizens-initiative/public/initiatives/ongoing/details/2013/000003> accessed on 24 July 2013. See also Rainer Bauböck, Philippe Cayla and Catriona Seth (eds.), 'Should EU Citizens living in other Member States vote there in national elections?' (2012) EUI Working Paper RSCAS 2012/32.

to a terminological summary of existing rights, but as a result of subsequent legislation and case law it is increasingly taking on a meaning of its own as a relationship between individuals and the Union. "European citizenship does now allow individuals a multiplicity of associative relations based on manifold economic, social, cultural, scholarly, and even political activities, irrespective of the traditional boundaries of the European nation-states, without binding individuals to a particular nationality."[419]

As regards citizens' rights, however, it is now clear that European Union citizenship can successfully be cited as law: Eman and Sevinger (at that time members of the Aruban Parliament, now respectively Prime Minister and Minister in the government of Aruba, an autonomous part of the Kingdom of the Netherlands) did so in Dutch courts when they contested their exclusion from the right to vote in European Parliament elections (which also affected most other Dutch nationals resident in the Caribbean countries of the Kingdom). A preliminary ruling by the Court of Appeal put an end to the discriminatory restriction on their European citizens' rights.[420]

The status as a European citizen gradually takes shape as a legal status in its own right. As regards family reunification it sometimes gives mobile EU citizens a stronger legal position than static citizens in 'wholly internal' situations.[421] Even where some would see the situation as wholly internal, however, in a judgment of 2 October 2003 the Court of Justice ruled that a European citizens' right to live and work elsewhere in the Union with the same rights as in his state of origin was affected. The case was a dispute between Carlos Garcia Avello and Belgium regarding an application to change the surname of his children, who hold both Belgian and Spanish nationality. Under Spanish law they could take a name combining the father's and mother's names, but not under Belgian law. The Court ruled that the relevant treaty provisions (currently Articles 18 and 20 of the Treaty on the Functioning of the EU) preclude "in circumstances such as those of the case in the main proceedings, the administrative authority of a Member State from refusing to grant an application for a change of surname made on behalf of minor children resident in that State and having dual nationality of that State and of another Member State, in the case

---

[419] Barnard (n. 58) 477.
[420] Case C-300/04 *Eman and Sevinger v College van burgemeester en wethouders Den Haag* [The Hague municipal executive] [2006] ECR I-8055.
[421] Jessurun d'Oliveira (n. 377) 118–9; Jo Shaw, 'EU citizenship and the edges of Europe' (2012) University of Edinburgh CITSEE Working Paper 2012/19 6–7.

where the purpose of that application is to enable those children to bear the surname to which they are entitled according to the law and tradition of the second Member State".[422]

Other judgments by the Court also indicate that European citizenship has fairly far-reaching consequences. In the *Ruiz Zambrano* case the Columbian parents of children who were born in Belgium and consequently held Belgian and European citizenship, received protection in their claim to be granted a right of residence as third-country nationals as well as a work permit. Otherwise the young European citizens would have had to leave the territory of the Union in order to accompany their parents. The Court ruled that "citizenship of the Union is intended to be the fundamental status of nationals of the Member States (...). In those circumstances, Article 20 TFEU precludes national measures which have the effect of depriving citizens of the Union of the genuine enjoyment of the substance of the rights conferred by virtue of their status as citizens of the Union".[423] This ruling is significant because it shows that the rights of a European citizen are no longer limited to situations of free movement between the Member States: the children had never left Belgium. More recent case law however makes clear that an assessment of individual situations can justify a more restrictive approach on the part of a Member State.[424]

The creation of European citizenship acknowledges a permanent legal – as a matter of fact constitutional – relationship between the citizen and the European Union, giving rights that cannot be taken away from him. In a judgment of 2 March 2010, the Court of Justice substantially strengthened the autonomy of European citizenship by ruling that member states wishing to revoke the nationality of their own nationals – as happened to Jakob Rottmann in Bavaria –, although they have the power to do so, need to take account of the requirement to protect European citizenship (derived from nationality). "It is not contrary to European Union law, in particular to Article 17 EC, for a Member State to withdraw from a citizen of the Union the nationality of that State acquired by naturalization when that nationality was obtained by deception, on condition that

---

[422] Case C-148/02 *Garcia Avello v Belgium* [2003] ECR I-11613.

[423] Case C-34/09 *Ruiz Zambrano* [2011] ECR I-1177, para. 41–42. The Court thus confirmed what it had said about the fundamental status of EU-citizenship in "inter alia, Case C-184/99 *Grzelczyk* [2001] ECR I-6193, para. 31; Case C-413/99 *Baumbast and R* [2002] ECR I-7091, para. 82; *Garcia Avello* (n. 422) para. 22; Case C-200/02 *Zhu and Chen* [2004] ECR I-9925 para. 25; Case C-135/08 *Rottmann* [2010] ECR I-1449, para. 43."

[424] Case C-256/11 *Murat Dereci and Others v. Bundesministerium für Inneres* [2011]; Case C-356–357/11 *O and S v Maahanmuuttovirasto* [2012].

the decision to withdraw observes the principle of proportionality."[425] Comparing the European Court's judgment with the infamous Dred Scott decision of the United States Supreme Court in the last years before the abolition of slavery,[426] Mann and Purnhagen support "the ECJ's more balanced, middle-of-the-road approach – to give Member States great latitude of judgment in determining who their 'people' are but at the same time to affirm the general applicableness of European Union law". They regret however the lack of guidance in the ruling with respect to the appropriateness of the decisions to be taken by the Member States.[427] Also Federico Fabbrini underlines that the ECJ requires the Member states to comply with EU law when exercising their power in citizenship affairs.[428]

This indicates that citizenship of the Union is a status that cannot be taken away from people arbitrarily any more than their nationality. The protection of the right – in some cases enhanced in relation to the domestic right – to marry a bride or bridegroom from another country points to a relationship between EU citizenship and human rights, and it goes without saying that this also applies to the exercise of political rights by EU citizens. Nonetheless, EU citizenship only comes into play as a fall-back provision if national citizenship fails, and it lacks a connection with a fully fledged common political discourse. The European Union is unable to lay down rules on its acquisition. As Shaw rightly points out, the real problem, then, is that European citizenship has had its wings clipped internally. This situation contributes to the fact that "EU citizenship is simply not perceived as being relevant to the democratic and other challenges that almost all the Member States are facing".[429]

The longer this situation persists while the European Union remains aloof from the problems of acquiring and losing the nationality of a

---

[425] *Rottman* (n. 423).

[426] *Dred Scott v Sandford*, 60 US 393 (1857).

[427] Dennis-Jonathan Mann and Kai P. Purnhagen, 'The Nature of Union Citizenship between Autonomy and Dependency on (Member) State Citizenship. A Comparative Analysis of the Rottmann Ruling, or: How to Avoid a European Dred Scott Decision?' (2011) Amsterdam Law School Research Paper no 2011–46; (2011) Amsterdam Centre for European Law and Governance Research Paper no 2011-09 <http://papers.ssrn.com/sol3/papers .cfm?abstract_id=1964269> accessed 24 July 2013.

[428] Federico Fabbrini, 'La Corte di giustizia europe e la cittadinanza dell'Unione: Corte di giustizia dell'Unione europea, grande sezione, sentenza 2 marzo 2010, Causa C-135/08 (Commento)' (2010) 7 *Giornale di diritto amministrativo* 702.

[429] Ibid. 14.

member state,[430] the more apparent the flip side of inclusion in EU citizenship becomes apparent, namely the exclusion of long-term legally resident so-called third-country nationals.[431] From the point of view of equal treatment – an essential feature of all human rights – this aspect of EU citizenship is controversial. D'Oliveira rightly asks: "Does there not come a point where maintaining a distinction between nationals of member states and the remainder of the lawful permanent population amounts to (…) illegal discrimination on the basis of nationality?"[432]

The potential of European Union citizenship as transnational citizenship still remains to be realized fully, then.[433] Experiences of inequality in relation to primary state-based nationality and the oft-discussed weaknesses of the democratic process in the European Union again show that half-hearted constitutional reforms are not a lasting solution. There can be no doubt that the creation of European citizenship in 1991–93 with the Treaty of Maastricht was designed to bring about a constitutional reform of this kind, a *refondation du projet européen* that would, among other things, respond to the democratic deficit experienced.[434] It was not possible to reason out European citizenship adequately, however, as many of those who were made into European citizens – without having asked for this – had no experience to lend sense and meaning to its transnational nature for them. National political leaders lacked the courage and willingness to give the European Union credit for the advantages experienced by all their electors instead of claiming them for themselves. This led to a situation where entirely unnecessary assurances on the nature of European citizenship had to be given to Danish voters in 1992 so as to induce them to agree to the Maastricht Treaty (for example that European citizenship did not result in an entitlement to Danish nationality).[435]

The persistent weaknesses of European citizenship are gauged by others too in terms of what it could and – if constitutional reform were to

---

[430] Vonk (n. 265) 96, points to "the lack of EU Competence to lay down the conditions on acquisition and loss of Member State nationality – and there are no signs that the EU aspires to develop such a competence".

[431] Willem Maas, 'Migrants, states, and EU citizenship's unfulfilled promise' (2008) 12 *Citizenship Studies* 583.

[432] Jessurun d'Oliveira (n. 286) 119.

[433] Cf. Annette Schrauwen, 'European Union in the Treaty of Lisbon: any change at all?' (2008) 25 *Maastricht Journal of European and Comparative Law* 55.

[434] Paul Magnette, *La Citoyenneté Européenne. Droits, politiques, institutions* [European citizenship. Rights, policies, institutions] (Éditions Européennes 1999) 125–33.

[435] Ibid. 155.

become more dynamic – should mean.[436] Further developments will depend to a large extent on the perceived value of EU citizenship as transnational citizenship. It has already taken on a life of its own in European Union Court of Justice case law, increasing its importance in relation to nationality of the member states,[437] with a proportionate decline in the importance of national citizenship. The power of states to reserve public offices for their own nationals is interpreted strictly by the European Court of Justice; the free movement of EU citizens means that being a national of one of the member states makes hardly any difference now within the Union, and the effect of the European Arrest Warrant is that the territory of their own state no longer provides a hiding place for suspects and convicted criminals.[438]

EU citizenship has the potential to become the mainstay of the full and unimpeded enjoyment of human rights transnationally, just as national citizenship did two centuries ago. In the development of substantive rights law, e.g. on the right to vote, family life and the protection of social rights, it is increasingly clear that European citizenship is bound up with the protection of human rights. The importance of this new institution, a transnational citizenship, should therefore not be underestimated.

Citizenship of the Union is similar to nationality but more comprehensive, and it creates new connections that are important to the proper understanding of citizens' rights: it is an original legal solution to providing fair treatment for people who are no longer economically and socially linked to just one member state. Under the entitlement to diplomatic and consular protection (Article 20 (2c) of the Treaty on the Functioning of the EU and Article 46 of the Charter) European citizenship also has a meaning outside the territorial jurisdiction of the Union treaties. In her book on the effects of EU citizenship Flora Goudappel explains how this new status encompasses economic, social and political rights. Safeguarding the rights of EU citizens is thus a step towards the acceptance of transnational citizens' rights, although it immediately raises the question of the flip side: the position of those who are not (or not yet) EU citizens but are legally resident in the EU. Here we see the complementary significance of the EU Directives on the position of third-country nationals and asylum seekers and refugees.

---

[436] See the discussions by Eijsbouts, Jurgens and Jessurun d'Oliveira in *Europees burgerschap* (n. 286).
[437] Vonk (n. 265) 161.
[438] Kochenov (n. 376) 333.

The European Commission is making efforts to achieve increasing acceptance of EU citizenship and even proclaimed a "European Year of Citizens 2013".[439] In a report published in 2010, the Commission identified the obstacles that EU citizens encounter and the discrepancies between the rules on EU citizenship and what happens in practice. The Commission formulated 25 action points to make EU citizenship more effective, including removing linguistic and bureaucratic obstacles.[440] In its "2013 EU Citizenship Report", the Commission evaluated the 2010 action points and presented 12 new key actions.[441] Some of these actions, like safety on the roads, important as they may be, have only a distant relationship with citizenship and citizens' rights. Much more focused on the legal rights of the European Citizen is the Commission's Report, presented on 8 May 2013 under Article 25 of the Treaty on the Functioning of the European Union "On progress towards effective EU Citizenship 2011–2013".[442]

For European citizenship, as to its basic idea, "the only way is up", according to Annette Schrauwen.[443] Nevertheless, although it has now been in existence for twenty years, it receives shabby treatment in the political discourse – even worse than the euro – and not just in the Netherlands. Nationals of the country concerned take advantage of their range of movement within Europe to their hearts' content, bringing them great economic benefits, but when workers from other member states make use of their rights the tone of the political debate turns negative. Jürgen Habermas has put forward various explanations for this. Governments are seen as representing collective state sovereignty, standing up for – supposedly – national interests in Brussels, but it is not yet the case that European citizens exercise the sovereignty of the people under uniform voting rights in a truly European party system.[444] As long as there is no political vision and will to strengthen the European project

---

439   <http://europa.eu/citizens-2013> accessed on 23 July 2013.
440   See European Commission, EU Citizenship Report 2010: Dismantling the obstacles to EU citizens' rights (European Commission 2010).
441   European Commission, EU Citizenship Report 2013. EU Citizens: Your Rights, Your Future (European Commission 2013).
442   European Commission, 'Report from the Commission to the European Parliament, the Council, the European Economic and Social Committee and the Committee of the Regions under Article 25 TFEU on the Progress towards Effective EU Citizenship 2011–2013' COM (2013) 270 final.
443   Annette Schrauwen, *Burgerschap onder gedeeld gezag* [Citizenship under Shared Authority] (inaugural adress University of Amsterdam, oratiereeks.nl 2013) <www.oratiereeks.nl> accessed 30 July 2013.
444   Jürgen Habermas, *Zur Verfassung Europas. Ein Essay* [On the European Constitution. An essay] (Suhrkamp 2011) 73, 77.

institutionally in the face of the euro crisis,[445] we cannot expect European citizenship to be nurtured by the "solidarity of citizens who are willing to stand up for one another".[446]

Although we may conclude that European citizenship widens the inclusiveness of the legal systems of the Member States, the other side of the coin is the exclusion of third-country nationals. In 2011, 6.6 % of the population of the European Union Member States consisted of foreigners, including EU citizens from other Member States.[447] For them European citizenship – as long as it has not been transformed into a legal status in its own right – remains off limits unless they are able to acquire the nationality of one of the Member States. So far third-country nationals permanently and lawfully resident in the European Union have been precluded from acquiring citizenship of the Union on the basis of their legal status in the Union. The limitations on and obstacles to the acquisition of the nationality of one of the member states differ considerably. (While some Member States may be more generous with respect to naturalization, the consequences for other Member States may convince them in the end that it is better to have common European standards for naturalization in view of the ex lege acquisition of EU citizenship.) Third-country nationals migrating legally within the Union are moreover at a strong structural disadvantage, as the continuous period of residence – a customary requirement for naturalization everywhere – is counted separately for each member state. The timer goes back to zero when a person migrates between member states.

Gradually the rights of third-country nationals have been better regulated and strengthened in European legislation and case law, e.g. in the area of family reunification. Nevertheless they ultimately remain aliens as far as European Union law is concerned.[448] European policy on third-country nationals, like national policies on integration, is two-faced (see § 2.2). In line with the Hague Programme for the Area of Freedom, Security and Justice for the 2004–2009 period, the Council of Ministers for Justice and Home Affairs unanimously agreed "Common Basic Principles for

---

[445] Ibid. 79.
[446] Ibid. 76: "Solidarität von Bürgern, die bereit sind, füreinander einzustehen".
[447] See *Eurostat - Statistics in focus* 31/2012 <http://epp.eurostat.ec.europa.eu/cache/ITY_OFFPUB/KS-SF-12-031/EN/KS-SF-12-031-EN.PDF> accessed on 19 August 2013: "In 2011 there were 33.3 million foreign citizens resident in the EU-27, 6.6% of the total population. The majority, 20.5 million, were citizens of non-EU countries, while the remaining 12.8 million were citizens of other EU Member States."
[448] Barnard (n. 58) 478 and 541.

Immigrant Integration Policy"[449] on 19 November 2004. These are based
on the principle that integration is a "dynamic, two-way process of mutual
accommodation", whereby immigrants are expected to have respect for
the "basic values of the EU" and a knowledge of the receiving society's
language, history and institutions, and for their part immigrants are entitled to practice their own cultures and religions and to take part in the
democratic process at national level. The current Stockholm Programme
2010–2014, in the brief section on integration, also includes a call "to
enhance democratic values and social cohesion in relation to immigration
and integration of immigrants and to promote intercultural dialogue and
contacts at all levels".[450]

Although European policy on third-country nationals has increasingly
been implemented so as to legitimize restrictions, European Union law
itself still has corrective mechanisms, in particular because it is based on
general principles such as the requirement of proportionality and fundamental rights, enforced by the European Union Court of Justice.[451] These
constitutional norms, however, are insufficient to achieve a constitutional
relationship with immigrants, i.e. to make European citizenship accessible to them, in the long run, maybe at some time as a corollary of a political Union.

The 2005–2010 European Commission agenda for the implementation
of the Common Basic Principles did acknowledge that the issue of the
participation of immigrants in the democratic process needed to be
mapped out. The closing sentences of the agenda read as follows: "Such a
mapping exercise will contribute to ongoing reflections at EU level on
the value of developing a concept of civic citizenship as a means of promoting the integration of immigrants who do not have national citizenship. Problems of identity lie at the heart of the difficulties which many
young immigrants in particular seem to face today. Further exploration
of these issues at EU level may therefore be helpful."[452] What is lacking,
however, is the consistent implementation of an EU policy to this effect.

---

[449] *Immigrant Integration Policy in the European Union* app no. 14615/04 (Council
Conclusions, 19 November 2004).
[450] The Stockholm Programma – an open and secure Europe serving and protecting
citizens, 4 May 2010, [2010] OJ C 115/01, para. 6.1.5.
[451] Barnard (n. 58) 449 and 457.
[452] Communication from the Commission to the Council, the European Parliament,
the Economic and Social Committee and the Committee of the Regions: 'A Common
Agenda for Integration. Framework for the Integration of Third-Country Nationals in the
European Union' COM (2005) 389.

While the Commission has continued the work by presenting a constructive new European Agenda for the Integration of third-country nationals under the slogan "The Way Forward" in 2011,[453] it no longer poses questions regarding the acquisition of national or European citizenship. Active citizenship is understood mainly in the social sense. However committed the Commission shows itself to be to strengthening the position of third-country nationals, making many worthwhile proposals to this end, the political tide in a number of member states has evidently made it necessary to mark time in this area. For the time being, the road to European citizenship third-country nationals will have to follow will go through the acquisition of national citizenship, which reflects the present condition of the European Union of "shared sovereignty" and "dual democracy".[454]

Once the European Union project has overcome the current monetary and confidence crisis, citizenship may provide a jumping-off point for restarting the political and legal discourse on the Union. We are seeing two trends in the development of European citizenship, as recently discussed in the *European Constitutional Law Review*:[455] one where – in line with the case law of the EU Court of Justice – member states are required to take account of the consequences of their nationality decisions for EU citizenship (Gerard-René de Groot and Anja Seling), and another where the independence of EU citizenship is advocated so as to reduce this dependency on domestic law (H.U. Jessurun d'Oliveira). These two approaches have one thing in common: in periods of migration – within the EU itself to begin with – European citizenship provides a normative framework for fundamental rights for people on the move. The political climate is however at present not favourable: according to Jo Shaw, "the equality that is supposed to underlie the free movement rules seems to be increasingly under threat from all sides."[456]

Jo Shaw sees a decoupling process taking place, with active participation ultimately becoming the deciding factor in European citizenship:

---

[453] Communication from the Commission to the Council, the European Parliament, the Economic and Social Committee and the Committee of the Regions, 'European Agenda for the Integration of Third-Country Nationals' COM (2011) 455.

[454] Roger Schütze, *European Constitutional Law* (CUP 2012) 71–77.

[455] Hans Ulrich Jessurun d'Oliveira, Gerard-Réne de Groot and Anja Seling, *'Janko Rottman v. Freistaat Bayern C-315/08'* [ECJ 2 March 2010] 7 *European Constitutional Law Review* 138 (Double note 'Decoupling Nationality and Union Citizenship?' and 'The Consequences of the Rottmann Judgment on Member State Autonomy – The European Court of Justice's Avant-Gardism in Nationality Matters').

[456] Shaw (n. 421) 12.

"a form of post-national membership radically different from a (nation) statist concept of citizenship".[457] The EU citizens' "double status", which is the very essence of this transnational citizenship, reflects the "multilevel constitutionalism of the EU"[458] – and maybe even its cultural identity of exchanges, translations and interpretations across borders.[459] In this line of thought, national and European citizenship retain their value and importance alongside each other. J.H.H. Weiler also advocates the parallel recognition of national citizenship, in his view based on "a strong sense of cultural identification and belonging", and citizenship derived from the European legal system, based on "shared values which transcend ethno-national diversity".[460]

The development of the law on European citizenship has anyway taken on a life of its own, in spite of the opposition to European integration that has been whipped up. My conclusion, then, is that the acceptance of a transnational citizenship such as European citizenship offers pioneering prospects, even though it is of course restricted to European Union citizens. Transnational citizenship bridges the gulf between citizenship that is tied to a single state and people's lives, which unfold across state borders.

---

[457] Jo Shaw, 'Citizenship of the Union. Towards Post-National Membership?' in Academy of European Law (ed.), *Collected Courses of the Academy of European Law, vol. VI book 2* (Kluwer Law International, 1998), cited by Barnard (n. 58). In his recent book, Nico Krisch discusses the problems with respect to "foundational" constitutionalism in an emerging postnational global context. These developments contribute to the relevance of transnational citizenship, and also to a right to make reasonable choices about one's one citizenship. See Krisch (n. 194).

[458] Christian Calliess, 'The Dynamics of European Citizenship: From Bourgeois to Citoyen' in Allan Rosas, Egils Levits and Yves Bot (eds.), *The Court of Justice and the Construction of Europe. Analyses and Perspectives on Sixty Years of Case-law / La Cour de Justice et la Construction de l'Europe. Analyses et Perspectives de Soixante Ans de Jurisprudence* (T.M.C. Asser Press/Springer 2013) 431; cf. on the constitutional ambiguity inherent in European citizenship also Espend D.H. Olsen, 'European Citizenship. Mixing Nation State and Federal Features with a Cosmopolitan Twist' (2013) 14 *Perspectives on European Politics and Society* 1.

[459] Étienne Balibar, *We, the People of Europe? Reflections on Transnational Citizenship* (transl. from French *Nous, citoyens d'Europe: Les Frontières, l'État, le peuple* 2001, Princeton UP 2004) 234–235.

[460] J.H.H. Weiler, 'To be a European citizen – Eros and civilization' (1997) 4 *Journal of European Public Policy* 495.

CHAPTER FOUR

THE HUMAN RIGHT TO BE A CITIZEN

4.1 *Citizenship, Self-Determination and Human Rights*

We have already pointed out that citizenship is required for the enjoyment of political rights. With this in mind I shall finally explore the relationship between citizenship – based on its political significance – and human rights in more detail. Two decades ago, just after the collapse of the Soviet system, Thomas Franck wrote about "The Emerging Right to Democratic Governance",[461] thus opening up a dimension of human rights that had been avoided during the Cold War, since any attempt to find common ground with the Communist states with respect to constitutional questions had been doomed to failure. The human rights covenants passed by the United Nations General Assembly in 1966 and subsequently signed by many states include (a) rights that must be observed by states immediately (International Covenant on Civil and Political Rights [ICCPR], Article 2) and (b) rights whose "progressive realization" is required (International Covenant on Economic, Social and Cultural Rights [ICESCR], Article 2). Although these conventions are silent on the subject of the democratic constitution – which rather dates them –, the International Convention on the Elimination of All Forms of Racial Discrimination (Article 5) and the Convention on the Elimination of All Forms of Discrimination against Women [CEDAW] (Article 7) do address specific aspects of citizenship.

The common "essential bottom line to be respected under all circumstances, even in times of shrinking resources, is that of non-discrimination", which the treaties require to be observed immediately and in full.[462] The ban on discrimination has a direct effect on the organization of constitutional systems, e.g. by requiring equal access to the political system for men and women, and affects 'political rights' in the sense of those

---

[461] Thomas M. Franck, 'The Emerging Right to Democratic Governance' (1992) 86 *American Journal of International Law* 46. See also Gregory H. Fox and Brad R. Roth (eds.), *Democratic Governance and International Law* (CUP 2000).

[462] International Covenant on Civil and Political Rights (n. 157) arts. 2 and 26; International Covenant on Economic, Social and Cultural Rights (adopted 16 December 1966, entered into force 3 January 1976) 993 UNTS 3 (ICESCR), arts. 2 and 3; cf. Boven (n. 329) 175.

human rights that make the political discourse possible (freedom of speech, assembly and association) and the citizens' rights set out in Article 25 ICCPR, including the right to vote (see § 3.2). At the same time, it is a legal principle for the organization of society and the functioning of the economy. To the same extent to which the democratic participation of the citizens in the public discourse and elections is a source of legitimation, exclusion from citizenship affecting members of the population has a delegitimizing effect.

In the same vein, socio-economic obstacles to the exercise of citizens' rights have such a delegitimizing effect. As Theo van Boven points out, the rights under the ICESCR cannot be dismissed as a side issue. "Over the years, as the human rights discourse became part of processes towards widening categories of entitlements and beneficiaries and linking human rights to the promotion of peace, security, and sustainable development, as well as preserving a healthy environment, a comprehensive human rights approach has evolved, encompassing the broad and interlinked scale of civil, political, economic, social, and cultural rights."[463] Equality of dignity and rights pertains to the entirety of human rights, so it was important and even necessary to think in terms of generations of human rights, recognizing the interrelationships and transitions between them: freedoms, social rights and collective rights of communities such as the right to development.[464]

The old-fashioned view that international law has nothing to say about giving and withholding citizenship is fading (see also § 3.1). There is a trend for this to be more and more the case, resulting from the human rights perspective. The increasing involvement of international law in democracy is strengthening this trend, as citizenship is the key to democratic participation, even in countries where democracy is still in its infancy. The relationship between democracy and international law is a complex one. The recognition of a universal right to democratic governance will bring citizenship unequivocally within the ambit of human rights.

An indirect step in this direction was the acknowledgement in 1966 of the collective right to self-determination in the identically worded Article 1 (1) of the ICCPR and Article 1 (1) of the ICESCR: "All peoples have the

---

[463] Boven (n. 329) 176.
[464] Arjun Sengupta, 'Development Co-operation and the Right to Development' in Morten Bergsmo (ed.), *Human Rights and Criminal Justice for the Downtrodden. Essays in Honor of Asbjørn Eide* (Martinus Nijhoff Publishers 2003).

right of self-determination. By virtue of that right they freely determine their political status and freely pursue their economic, social and cultural development." The collective right to self-determination, recognized in Article 1 (1) ICCPR and Article 1 (1) ICESCR appeared, when this provision was laid down, to be a politically necessary confirmation of decoloniza-tion but falling outside the proper subject of the covenants. Julie Debeljak, however, regards the right set out in this clause as "the essence of democ-racy", since "self-determination is the right of a people to determine its political status collectively". Democracy depends on human rights, as Debeljak puts it, both as collective rights and as seen from the point of view of citizens' individual legal status. The democratic rights of citizens are a spin-off: "This includes the right to free, fair and open participation in the democratic processes of government", hence the need for "addi-tional rights" such as "the right to vote and the right to run for public office".[465] These rights in turn presuppose freedom of speech, freedom of assembly, personal freedom and due process, but also fundamental eco-nomic, social and cultural rights. In relation to these rights, citizens' rights are confined to nationals only because by their nature they presuppose a specific relationship with the state in question. But that does not make them a dispensable accolade, a bonus, or something that puts you 'one step ahead'.

As early as in 1992 Franck viewed the right to self-determination as the decisive anchor-point – followed by free expression and free elections – for the recognition of the democratic principle in international law.[466] In 1993, the Vienna Declaration of Human Rights affirmed the relationship between the right to self-determination and the different generations of human rights, including the democratic principle: "Democracy, develop-ment and respect for human rights and fundamental freedoms are inter-dependent and mutually reinforcing. Democracy is based on the freely expressed will of the people to determine their own political, economic, social and cultural systems and their full participation in all aspects of their lives."[467] The historical and cultural conditions for the development of a coherent view on citizenship and human rights are obviously not the

---

[465] Julie Debeljak, 'Rights and Democracy. A Reconciliation of the Institutional Debate' in Tom Campbell, Jeffrey Goldsworthy and Adrienne Stone (eds.), *Protecting Human Rights. Instruments and Institutions* (OUP 2003) 149.

[466] Franck (n. 461) 52: "Self-determination is the historic root from which the demo-cratic entitlement grew."

[467] Vienna Declaration and Programme of Action, UNGA A/CONF.157/23 (12 July 1993) para. I.8.

same all over the world. The acceptance of the right to self-determination was a catalyst for political developments in parts of the world like the Middle-East and Africa, where the Western idea of individual rights was not at home. Abdullahi Ahmed An Na'im, arguing from an Islamic scholarly point of view, emphasizes the importance of democratic citizenship in a secular state as a precondition for the freedom to live a life in conformity with the values and principles of a faithful person.[468]

Daniel Halberstam has dissected the "constitutional idea of limited self-governance" into "three primary values", "'voice', 'rights' and 'expertise'".[469] In a democratic constitutional context, "the people are not only the object but also the authors of the law to which they are subject."[470] It is in the connection between 'voice' and 'rights' that we find the essence of the political rights associated with citizenship. But the rules that are thus legitimized are not confined to the life of the state, they also – indeed primarily, from a historical perspective – relate to civil society, trade, the law of persons and family law, and all the other areas of codification where the citizenry subjected itself to new rules after the French Revolution. Merely identifying the right to be a citizen with certain specific fundamental rights related to a person's own state, such as the right to take part in elections and not to be deported from his or her own country, is not enough: the relationship between citizenship and the specific rights associated with it is not just a question of the political system but of the entirety of social and economic relations organized by that system (*bürgerliche Gesellschaft* – civil society – and the *Bedürfnisse* – needs – regulated by it[471]). Étienne Balibar emphasizes that the "genesis of the modern citizen" has a wide range. Citizenship is "not purely a question of autonomy in the Rousseauian and Kantian sense (being oneself the author of the law to which one conforms), but also of autonomy or independence in the Spinozist or Lockean sense: 'self-ownership,' ownership of the actions of one's body and the thoughts of one's mind."[472]

---

[468] Abdullahi Ahmed An-Na'im, *Islam and the Secular State. Negotiating the Future of Shari'a* (Harvard UP 2008) 84: "constitutional and human rights norms enable citizens to exchange information, organize and act publicly to promote their own vision of the social good, and protect their rights."

[469] Halberstam (n. 53) 171.

[470] Benhabib, *Another Cosmopolitanism* (n. 29) 148.

[471] Cf. Ludwig Heyde, 'Behoefte en vrijheid. Hegels begrip van het economische in de Grundlinien der Philosophie des Rechts' [Need and freedom: Hegel's concept of economy in Elements of the Philosophy of Right] (1977) 39 *Tijdschrift voor Filosofie* 286.

[472] Balibar (n. 459) 197.

Democracy, then, is not just having a voice in the state as the body politic but in the whole of society organized by the law: the society in which all the other human rights – of assembly and association, of freedom of religion and property, of freedom of education and social security, to name but a few – operate. Fundamental rights are not just about freedoms in relation to the state and the restrictions that the government needs to comply with, but the whole organization of social life. This interplay between the way fundamental rights work is the true meaning of the three so-called "generations of human rights".[473] The previous sections showed how statelessness, by denying citizenship, has a negative and sometimes even destructive effect on participation in the society in which those affected by it live, and what a dynamizing effect the acquisition of citizenship has, even in the skeletal form of European citizenship.

In the case of all fundamental rights, it is people's life situations that reveal what real meaning the recognition of those rights has for them.[474] This is more than a question of the government's responsibility for preventing iniquities; it also applies the other way round: without citizens' rights, situations of social and economic disadvantage and deprivation of rights are all the more intractable, as experience shows. The true value of texts, however mellifluous, is determined by socio-economic and administrative conditions – the aspect of human rights that Bas de Gaay Fortman focuses upon in his work[475] –, but at the same time these rights are a necessary jumping-off point in the struggle against deprivation. Citizenship, in the origin of these rights and the fight for their recognition, is bound up with participation in social and economic life, culture and science. The civil rights movement in the USA, like other past and present emancipation processes, was about being a free and equal subject in politics and civil society and therefore, in their full sense, about human rights.[476]

---

[473] The expression was coined in a speech at the International Institute for Human Rights in Strasbourg by Karel Vasak, 'A 30-year struggle. The sustained efforts to give force of law to the Universal Declaration of Human Rights' [speech at the International Institute for Human Rights in Strasbourg] (1977) XXX *The UNESCO Courier* 11, 29, 32.

[474] This is the subject of my article 'Werking en verwerkelijking van grondrechten' [The operation and realization of fundamental rights] in Ludwig Heyde and others (eds.), *Begrensde vrijheid. Opstellen over mensenrechten* [Limited freedom. Essays on human rights] (presented to Prof. D.F. Scheltens on his retirement as Professor at the Catholic University of Nijmegen, W.E.J. Tjeenk Willink 1989) 128–45.

[475] Bas de Gaay Fortman, *Political Economy of Human Rights. Rights, Realities and Realization* (Routledge 2011).

[476] Cf. Thomas F. Jackson, *From Civil Rights to Human Rights. Martin Luther King, Jr., and the Struggle for Economic Justice* (University of Pennsylvania Press 2007).

Citizens' rights have thus turned out to be vital in a much broader context than just as political rights in the world of the twenty-first century, where so many people are on the move, to the cities in their own countries, to other countries, as economic migrants, refugees or loved ones, or as profiteers, criminals, or victims; and it is not always possible to establish with certainty what is making people move.[477] We saw in the previous chapter when discussing the problems of stateless persons that they lack more than just a proper passport. From the other side, as it were, we saw the same correlation in the reason for placing the rights originally intended solely as reciprocal economic freedoms of the nationals of the member states in the broader context of European *citizenship*. It is clear that the legal system can no longer be based – if indeed this was ever the case – on the unquestioned congruency of state and nationality. In the wake of twentieth-century nationalism, the smooth integration of *étrangers* in the French legal system at the time of the Revolution has given way to strict criteria for admission and the granting of civil rights. Meanwhile, gigantic holes have been punched in this by political and socio-economic facts, or by consequences that these same states have had to attach to the ban on the *refoulement* of refugees and the obligations to protect people against inhuman or humiliating treatment and to respect family life.[478] The protection of human rights, then, affects migration, and not just in the case of refugees.

Worldwide this is leading to the need to deal with the mismatch between population mix and nationality, i.e. the ill-boding lacuna in the implementation of human rights insofar as this depends on nationality. Human rights – while there is a hard core of protection against systematic abuse – only have the prospect of development once 'voice' – i.e. a say in one's own life – is combined with an ethos in which rights are optimized. We know from Amartya Sen that it depends on that voice and those rights whether people have food,[479] education for their children and a roof over their heads. The redefinition of citizenship leads us to the question of whether it could be regarded less as tied to the state and more in terms of human rights.

This brings us back to political rights. It is vital, not just from the perspective of the relationship between citizens and their states but as regards

---

[477] Cf. International Organization for Migration (IOM), *International Migration Report* (IOM 2010) for the discussion regarding 'mixed migration flows'.

[478] Convention for the Protection of Human Rights and Fundamental Freedoms (European Convention on Human Rights, as amended) (ECHR) arts. 2 and 8.

[479] Sen, *The Idea of Justice* (n. 224) 389–390.

the entirety of human rights, that the importance of democracy as a *constitutional system* is recognized in the international political discourse. In international *Realpolitik* there was until recently an acceptance – to prevent even worse things from happening – of semblances of democracy where political rights were assigned to population groups rather than individuals – as if there *could* be such a thing as democracy without rights. The argument was often couched in terms of internal and international peace, the positive effects of which on human rights and citizens' rights were supposed to be a by-product, as it were, but this was never proven.[480] However, democracy and the rule of law are not available separately.[481] It is the citizens' rights concerned with participation in public life that make a state a democracy. The protection of human rights requires a constitutional order to be effectuated with legislative powers and an independent judiciary. Since a democratic polity governed by the rule of law cannot exist without citizens, citizens' rights have to be part and parcel of the fundamental rights. The constitutional fact that their enjoyment is confined to nationals creates a rift between the source of legitimation of public powers (the "voice" in Halberstam's terminology) and the addressee of the democratic legitimation, i.e. the population as a whole. To the extent that people subject themselves temporarily and voluntarily to a jurisdiction that is not theirs, such a discrepancy appears to be acceptable, but with respect to permanent residents, denial of citizens' rights amounts to exclusion from the process of realization of human rights. Hence the expression "denizens", who should in the view of T. Alexander Aleinikoff enjoy certain rights approaching – but not identical with – citizens' rights.[482]

The entirety of human rights recognition and protection, described in the first chapter of this book as the historical outcome of civil emancipation, forces us to conclude that both democratic constitutionality and human rights require the recognition of the right to be a citizen for every member of the society who is able and willing to assume the reciprocal responsibilities of citizenship (the "office" of being a citizen, see § 2.2 *in fine*).

---

[480] Cf. the controversial idea, interpreted in various ways, that "international law includes a right to democratic government." See Charles R. Beitz, *The Idea of Human Rights* (OUP 2009) 174.

[481] Ernst M.H. Hirsch Ballin, 'De rechtsstaat, wachten op een nieuwe dageraad?' (2011) 87 *Nederlands Juristenblad* 71; cf. Jürgen Habermas, 'Über den internen Zusammenhang von Rechtsstaat und Demokratie' [On the internal relationship between the constitutional state and democracy] in Menke and Raimondi (n. 35) 442–53.

[482] Aleinikoff (n. 292) 147–148.

This is why democracy and the constitutional state are intrinsically inter-connected and interwoven. Just as the constitutional state exists by and for everyone, majority democratic decision-making must never be sepa-rated from responsibility for society as a whole. Excluding people from citizenship and citizens' rights does even more violence to the underlying social cohesion ("We the people") that carries, as it were, the state.

If we sum up what such a universal right to be a citizen means in reality, then, the notion that states are free under international law to decide whether to organize themselves as democracies is no longer tenable. This also answers the key question posed at the start of this book, how in our era citizens' rights can once more bridge the gap between the universality of human rights without distinction and the political and social setting in which people participate in a democratic society. Our approach requires the *legal recognition as citizens* of those members of a society who are ready to assume the ensuing rights and responsibilities. Under interna-tional law, in force of the principles of democratic self-governance and equal respect due to anyone everywhere, states should restate their "sover-eign" power to recognize, give or withhold citizenship as an *obligation* mir-roring the human right to citizenship in the state – or, depending on someone's existential situation, in *a* state – where he or she is at home.

Statehood is in this view definitely not irrelevant, but – in accordance with the universal primacy of human rights – its legitimacy is dependent on the extent to which it serves and protects its citizens. Here is the com-mon ground of our view with value-cosmopolitanism, but also the differ-ence with cosmopolitanist views that would ignore the importance of constitutional relations between human beings and *specific* states. Only "a few political cosmopolitans", emphasizes Kwame Anthony Appiah, "say they want a world government."[483] The cosmopolitanism defended by Appiah is rather a moral quality, requiring understanding and practical "kindness to strangers".[484] Immanuel Kant views the "ius cosmopoliticum" (*Weltbürgerrecht*) as the fruit of a legal principle,[485] requiring all nations on earth to live under a common arrangement of peaceful coexistence and cooperation, but a cosmopolitan law in this would not by itself create

---

[483] Kwame Anthony Appiah, *Cosmopolitanism. Ethics in a World of Strangers* (W.W. Norton 2006) 163.

[484] Ibid. ch. 10.

[485] Immanuel Kant, 'Metaphysik der Sitten, Erster Teil. Metaphysische Anfangsgründe der Rechtslehre. Das öffentliche Recht' in Immanuel Kant, *Zum ewigen Frieden und Auszüge aus der Rechtslehre. Kommentar von Oliver Eberl und Peter Niesen* (first published 1797, Suhrkamp 2011) para. 63.

identical rights for citizens all over the world. The only right that Kant conceives of is a "Weltbürgerrecht" – a cosmopolitan right – to universal hospitality.[486] Seyla Benhabib builds on this legacy in her search for "cosmopolitan norms" that "go beyond liberal international sovereignty"[487] and justify punishing crimes against humanity.[488]

Pierik and Werner discuss "the ideal world of moral cosmopolitanism"[489] as a framework for a wide range of international rights and institutions, incorporating "notions such as 'the common bonds' and the 'shared heritage' of all peoples, the idea of human dignity, or the notion that environmental protection is a 'common concern of humankind.'"[490] The understanding that "immigrants should be placed on the road to citizenship"[491] also fits into this framework.

Cosmopolitanism as a moral concept reminds us that differences according to someone's citizenship are questionable. While it is inconceivable that 'world citizenship' will be recognized as the right of everyone to exercise citizens' rights in their chosen place, in terms of moral concepts it does make two things clear: (a) that the inevitable negative side of citizenship of a state – the exclusion inherent in any specific inclusion – requires *justification*, and (b) that no-one must be excluded from having an *appropriate* nationality. States have the right to apply procedures and criteria here, but these must not result in people not being able to acquire citizenship in the society/societies that they may regard as their home(s).

A true world citizen is aware not only of humanity but also of its many manifestations. States – complemented both by infrastatal regional authorities, closer to real life problems, and by unions of states with common objectives such as the European Union – are necessary to justice, peace and prosperity. Recognizing the right to be a citizen as a human right places citizenship at the center of human rights. Although citizenship is more limited in scope than being human – a person is only a citizen in relation to a particular state – this is not a limitation of human rights but a strengthening. Taking the citizen as the point of reference means that (a) every state must be willing, and must provide a procedure, to

---

[486] Immanuel Kant, 'Dritter Definitivartikel zum ewigen Frieden' in Kant, *Zum ewigen Frieden* (n. 485) 30–3.
[487] Benhabib, *Another Cosmopolitanism* (n. 29) 24.
[488] Ibid. 21.
[489] Pierik and Werner (n. 28) 3.
[490] Roland Pierik and Wouter Werner, 'Can cosmopolitanism survive institutionalization?' in Pierik and Werner (n. 28) 277.
[491] Jorge M. Valadez, 'Is immigration a human right?' in Pierik and Werner (n. 28) 238.

make citizenship accessible to those whose role in society qualifies them for it, so that no-one is unjustifiably excluded *de jure* or *de facto*, and (b) the fundamental rights to which citizens are entitled are gauged by the dynamics of and interplay between the three generations of human rights. It is because of the importance of states for administering justice and organizing solidarity between citizens that national citizenship cannot be replaced by a transnational model.[492]

Radical cosmopolitanism would do away with any difference between being the citizen of one state or that of another, whereas in our view questions have to be answered about the way in which states share the responsibility of leaving no one devoid of appropriate citizenship. International agreements about reducing statelessness are definitely important, however inadequate unless states recognize actual defects, especially when states fail to recognize de facto statelessness (see § 3.4). If someone's nationality has become irrelevant, the person concerned should have the right to apply for a relevant and effective nationality and the state of the person's original nationality should, where necessary, cooperate with renunciation.

Becoming the citizen of a state should in this sense be liberalized, but that does not make it a matter of choice. The state has the right – and as regards its existing citizens the duty – to assess in well-ordered administrative proceedings whether or not someone's bonds with society justify and require his recognition as a citizen: social cohesion can be damaged both by over-inclusion and by under-inclusion.[493]

The importance of origin – being born as a resident of the country (*ius soli*) or being the child of a citizen (*ius sanguinis*) – is sufficient to justify citizenship *ex lege*. Someone's ability to use a common language (some societies have one; other societies are multilingual) and to understand the society's institutions as a rule require no further legal obligations, since family and school will play their role; additional testing would affront the shared understanding of belonging to the same people or even be detrimental to a person's human right to be a citizen. In other cases, where the existence of a ius nexus has to be established, the granting of citizenship

---

[492] While emphasizing the primacy of a post-national model in her view, Yasemin Nuhoğlu Soysal does not overlook that "the responsibility of providing and implementing individual rights lies with national states" (*Limits of Citizenship. Migrants and Postnational Membership in Europe* (The University of Chicago Press 1994) 143).

[493] David Goodhart (see § 3.6, text to n. 411) warns against the risks of over-inclusion, which would be detrimental to solidarity, Doug Saunders (see § 2.1, text to n. 88) against the risks of under-inclusion, hampering the integration process.

("naturalization") has to be related to relevant life events (such as marriage, adoption or asylum) or to be applied on the basis of an individual assessment. An assessment is, however, not the same as an exam. The integration tests that in recent years have been introduced in the Netherlands and some other countries are at risk of going beyond what is necessary with respect to the granting of citizenship, either because they amount to an opinion test in breach of fundamental freedoms, or because they exclude people with impairments or learning difficulties. The assessment should therefore retain the character of an administrative decision about the aforesaid qualification for citizenship, i.e. being a member of society who is able and willing to assume the reciprocal responsibilities of citizenship. Legal and moral responsibilities as a citizen are not the same for everyone, but depend on what someone can reasonably be asked to contribute. A person with a physical disability does not have to do military service, a person with political talents ought to consider getting involved in democratic decision-making processes. Having been a (legal) resident for a sufficiently long period can be a precondition for obtaining citizenship on the basis of an individual assessment, or a reason for omitting further assessments.

Such a human right to be a citizen of the state where someone is effectively at home will go beyond the existing norms about nationality. It is also more than being protected against statelessness, since it focuses on the human-rights dimension of the constitutional relationship between person and state. It will reflect a major change in international legal development since the last decades of the twentieth century. This development in international law has meant that persons – human beings – have gained a place of their own, not only in their citizenship but also in their individuality.[494] Andrew Fagan meanwhile points out that a one-sided emphasis on "cosmopolitan principles" as the basis for human rights shows the state in too much of a negative light, as if it primarily constitutes a threat to human rights. This is to misconstrue "the state's capacity to protect human rights"[495] and – I would add – the state as a framework within which citizens decide on their political destiny in a democratic process. The proper operation of the international legal order stands and falls with democracy and accountability at national level – and this is exactly what the core rights of the citizens are about. Human rights must be implemented in

---

[494] Hirsch Ballin, *Wereldburgers* (n. 268).
[495] Fagan (n. 69) 77.

and by the state: this is the current meaning of the relationship set out in the *Déclaration* between human rights, citizens' sovereignty and citizens' rights.[496]

Recognition of a human right to be a citizen will also stress the importance of strict limitations on "denationalization" or "denaturalization".[497] According to Article 15 (2) of the Universal Declaration on Human Rights, "No one shall be arbitrarily deprived of his nationality nor denied the right to change his nationality." Some treaties and constitutions already contain limitations on the revocation of citizenship, limiting the power to apply such measures to situations of fraudulent acquisition or a manifest breach of trust. Article 7 of the European Convention on Nationality (a Council of Europe Treaty signed on 6 November 1997) allows states to revoke citizenship in situations of fraudulent acquisition, voluntary foreign military service or "conduct seriously prejudicial to the vital interests of the State party", but (with the exception of the cases of fraud) only if the person concerned would not thereby become stateless. Nevertheless, this convention still allows for the revocation of citizenship on the mere ground of acquisition of another nationality, a measure which in many cases infringes upon the human right, as recommended here, to be a citizen where someone is at home, possibly in more than one country at different moments.

4.2 Gender and Citizenship

Recognition of a human right to citizenship and establishing the limits of the state's demos is thus "not merely a matter of the 'inside/outside' distinction; it is in the first place about the status of the so-called 'others' within the *demos* itself."[498] Obviously it is difficult for many people to accept that they are really equal in dignity with any other human being and therefore have no innate entitlement to more power in state and society than others. Notwithstanding the public endorsement of equal citizenship, inequalities continue to find a dubious justification in the idea that some people are entitled to more power, not because of what they *do* but because of who they *are* as to their sex, ethnicity or religion. People have different abilities, but what counts in the end is the way they use

---

496 Jaume (n. 38).
497 Cf. Manly and Van Waas (n. 361) 63.
498 Benhabib, *Dignity in Adversity* (n. 337) 165.

their abilities, and not abuse them. The equation of statehood with being a nation with a supposedly distinctive ethnical and cultural "identity" has often served as a justification for exclusion from citizenship. Another dangerous motive for exclusion from citizenship is the attribution of distinctive qualifications to male subjects. These two patterns of exclusion are related, just like their reverse. The increased acceptance of dual nationality is due partly to the acceptance of equal rights for men and women in family law and in migration law concerning family reunification. At the same time, removing obstacles to multiple nationality also puts women in a better position to go their own way, e.g. to decide about their future after the dissolution of a marriage through divorce or death: the dependence of women upon their husbands' economic and legal position can thus be reduced.[499]

The importance of citizens' rights to emancipation can be seen par excellence in the case of those who are excluded from social and political participation by virtue of their gender. Limiting full citizenship to persons of the male sex has a long history and has by no means ended. The arguments put forward were often based on biologism, but the real explanations, as always, were related to socio-economic empowerment and disempowerment in a legal guise.

Technological development, industrialization and urbanization were critical to the equal rights movements of the nineteenth and twentieth centuries.[500] Here again citizenship – despite its inherently inclusive purport – was used as a means of exclusion. Excluding women was thus a kind of second-degree exclusion, as it turned them into second-class citizens within their (often still nationally delineated) communities. This is why the exclusion affected not only their right to vote – in the Netherlands up to less than a century ago – but also their legal status under civil law – in the Netherlands up to less than sixty years ago – in that married women had no legal capacity and were obliged to leave civil service posts upon marriage. This discrimination in terms of citizens' rights not only violates the constitutional requirement of equal treatment but also affects the place in society associated with citizenship. Women must be able to be the

---

[499] Betty de Hart considers inter alia the position of women in migration law and nationality law in her PhD thesis *Onbezonnen vrouwen. Gemengde relaties in het nationaliteitsrecht en het vreemdelingenrecht* [Impetuous women. Mixed relationships in nationality law and aliens law] (Aksant 2003) 78–83.
[500] Rosalind Rosenberg, 'The "Woman Question"' in Richard W. Bulliet (ed.), *The Columbia History of the 20th Century* (Columbia UP 1998).

personal reference point of relationships in socio-economic and cultural life, and this is why their emancipation, just like the emancipation of Jews and others, began there.

Even many of the most enlightened and learned thinkers at the time of the French Revolution did not yet realize that women are entitled to equal protection of their citizens' rights. The principles of the French Revolution were subject to "permanent, self-radicalizing redefinition": "What not long before had been seen as an enormous step forward in the achievement of equality – equality of rights with all male residents – soon afterwards turned out to be a form of social suppression of natural rights", as Christoph Menke put it in his introduction to a pamphlet, published by Olympe de Gouges in 1791.[501] She demanded a *Déclaration des Droits de la Femme et de la Citoyenne*, but was guillotined two years later.[502] Her treatise and her actions were the starting point for a long struggle for the citizens' rights of women – especially the rights to vote and to stand for election – that in many parts of the world is not over yet. Although equal treatment of men and women is solidly anchored in the Dutch constitution and several treaties with direct effect in the Dutch legal order, in recent years the right to stand for election was the subject of one of the few court rulings on citizens' rights. The *Staatkundig Gereformeerde Partij* (a small orthodox reformed political party) used, according to its religious principles, to accept only male members of the party as candidates in parliamentary elections. In 2010, the *Hoge Raad der Nederlanden* (Court of cassation of the Netherlands) ruled that the prohibition of discrimination with respect to the right to be elected to Parliament cannot be restricted by the freedom of religion.[503] This judgment was based on Article 7 (a) and (c) of the Convention on the Elimination of All Forms of Discrimination against Women (CEDAW), which provisions of the convention have direct effect in the national legal order of the Netherlands:

---

[501] Menke and Raimondi (n. 35) 19.

[502] See Menke and Raimondi (n. 35) 54–57.

[503] See HR 9 April 2010 *LJN* BK4547 for the judgment of the Dutch Court of Cassation regarding the SGP, based on the Convention on the Elimination of All Forms of Discrimination against Women, UNGA A/RES/34/180 (18 December 1979) art. 7. This judgment overruled the verdict of the Afdeling bestuursrechtspraak van de Raad van State [Administrative Jurisdiction Division of the Council of State], the highest tribunal in an administrative law case, regarding the subsidization of the SGP, see ABRvS 5 December 2007 *LJN* BB9493 *AB* 2008, 35.

States Parties shall take all appropriate measures to eliminate discrimination against women in the political and public life of the country and, in
particular, shall ensure to women, on equal terms with men, the right:

    (a) To vote in all elections and public referenda and to be eligible for
          election to all publicly elected bodies;

    (b) To participate in the formulation of government policy and the
          implementation thereof and to hold public office and perform all
          public functions at all levels of government;

    (c) To participate in non-governmental organizations and associations
          concerned with the public and political life of the country.

The judgment of the *Hoge Raad* was confirmed in a decision of the ECHR
of 10 July 2012. The Court considered, *inter alia*, "that the advancement of
the equality of the sexes is today a major goal in the member States of the
Council of Europe. This means that very weighty reasons would have to be
advanced before a difference of treatment on the ground of sex could be
regarded as compatible with the Convention".[504]

These judgments are a rare example of Dutch case law about citizens'
rights. In an international perspective, gender discrimination with respect
to political rights is a persistent problem. In the opinion of Saskia Sassen,
globalization and migration will also induce changes with respect to the
economic position of Third World women.[505] Such changes have "given
considerable economic and social power to women in many otherwise
traditional communities."[506] In the long run, this will translate into a different view on political participation and the enjoyment of civil rights by
women.

Charles Beitz points out that CEDAW, signed in 1979, is "significantly
more ambitious" than the ICCPR and ICESCR.[507] The recognition of wom-
en's rights in this way also acts as a lever in achieving broader recognition
of the right to be a citizen and safeguarding the ability to exercise the associated rights. Nowadays it is generally accepted that sex-based discrimination in citizens' rights is not only intrinsically unfair, it also stands in the
way of the political and social dynamics of these rights. The norms laid
down in CEDAW are compared to older human rights treaties more in line
with the now acknowledged relationship between the first, second
and third generations of fundamental rights. States are accepting the

---

[504] *Staatkundig Gereformeerde Partij (SGP) v The Netherlands* App no 58369/10 (ECtHR,
10 July 2012) para. 72.

[505] Sassen (n. 183) 130.

[506] Saunders (n. 88) 283.

[507] Beitz (n. 480) 186.

obligation to improve social and cultural behavior patterns in favor of women.[508] Compared with a century earlier, since the end of the twentieth century the proportion of women migrants, owing to both family reunification and migration on their own initiative, has increased sharply, which can facilitate integration, provided that suitable policies are adopted.[509] Gender equality also results in greater acceptance of dual citizenship.[510] Worldwide migration from rural areas to the cities is partly due to – and benefits – a growing awareness of the equal position to which women are entitled. Something similar is in fact true of all sorts of tribal, ethnic and religious differences, which are losing their importance in the cities. The history of 19th century Jewish emancipation – which was partly owed to remarkable women like Rahel Varnhagen von Ense – is under quite different conditions another example of this pattern of experiences.[511]

4.3 *Conclusions*

The relevance of the subject of this book is determined by two epochal changes. The first is that citizenship marks the end of the subjection of people to the political, tribal, ethnic or religious entities to which they have been subordinated for centuries, based on a specific single identity: a citizen is not an obedient subject. The second is that the worldwide, continuing and intensified process of migration brings with it an intrinsic interest on the part of society and the migrants to be included in that society's legal, political and socio-economic organization on the basis of elementary reciprocal respect under human rights law. Requirements may be laid down here for migrants, not to keep them out right from the start, let alone to humiliate them or turn them into second-class citizens, but to ensure reciprocity between the polity and citizenship.

This is the practical value of our topic. The situations where the right of citizenship has to be realized and enforced reflect these epochal changes. Migrants have often been men and women who want to make a difference by not taking the background that they come from for granted but seeking out and entering into fresh connections – "exceptional people",[512] in other

---

[508] On this subject, ibid. 187.

[509] Cf. Giovanni Gozzini, *Le migrazioni di ieri ed oggi, Una storia comparata* [Migrations in the past and present. A comparative history] (Bruno Mondadori 2005) 89–91.

[510] Vonk (n. 265) 156.

[511] Goldfarb (n. 42) 107.

[512] The title of Goldin, Cameron and Balarajan (n. 74) 176.

words, who are expected to contribute to more expansive, dynamic value communities in their arrival cities. The protection of the right to be a citizen is important for everyone, but given the widespread use (or abuse) of legal powers related to citizenship as a means of exclusion, the most urgent questions concern the legal inclusion of migrants and the protection of citizens' rights without discrimination. Obviously though, not all migrants are ready to become co-responsible citizens. They may be unable or unfit to take up such an active role, or their sheer number may jeopardize the chances of successful integration. It is therefore justified to maintain an immigration policy, with an admission policy based on reasonable requirements.

Citizenship has been off limits for most of the international systems designed to protect human rights, although there has – for over more than half a century – been talk of a political "right to have rights", as Hannah Arendt put it, a "right to membership in a political community".[513] Only the position of stateless persons has resulted in any action, but, as we have seen, with wildly inadequate results. The underlying problem is that a host of states do not automatically regard it as their responsibility to recognize as nationals those who – sometimes with a permanent residence permit – belong to their society and participate in it, or would like to if they were given the opportunity. It is sensible to make the acquisition of nationality on this basis conditional upon the ability to communicate and participate, and there is nothing against celebrating it with a ceremony. Unfortunately, even in countries such as the Netherlands with a long history of immigration, in recent years we have heard official demands for a kind of 'conversion' on the part of new citizens, instead of integration and participation.[514] The compulsory communal consumption of herrings and curly kale at naturalization ceremonies, along with benign pressure to say how 'tasty' they are, has been a relatively innocuous expression of this, but more serious has been the casual way in which some politicians have sought to have nationality granted only under heightened conditions. No more than any other public law decision should this be represented as a favour that could just as freely have been withheld as granted. A genuinely decisive step would be to make the acquisition of nationality non-discretionary. So as to regulate the reciprocal rights and duties of the citizen and the state (see § 3.1), the human right set out in Article 15 of the

---

[513] Benhabib, *Dignity in Adversity* (n. 337) 62.
[514] (n. 120) 8.

Universal Declaration of Human Rights should be included in the ICCPR after all, together with the right to renounce one's citizenship.

In the course of our analyses, we have seen in various contexts that states should not arbitrarily decide on citizenship as they see fit. The conclusions can be summarized in the following points.

- The "iteration" of the centuries-old concept of citizenship has lent a new dimension to constitutional thinking. The constitution of the modern state can no longer be interpreted in categories of authority and ties; instead it is characterized by citizens' say in decision-making, their rights and the substantive qualification of institutions, which are thus dependent on a permanent process of legitimization. Citizens' rights are the essential connecting link between human rights and life "in a democratic society", when this society has become urban, pluriform and dynamic. Against the background of a human rights ethos, citizenship is a personal entitlement to the progressive realization of solidarity in a commonwealth defined by reciprocity of rights and obligations.
- In the urbanizing, multicultural societies of the late twentieth century and the beginning of the twenty-first century norm-free coexistence on the one hand and a desire to assimilate immigrants on the other may give way to a different approach: to link the multicultural reality with the constitutional concept of citizenship. For multiculturalism to have a positive effect on society as a whole, more is needed than just living side by side: multiculturalism cannot be separated from a normative constitutional setting in which fundamental rights are guaranteed to every citizen. Acceptance, appreciation and mutual recognition of cultural diversity are committed to active, open citizenship. Citizenship offers an institutional response, instead of the ideological reactions to the multicultural realities of our time.
- Every polity defines and redefines itself through processes of constitutional change that derive their legitimacy not only from the citizens' voting results but also from the shared understanding among the citizens that the polity respects and protects the individual citizens and their community life. States ought no longer to have unrestrained control over the nationality of their subjects; instead they should take reasonable decisions on citizenship aspirations.
- A natural right to be a citizen, born free, requires the *legal recognition as citizens* of those members of a society who are ready to assume the ensuing rights and responsibilities. Under international law, in force of the principles of democratic self-governance and equal respect due to

anyone everywhere, states should restate their "sovereign" power to recognize, give or withhold citizenship as an *obligation* mirroring the human right to citizenship in the state – or, depending on someone's life existential situation, the state – where he or she is at home, which can change during the course of a person's life.

· Granting nationality is not a favour that can be arbitrarily bestowed or denied; it must be seen in the context of "an implicit two-way contract" that complies with the idea underlying citizenship. As regards the rights and obligations associated with citizenship, states should also recognize the right – as a human right – to renounce (change) nationality (under the condition of not living in the country concerned). This freedom should also be the guiding principle when it comes to the possibility of retaining a nationality.

· Migration confronts people not only with the diversity of their fellow citizens' identities but also sets everyone the task of accepting diversity as a characteristic of citizenship itself. In the migration patterns of our times people often do not leave their house and home for good, never to return, forgetting their families. Citizenship must not be confined to those who are merely 'insiders'. Multiple nationality is the legal reflection of the social reality that people's involvements in a society and its system of law and order can be multiple. This will have an increasing influence on nationality and the exercise of citizens' rights in the twenty-first century. It needs to be recognized that multiple nationality, with the associated citizens' rights, can in fact be a positive factor in relations with co-citizens after moving from one life situation to another.

· While citizenship is legally grounded in ties with a state, as political power remains predominantly organized at that level,[515] the effects of twenty-first-century citizenship are just as transnational as life itself. European citizenship, additional to and not replacing national citizenship, is a useful and fitting legal institution under these circumstances.

· As nationality incorporates the right to citizens' rights, a human right should be recognized not only to a nationality but also to the nationality, with its associated rights, that is appropriate to everyone's social situation.

Once nationality ought no longer to be granted and taken away arbitrarily, citizens should also be able to find protection in their right to citizenship. In Europe, there has in fact been a realization since the end of the Second

---

[515] Crouch, *Post-Democracy* (n. 248).

World War that human rights need to be protected in the context of the democratic constitutional state, as shown particularly by the conventions and work of the Council of Europe. This can be seen in the European Convention for the Protection of Human Rights and Fundamental Freedoms (ECHR) in the requirement that any restriction of rights must be "necessary in a democratic society".[516] A recent judgment which would seem to constitute a step towards recognition of the right to a nationality under the ECHR was in the Genovese v. Malta case: "the concept of "private life" is a broad term not susceptible to exhaustive definition. It covers the physical and psychological integrity of a person. It can therefore embrace multiple aspects of the person's physical and social identity (...). The provisions of Article 8 do not, however, guarantee a right to acquire a particular nationality or citizenship. Nevertheless, the Court has previously stated that it cannot be ruled out that an arbitrary denial of citizenship might in certain circumstances raise an issue under Article 8 of the Convention because of the impact of such a denial on the private life of the individual (...)."[517]

Article 3 of the First Protocol to this convention requires the contracting parties "to hold free elections at reasonable intervals by secret ballot". Article 3 of the Fourth Protocol guarantees among other things the freedom of nationals to enter the territory of their own state. The relationship between democracy and human rights is also discussed in the case law of the European Court of Human Rights. The fact that prisoners in the United Kingdom lose the right to vote led to a judgment by the Court – attacked by British and Dutch neo-democrats[518] – condemning this automatic restriction on citizens' rights.[519]

Migration places people in a personal transitional situation. Under a host of systems, including the Dutch one, people who cross the border as aliens with no legal residence rights are in principle thrown back upon the most basic protection of fundamental rights (the prohibition on

---

[516] See Anika Logemann, *Grenzen der Menschenrechte in demokratischen Gesellschaften. Die "demokratische Gesellschaft" als Determinante der Grundrechtsschranken in der Europäischen Menschenrechtskonvention* [Limits of human rights in democratic societies. The 'democratic society' as a determinant of human rights limitations in the European human rights convention] (Nomos 2004).

[517] *Genovese v Malta* App no 535124/09 (ECtHR, 11 October 2011).

[518] By this I mean those who, citing democracy, demand that the law and policies should reflect the will of the majority, unhindered by courts and minority rights. This movement includes populism, but it is broader-based and often more sophisticated in its expressions.

[519] also mentioned in (n. 293) § 3.1.

degrading treatment, the protection of life, access to the courts) with no possibility of participation whatsoever: they are and are not regarded as members of Dutch society. While their residence permit applications are under consideration they are granted provisional rights, as it were. As soon as they come under the jurisdiction of the arrival state they have rights other than those dependent on citizenship. Once a residence permit is granted, the situation changes: the 'limitation' (to use the Dutch legal terminology) attached to this determines the extent of the rights that they can exercise. A resident alien who is issued with a permanent residence permit has a legal status on the way to citizenship. A human rights interpretation of this status requires a recognition of rights geared to the person's life situation and ability to participate. This is indeed the case with the EU-law status of third-country nationals, as outlined in § 3.5. In a judgment of 18 July 2012, the German Federal Constitutional Court ruled that the social security benefit paid to asylum seekers whose cases are under consideration must not fall below the universal social minimum in Germany,[520] and the idea is gradually gaining ground that they must not be excluded from employment on a long-term basis either.

However valuable it may have been, the realization in the second half of the twentieth century that human rights are by their very nature universal has meanwhile had a negative side-effect: the citizens' rights associated with nationality are now being treated as a separate issue. Their substance is now left to the sovereignty of national states, except where there is no real basis for a relationship between the state and citizens, or where naturalization policy is used to conduct foreign policy (as with the granting of Hungarian nationality to ethnic Hungarians in the areas lost to neighboring states under the Treaty of Trianon).[521]

The concept of nationality therefore needs to be re-interpreted with a deeper understanding of its actual significance – far more than is customary at present, and more than many politicians are willing to acknowledge – as the anchoring of human rights *in relation to the state and society.* In other words: since state and society cannot be viewed as separate from other states and societies, and human beings even less, the nationality should rather be defined in view of inclusion rather dan exclusion (sc. of foreigners). The importance of this is corroborated by the experiences

---

[520] Bundesverfassungsgericht 18. Juli 2012, 1 BvL 10/10 and 1 BvL 2/11, see <www.bundesverfassungsgericht.de/entscheidungen/ls20120718_1bvl001010.html> accessed on 21 July 2013.
[521] This legislation was mentioned in § 3.1 as an example of over-inclusion.

that led to civil revolutions in the eighteenth and nineteenth centuries and equally by those surrounding worldwide migration in the twentieth and twenty-first centuries. A democratic constitutional state must be willing to grant the rights associated with nationality to those who are in that society the fellows of its established citizens. Combating exclusion from citizenship – on which I have formulated my conclusions – will enable citizens' rights to become the cement of political and socio-economic life once more.

Without the right to reside in a country safely, remain there and participate in political decision-making – hence over the laws that apply to everyone – the protection of universal human rights will continue to be deficient precisely where it needs to be put into practice in people's actual experience. Citizens' rights are the essential connecting link between human rights and life "in a democratic society".[522] These constitute not only political rights but also the basic right of citizens to subjectivity under the law and respect for the entirety of human rights reflecting the sacrality of the person – not as an individual who turns his back on his fellow men but as a πολιτικόν ζωιον.[523] Being a citizen in a democratic polity is different from being a subject, living under the authority of a ruler or a ruling group. But the institution of citizenship is not self-sufficient: it has – according to Otfried Höffe, a philosopher of law in the Aristotelian and Kantian tradition – "to be infused with life" from civic virtues.[524] A "sense of state citizenship" is an essential part of these virtues, similar "to the French understanding of *citoyenneté*: the affiliation to a community that includes the willingness to accept responsibility."[525] The modern citizen "must usually be simultaneously a working subject, or an economic citizen (*bourgeois* in a wider sense so as to include employees and workers), and a citizen of the state (*citoyen*)"[526] with a "participatory sense" among "a considerable number of citizens".[527] Civic virtues should contribute to social cohesion through a "spirit of cooperation",[528] rooted in a "sense of law",

---

[522] Here I am using the words in the refrain of the limitation clauses in the ECHR.

[523] "'ο ἄνθρωπος φύσει πολιτικόν ζωιον" in Aristoteles, Πολιτικά (——) para. 1253 α 2–3.

[524] Otfried Höffe, *Democracy in an Age of Globalisation* (Springer 2007) 133, 153: "Civic virtues" concern "responsibilities that cannot be accomplished by democratic institutions alone".

[525] Ibid. 144.

[526] Ibid. 145.

[527] Ibid. 146.

[528] Ibid. 153.

a "sense of justice" and "tolerance".[529] This will – hopefully – bring the "ethos of human rights" to life and in that sense show the way to a practical answer to Böckenförde's aporia of the liberal constitutional state.[530] The full effect of the right to be a citizen must therefore be felt in the manifold social, economic and cultural dimensions of civil society.

---

[529] Ibid. 154.
[530] Text to n. (205) in § 2.5.

EPILOGUE: RECIPROCAL RECOGNITION AND DEMOCRACY

In troubled times, it can be helpful to step back before moving on and ask what path we have travelled so far. This is just as true of the current uncertainties affecting the democratic political system in countries, especially in Western Europe, that viewed themselves as the cradle of tolerant, pluralistic political communities. The growing interconnectedness of societies and people does not mean that the majority of people are effectively on the move. However, this cannot justify the nostalgic claim for "nation-states" as a culturally more or less homogeneous polity. Everyone's life will be influenced and to some extent transformed by the twenty-first century realities of worldwide communication, travel and transport, alongside ongoing migration and urbanization. It is contradictory to claim that serious problems come with migration and to contend at the same time that the nation-state can remain unchanged in its basic features. The revolution of the human rights created constitutional systems in which citizenship cannot be defined exclusively from the standpoint of the ruler or a ruling group. It is citizens who define and continuously redefine the constitutions that bind them together.

Although only a relatively small part of the population has personally participated in migration, the realities of migration, diversity, travel and communication create a "world on the move". Exclusion from citizenship and from democratic participation on the basis of differences in origin is in the end incompatible with human rights and fundamental democratic principles. Citizenship has to be viewed as the institutional expression of a reciprocal relationship, i.e. a requirement and entitlement at the same time. In a constitutional framework defined by human rights, the democratic process ought to result in citizens laying down the law for themselves. Human rights are those of the people who, reasoning in freedom, appoint the democratic authorities. This is what distinguishes modern polities from tribal political entities; and since the interests and values that bind people together have to be viewed in layers – the national interest community is by no means the only relevant interest community – different constitutional layers are in play here. The fact that most people in the European Union view "their" state as the most important political level results from the importance of solidarity within a state, at present alongside other – e.g. regional and supranational – structures of institutionalized solidarity. Notwithstanding the legal doctrine that the state defines its citizenship, it is citizens who continuously define and redefine their constitutions.[531]

Historically, the creation of cities was the decisive factor here. Urbanization has brought people together who were different, seen from a tribal point of view, but who increasingly determined their own identities. The colonization of the Third World from these cities resulted in the dissemination of European culture to other parts of the world, followed in the twentieth century by migration in the opposite direction. The constitutional standards of the rule of law are designed to ensure that citizens can have faith in the institutions of the state and other polities. The organs of a democratic state under the rule of law must therefore always consider the consequences of their decisions for people in their actual life situations. This (to use Böckle's term) is the requirement of an *Ethos der Menschenrechte* (human rights ethos),[532] an ethos of the community which cannot be met with merely abstract safeguards but only with empathetic and compassionate application of the law, always taking into account the respect due just as much to the most vulnerable fellow citizen as to the proudest.[533] Particularly in times of socio-economic and – migration-related – socio-cultural upheaval it is vital to maintain and if possible strengthen that trust.[534]

Without the right to reside in a country safely, remain there and participate in political decision-making – hence over the laws that apply to everyone –, the protection of universal human rights will continue to be deficient precisely where it needs to be put into practice in people's actual experience. As Amartya Sen has written in his discussions of freedoms and capabilities, real ways of enforcing entitlements – determined by social and economic and administrative factors – are crucial when it comes to human rights and freedom.[535] Citizens' rights provide the

---

[531] Krisch (n. 194) 266: "the potential for transboundary communication (is) still so underdeveloped that a strong form of democracy beyond the state remains hardly conceivable."

[532] Böckle (n. 207).

[533] A constitutional state thus needs to provide the setting for "empathy beyond tolerance": Martin Hartmann, 'Dulden oder Anerkennen? Varianten der Toleranzkritik' [Toleration or recognition? Variations of the criticism of tolerance] in Matthias Kaufmann (ed.), *Integration oder Toleranz? Minderheiten als philosophisches Problem* [Integration or tolerance? Minorities as a philosophical problem] (Karl Alber 2001) 132.

[534] Cf. Christine Goodall, 'The coming of the stranger: asylum seekers, trust and hospitality in a British city' (2010) UNHCR Research Paper 195.

[535] Sen, *Inequality Reexamined* (n. 254); Amartya Sen, *Development as Freedom* (Alfred A. Knopf 1999).

framework for inclusion and integration, as a reciprocal process, and must not therefore be regarded as a kind of nationality-dependent bonus on top of human rights. Unlike the later International Covenant on Civil and Political Rights (of 1966), the 1948 Universal Declaration of Human Rights states this clearly in Article 15: "(1) Everyone has the right to a nationality. (2) No one shall be arbitrarily deprived of his nationality nor denied the right to change his nationality". Whereas the enumeration of rights in the European Convention on Human Rights and Fundamental Freedoms has frequently been revised by so-called Protocols, the International Covenant on Civil and Political Rights has never been updated. In a future revision of the Covenant or any new treaty on nationality, both elements of the right to a nationality should be included: a human right not only to a nationality but also to the nationality, with its associated rights, that is appropriate to everyone's life situation, where he or she is at home – which can change during the course of a person's life.

Lastly I must say a few words about democracy under conditions of constitutional pluralism and the place of human rights there. Human rights means more than just statutory rights.[536] In international political relations, they are the reference point for diplomatic pressure and for the increasingly powerful effects of public opinion on the behavior of large corporations as well as states.[537] Citizenship is thus the gateway to safeguarding human rights within the context of the constitutional systems of states and other political unions. To be more precise, this is the case for two reasons: (a) because if limitations on people's residence rights and their access to the courts and legal assistance are not permitted they can also stand up for their other rights, and (b) because it provides the basis for democratic participation. From an agonist perspective, democratic action takes precedence. This is why Paulina Tambakaki, following on from Chantal Mouffe's work, regards citizenship as a lever in the human rights struggle. Citizenship constructs a collective 'we' within which the agonist debate is conducted,[538] and this collective identity provides scope for multicultural diversity.[539] Citizenship is therefore "a common form of political association or political identity that is held together by the principles of liberty and equality for all."[540] Because of their universality,

---

[536] Sen, *The Idea of Justice* (n. 224) 364–6.

[537] Richard Steenvoorde, *Regulatory Transformations in International Economic Relations* (Wolf Legal Publishers 2008).

[538] Paulina Tambakaki, *Human Rights, or Citizenship?* (Birkbeck Law Press 2011) 114.

[539] Ibid. 115.

[540] Ibid. 10.

human rights have a great "emancipatory potential",[541] but the deciding factor, says Tambakaki, is ultimately that citizenship needs to be shaped by "democratic practice".[542] Through the political exercise of citizenship, human rights are shaped in a particular constitutional context.

Overestimating democratic legitimacy is a permanent threat to the actual realization of human rights. The *Revolution der Menschenrechte* (human rights revolution) legitimizes government authority in that it is the *citizens* who want it and accept it: "We the people", to quote the celebrated opening words of the 1787 American constitution (and for that matter India's 1949 constitution). 'We' are *the citizens who bring the state to life together* through our fundamental rights (political rights and rights that protect diversity and individuality) and through the constitutional decision-making and accountability procedures.[543] But democracy is not a system under which the majority is permitted to impose its will on minorities, so that 'we the people' degenerates into 'we the majority' as opposed to 'them', the 'others'. There is no reason – as Andrew Fagan pointed out a few years ago – to regard democracy and the constitutional state as virtually synonymous and identical.[544] Ostensibly democratically following the will of the majority can take the form of 'majoritarianism': majorities may have an interest in laying down rules – citing the democratic legitimacy of majority decisions – that force those discriminated against to accept their fate.[545] This is the core of radical criticism such as that of William Paul Simmons. Simmons condemns the predominant legal practice as a system for the "silencing of the other".[546] He accuses the European Court of Human Rights of failing in its mission of ensuring that minorities are not discriminated against, by permitting states a 'margin of appreciation'.

Simmons' argument is conditioned by the view that even such rule-of-law institutions are the product of historical violence. Nevertheless, in the same year as he published his work, a few legal scholars, most notably in the United Kingdom, popped up claiming that the Court was in fact

---

[541] Ibid. 117.
[542] Ibid. 136.
[543] Cf. Honneth (n. 229) 470–1, 521 on the importance of "the political arena of public deliberation and decision-making", which must be geared to political 'Verständigung' (understanding, agreement). The theme of citizenship and democracy is also central to Tambakaki's recent book (n. 538) but it is interpreted there within the context of the political theory of 'agonism'.
[544] Fagan (n. 69) 95.
[545] Fagan (n. 69) 100–1.
[546] William Paul Simmons, *Human Rights and the Marginalized Other* (CUP 2011) 130ff.

interpreting the margin of appreciation too narrowly,[547] thus in their view undermining national democracy – a view diametrically opposed to that of Simmons. Their favorite example is the Court's ruling in the Hirst case that automatic loss of the right to vote when sentenced to a term of imprisonment constitutes a violation of the ECHR. Here we need to differentiate between two issues. One point is whether the Court should be relieved of cases that could be dealt with by full-fledged national constitutional courts. The other is whether it is permissible to restrict people's rights as citizens' (as is the nature of the right to vote) without establishing necessity and proportionality in each individual case.

In order to forestall such questions, legislatures need to provide scope for more detailed assessment of individual cases, and courts need to learn to view cases from the perspective of everyone who has a personal interest in the application of a rule. The greater the inroads that a measure makes into what Simmons – based on his experience with migrants on the American-Mexican border – refers to as their *proyecto de la vida* (life project), the more justification there is for viewing the case through the prism of human rights.[548]

I do not share Simmons' gloomy view that "even the most progressive human rights institutions (...) contain traces of their original violence", but that does not make his demand that every institution "must be constantly interrogated as to whether they are truly doing justice for the Marginalized Other" any less relevant.[549] The faith that legislative, administrative and judicial institutions need to vindicate day in, day out cannot be unconditional for any of these institutions. It is precisely by realizing the conditionality of the exercise of power by each one of them that a human rights ethos should be brought to life.

This is the context for the recognition of the human right to be a citizen: as a co-author of the rules that apply to everyone (the principle of reciprocity), but to which no-one's personal integrity must ever be sacrificed

---

[547] E.g. Michael Pinto-Duschinsky, *Bringing Rights Back Home. Making human rights compatible with parliamentary democracy in the UK* (with a foreword by Leonard Hoffmann, Policy Exchange 2011). This line of reasoning attracted some followers in the Netherlands, including Member of Parliament Joost Taverne, who in September 2012 presented a private bill aiming at a constitutional amendment repealing the automatic direct effect and primacy of treaties like the ECHR vis-à-vis Dutch legislation. See *Kamerstukken II* 33 359 (R 1986) nos. 1–3.

[548] This imagery has been borrowed from Janneke Gerards' *Het prisma van de grondrechten* (inaugural lecture Radboud Universiteit Nijmegen 2011); 'The Prism of Fundamental Rights' (2012) 8 *European Constitutional Law Review* 173.

[549] Simmons (n 546) 227.

(the principle of individuality). As I wrote on this subject in another context, "the single focus on general rules since the Enlightenment has led us to neglect the requirements of specific circumstances, requirements of which Aristotle and Aquinas were aware. (...) a legal culture alert to the individual places demands not only on the mindset of the administrator and the judge who 'applies' the rules; the legislative branch too must realize that it cannot comprehend everything and that it should allow scope for the judgment of those 'applying' the rules. (...) No rule can be adequately justified if general policy objectives are so decisive as to prevent sufficient consideration being given to their effect on the lives of individuals."[550]

A sustainable combination of democracy and the rule of law requires an understanding of the interrelationship between the individual, political and socio-economic dimensions of human rights. The development of citizens' rights over three centuries as outlined by Butenschøn – in the context of a national state increasingly linked to civil, political and social rights – has been followed in our era by complex relationships with states and societies that can change during the course of people's lives, resulting in the constant revision – "iterations" – of the rights associated with citizenship. By recognizing everyone's right to the citizenship in which they can make these rights a reality, citizens' rights once again – or still – bridge the gap between the universality of human rights and the political and social settings of people's lives.

It is people, exceptional people, who by their creativity and mobility claim rights for themselves and their children. They give civil society a new identity that transcends borders. The interlocking nature of lives and societies across national borders is bringing citizens' rights increasingly into the ambit of human rights, rights whose operation should not be dependent on a particular state.[551] The economic dominance of large corporations, with political offshoots, cannot be broken, but it can be effectively forced to take account of the freedom of people to share their lives with loved ones, of working conditions, of the protection of children and the environment – in other words of the interests regarded as the rights of every person. The human right to be a citizen is the mainstay of this, as it provides a home base in a state, which is entitled to be described

---

[550] Hirsch Ballin, *Law, Justice, and the Individual* (n. 109) 16.
[551] The separation between the rights of man and the rights of the citizen was on the one hand due to nationalism using nationality as an exclusion mechanism, but on the other it was intensified by the fact that human rights were universalized after the Second World War, whereas citizens' rights were not ready for this.

as a democratic constitutional state to the extent that it makes human rights a reality. Shared citizenship across differences in origin and varieties of culture is the most essential institution of a society based on mutual (and mutually safeguarded) trust, "a prepolitical condition for a functioning democracy where people and parties peacefully and confidently move in and out of government positions and where those in the minority position after an election do not need to fear unjust treatment by those in the majority position."[552]

Nothing gives people so much freedom as an institutional home that they can have faith in. Discrimination and exclusion of people on the grounds of ethnicity is the strongest incentive for them to strive for an independent state of their own, where the problems of discrimination and the exclusion of others often recur, however. The vicious circle can only be broken by observing the principle of unconditional equal respect for everyone's human dignity – the cornerstone of human rights protection – from the perspective of both democracy and the rule of law.

Citizenship is human dignity in constitutional terms. Migration not only confronts people with the diversity of their fellow citizens' identities but also sets everyone the task of accepting diversity as a characteristic of citizenship itself, with its associated rights: a citizenship that is appropriate to everyone's life situation, where he or she is at home – which can change during the course of a person's life: a natural right to be recognized as a citizen, born free.[553]

One may be proud to be a citizen. Human rights are often associated with giving shelter, protection for the downtrodden, non-discrimination. That is correct, but not enough. The constitutional core of a democracy is its legitimizing anchoring in the community of citizens: they share the responsibility for the future of their society. The traditional understanding of human rights was implicitly geared to a static society, where people can invoke rights in order to protect their interests. Human rights in the wider, profounder understanding of the Vienna Declaration on Human Rights are much more oriented to the future of society and – because of the manifest interdependence of peace, justice and the environment across borders – humanity. This is the driving force of respect for human dignity.[554]

---

[552] Gunnar Skirbekk, *Multiple Modernities. A Tale of Scandinavian Experiences* (The Chinese UP 2011) 183.

[553] Cf. Universal Declaration of Human Rights (n. 407) art. 1: "All human beings are born free and equal in dignity and rights. They are endowed with reason and conscience and should act towards one another in a spirit of brotherhood."

[554] From his experience as a member of the post-apartheid Constitutional Court of South-Africa, Justice Albie Sachs has made this same observation: "Respect for human

The worldwide significance of migration and urbanization, with which this book started, gives further evidence of this changing perspective of human rights.

Alongside the *synchronic* orientation of the protection of existing interests through enforcement of fundamental rights, a growing number of human rights disputes in domestic courts as well as supranational courts is related to the protection that individuals and communities seek for their *future*: the right of refuge in a safe country, the right for immigrants to have or make a living for themselves and their children, the right to education, the right to seek an educational environment consistent with the values that the parents want to pass on, the right to have dedicated institutions for minority cultures, protection of the environment as an element of the right to private life,[555] and other "third generation of human rights" requirements of sustainability.[556] This developmental perspective on human rights marks the individual right, as a citizen, to take part in the democratic process. Citizens are, in the constitutional context of a free discourse and decision-making process, the co-authors of the laws and policies for the future of their society.

It may be uncertain whether democratic processes dominated by the mass media and political marketing techniques will still be able to deliver sufficiently sustainable outcomes.[557] The best chance however of building a peaceful, just and sustainable future is to be found in the recognition of a human right to be a citizen, and of human rights to take part as a free citizen in the life of society, to be educated as a citizen and to be informed as a citizen. Recognizing that these rights do not come without continuous efforts and struggle may be the only antidote against

dignity is the unifying constitutional principle for a society that is not only particularly diverse, but extremely unequal. This implies that the Bill of Rights exists not simply to ensure that the 'haves' can continue to have, but to help create conditions in which the basic dignity of the 'have nots' can be secured." (Albie Sachs, *The Strange Alchemy of Life and Law* (OUP 2009)).

[555] *Taşkın and Others v Turkey* App no. 46117/99 (ECtHR, 10 November 2004).

[556] These issues are sometimes framed as questions of intergenerational justice. See Clark Wolf, 'Intergenerational Justice' in R.G. Frey and Christopher Heath Wellman (eds.), *A Companion to Applied Ethics* (Blackwell 2003); cf. Sen, *Development as Freedom* (n. 535).

[557] Ingolfur Blühdorn, *Simulative Demokratie. Neue Politik nach der postdemokratischen Wende* (Suhrkamp 2013); See also in English 'The sustainability of democracy. On limits to growth, the post-democratic turn and reactionary democrats' (Eurozine, 11 July 2011) <www.eurozine.com/articles/2011-07-11-bluhdorn-en.html> accessed 19 July 2013; 'Democracy and Sustainability: Opening the discursive arena – Struggling for an innovative debate' (*Friedrich Ebert Stiftung*, Series *Sustainability and Democracy*, 13 December 2012) <www.fes-sustainability.org/en/nachhaltigkeit-und-demokratie/democracy-and-sustainability> accessed 19 July 2013.

a seemingly problem-free equation of democracy with following demo-cratic procedures.

It is worth fighting for these rights. This was a demand that was heard not only when people in South Africa opposed having their nationality replaced with that of the 'homelands', or when black Americans, who were treated as second-class citizens, fought for their rights under the leader-ship of Martin Luther King; it is heard everywhere where people have found their place in society, which may not be the same as their society of origin, everywhere where people are willing to take a share in citizenship but are living in expectation of the recognition of their citizens' *rights*. Such rights are essential if we want the democratic constitutional state to remain the place where no-one is excluded from the discourse, where everyone can contribute freely to new activities, inspirational ideas, better justice, greater trust.

BIBLIOGRAPHY

—— '"Deutschland wünscht einen fairen Wettbewerb". Interview mit Angela Merkel in France 2' (*Bundeskanzlerin.de* 18 October 2010) <www.bundeskanzlerin.de/Content/DE/ Interview/2010/10/2010-10-18-merkel-france-2.html> accessed 4 May 2013.

—— 'Enemy Subjects - shall all be interned?' *Sunday Times* (Perth, 23 May 1915).

—— 'Guide de Genealogie: Naturalisations' [Guide on Genealogy: Naturalizations] <www .guide-genealogie.com/guide/naturalisations.html> accessed 20 July 2013.

—— *Holman Christian Standard Bible* (digital text edn, Holman Bible Publishers 2010).

—— *Putzger Atlas und Chronik zur Weltgeschichte* [Atlas and Chronicle of World History] (2nd edn, Cornelsen Verlag 2009).

Adjami M. and Harrington J., 'The Scope and Content of Article 15 of the Universal Declaration of Human Rights' (2008) 27 *Refugee Survey Quarterly* 93.

Adviescommissie voor Vreemdelingenzaken (ACVZ), 'Nederlanderschap in een onbegrensde wereld. Advies over het Nederlandse beleid inzake meervoudige nationaliteit' [Dutch nationality in a world without borders: Report on Dutch policy on multiple nationality] (2008) ACVZ.

Aleinikoff T.A., *Semblances of Sovereignty: The Constitution, the State, and American Citizenship* (Harvard UP 2002).

—— and Klusmeyer D., *Citizenship Today. Global Perspectives and Practices* (Carnegie Endowment for International Peace 2001).

Ambos K., *Internationales Strafrecht. Strafanwendungsrecht – Völkerstrafrecht – Europäisches Strafrecht* [International criminal law: sentencing law – international criminal law – European criminal law] (C.H. Beck 2006).

An-Na'im A.A., *Islam and the Secular State. Negotiating the Future of Shari'a* (Harvard UP 2008).

Antos G., '"Verständlichkeit" als Bürgerrecht? Positionen, Alternativen und das Modell der "barrierefreien Kommunikation"' in Karin M. Eichhoff-Cyrus and Gerd Antos (eds.), *Verständlichkeit als Bürgerrecht? Die Rechts- und Verwaltungssprache in der öffentlichen Diskussion* (Dudenverlag 2008).

Appiah K.A., *Cosmopolitanism. Ethics in a World of Strangers* (W.W. Norton 2006).

Arendt H., *The Origins of Totalitarianism* (first published 1948, Harcourt 1973).

—— 'Es gibt nur ein einziges Menschenrecht' [There is only one human right] in Christoph Menke and Francesca Raimondi, *Die Revolution der Menschenrechte. Grundlegende Texte zu einem neuen Begriff des Politischen* [The Human Rights Revolution: Basic Texts for a New Concept of the Political] (originally published 1949, Suhrkamp 2011).

Aristoteles, Πολιτικά (first published ± 350 BC, William Ellis trans., *Politics: A Treatise on Government*, 1912) <www.gutenberg.org/ebooks/6762> accessed 18 August 2013.

Ateş S., *Der Multikulti-Irrtum: wie wir in Deutschland besser zusammenleben können* [The multiculturalism mistake: how we can live together better in Germany] (Ullstein 2008).

Balibar E., *We, the People of Europe? Reflections on Transnational Citizenship* (James Swenson trans., Princeton UP 2004).

Balkin J.M., *Living Originalism* (The Belknap Press of Harvard UP 2011).

Barnard C., *The Substantive Law of the EU. The Four Freedoms* (OUP 2010).

Bauböck R., Ersbøll E., Groenendijk K. and Waldrauch H. (eds.), *Acquisition and Loss of Nationality: Policies and Trends in 15 European States. Vol. I: Comparative Analyses* (Amsterdam UP 2006).

Bauböck R., Cayla P. and Seth C. (eds.), 'Should EU Citizens living in other Member States vote there in national elections?' (2012) EUI Working Paper RSCAS 2012/32.

Beckwith C.I., *Empires of the Silk Road: A History of Central Eurasia from the Bronze Age to the Present* (Princeton UP 2009).
Bedorf T., 'Das Politische und die Politik. Konturen einer Differenz' in Thomas Bedorf and Kurt Röttgers (eds.), *Das Politische und die Politik* (Suhrkamp 2010).
Beek J.H. van de, *Kennis, Macht en Moraal. De productie van wetenschappelijke kennis over de economische effecten van migratie naar Nederland, 1960–2005* [Knowledge, power and morality: the production of scientific knowledge on the economic effects of migration to the Netherlands, 1960–2005] (Vossiuspers 2010).
Benhabib S., *Another Cosmopolitanism* (OUP 2006).
—— 'Transformations of Citizenship: The Case of Contemporary Europe' in Richard Bellamy and Antonino Palumbo (eds.), *Citizenship* (Ashgate 2010).
—— *Dignity in Adversity* (Polity Press 2011).
Beitz C.R., *The Idea of Human Rights* (OUP 2009).
Bellamy R. and Palumbo A., *Citizenship* (Ashgate Publishing 2010).
Blockmans W., *Metropolen aan de Noordzee. De geschiedenis van Nederland, 1100–1560*. [North Sea Metropolises: The History of the Netherlands 1100–1560] (Bert Bakker 2010).
Blok S., Dijkhoff K. and Taverne J., 'Verdragen mogen niet langer rechtstreeks werken' [Treaties should no longer be directly applicable] *NRC Handelsblad* (Rotterdam, 23 February 2012).
Blühdorn I., 'The sustainability of democracy. On limits to growth, the post-democratic turn and reactionary democrats' (*Eurozine*, 11-07-2011) <www.eurozine.com/articles/2011 -07-11-bluhdorn-en.html> accessed 19 July 2013.
—— 'Democracy and Sustainability: Opening the discursive arena – Struggling for an innovative debate' (*Friedrich Ebert Stiftung*, Series *Sustainability and Democracy*, 13 December 2012) <www.fes-sustainability.org/en/nachhaltigkeit-und-demokratie/ democracy-and-sustainability> accessed 19 July 2013.
—— *Simulative Demokratie. Neue Politik nach der postdemokratischen Wende* (Suhrkamp 2013).
Böckenförde E.W., *Recht, Staat, Freiheit* (2nd edn, Suhrkamp Verlag 2006).
Böckle F., *Ja zum Menschen. Bausteine einer Konkreten Moral* (Kösel 1995).
Bodelier R., *Kosmopolitische perspectieven. Reflecties op 'Human Development' en 'Human Security'* (Celsus juridische uitgeverij/Wereldpodium 2012).
Boeles P., Heijer M. den, Lodder G. and Wouters K., *European Migration Law* (Intersentia 2009).
Boll A.M., *Multiple Nationality and International Law* (Martinus Nijhoff 2007).
Bosniak L., *The Citizen and the Alien: Dilemmas of Contemporary Membership* (Princeton UP 2006).
—— 'Persons and Citizens in Constitutional Thought' (2010) 8 *International Journal of Constitutional Law* 9.
Bossuyt M.J., *Guide to the "Travaux Préparatoires" of the International Covenant on Civil and Political Rights* (Martinus Nijhoff 1987).
Boven T. van, 'Categories of Rights' in Daniel Moeckli, Sangeeta Shah and Sandesh Sivakumaran (eds.), *International Human Rights Law* (OUP 2010).
Bovenkerk F., *Etniciteit, criminaliteit en het strafrecht* [Ethnicity, criminality and the criminal law] (Valedictory lecture, University of Utrecht, Boom 2009).
Broeders D. and Engbersen G., 'The Fight against Illegal Migration: Identification Policies and Immigrants' Counterstrategies' (2007) 50 *American Behavioral Scientist* 1592.
Brood P. and Kubben R., *The Act of Abjuration: Inspired and Inspirational* (Wolf Legal Publishers 2011).
Brouwer J.H., Fokkema K., Gosses G. and Hoekstra J., *Specimina linguae Frisiae veteris* (E.J. Brill 1950).
Brownlie I., *Principles of International Public Law* (OUP 2008).
Búrca G. de, 'The ECJ and the international legal order: a re-evaluation' in Gráinne de Búrca and J.H.H. Weiler (eds.), *The Worlds of European Constitutionalism* (CUP 2012).

Burg W. van der, Schuyt C.J.M. and Nieuwenhuis J.H., *Multiculturaliteit en Recht* [Multiculturalism and Law] (Kluwer 2008) Handelingen Nederlandse Juristen-Vereniging 138–1.

Butenschøn N.A., 'Citizenship and Human Rights: Some Thoughts on a Complex Relationship' in Morten Bergsmo (ed.), *Human Rights and Criminal Justice for the Downtrodden. Essays in Honor of Asbjørn Eide* (Martinus Nijhoff Publishers 2003).

Calliess C., 'The Dynamics of European Citizenship: From Bourgeois to Citoyen' in Allan Rosas, Egils Levits and Yves Bot (eds.), *The Court of Justice and the Construction of Europe: Analyses and Perspectives on Sixty Years of Case-law / La Cour de Justice et la Construction de l'Europe: Analyses et Perspectives de Soixante Ans de Jurisprudence* (T.M.C. Asser Press/ Springer 2013).

Cameron D., 'Speech on the European Court of Human Rights' (Parliamentary Assembly of the Council of Europe, Strasbourg, 25 January 2012) <www.gov.uk/government/ speeches/speech-on-the-european-court-of-human-rights> accessed 20 June 2012.

Carrera S., *In Search of the Perfect Citizen? The Intersection between Integration, Immigration and Nationality in the EU* (Martinus Nijhoff Publishers 2009).

Centraal Bureau voor de Statistiek, *Jaarrapport integratie 2012* [2012 Report on Integration] (Centraal Bureau voor de Statistiek 2012).

Clark B., *Twice a Stranger: The Mass Expulsions that Forged Modern Greece and Turkey* (Harvard UP 2006).

Crawford J., *Brownlie's Principles of Public International Law* (8th edn, OUP 2012).

Crosby A.W., *The Measure of Reality. Quantification and Western Society, 1250–1600* (CUP 1997).

Crouch C., *Post-Democracy* (Polity 2004).

—— *The Strange Non-Death of Neoliberalism* (Polity Press 2011).

Dauvergne C., *Making People Illegal: What Globalization Means for Migration and Law* (CUP 2008).

Debeljak J., 'Rights and Democracy: A Reconciliation of the Institutional Debate' in Tom Campbell, Jeffrey Goldsworthy and Adrienne Stone (eds.), *Protecting Human Rights: Instruments and Institutions* (OUP 2003).

Dodds J.D., Menocal M.R. and Krasner Balbale A., *The Arts of Intimacy. Christians, Jews, and Muslims in the Making of Castilian Culture* (Yale UP 2009).

Dolidze A.V., 'Lampedusa and Beyond: Recognition, Implementation, and Justiciability of Stateless Persons' Rights under International Law' (2011–2012) 6 *Interdisciplinary Journal of Human Rights Law* 123; (2011) IGL&P Working Paper No. 2011/5, <http://ssrn.com/ abstract=1927033> accessed 31 July 2012.

Domingo R., *The New Global Law* (CUP 2010).

Donner A.M., 'Grondwetsstudie in Nederland 1848–1948' [Constitutional studies in the Netherlands 1848–1948] in *Tussen het echte en het gemaakte. Uit de geschriften van Prof. mr. A.M. Donner* [Between the real and the artificial: from the writings of Prof. A.M. Donner] (W.E.J. Tjeenk Willink 1986).

Duany J., *The Puerto Rican Nation on the Move: Identities on the Island and in the United States* (University of North Carolina Press 2002).

Duckett K., 'The meaning of citizenship: a critical analysis of dual nationality and the oath of renunciation' (2000) 21 *Immigration and Nationality Law Review* 717.

Dugard J., *International Law: A South African Perspective* (Juta & Cp. 2000).

Dunbar N., *The Devil's Derivatives: The Untold Story of the Slick Traders and Hapless Regulators Who Almost Blew Up Wall Street... and Are Ready to Do It Again* (Harvard Business Review Press 2012).

Edwards A. and Ferstman C. (eds.), *Human Security and Non-Citizens. Law, Policy and International Affairs* (CUP 2010).

Engelen E., 'Towards an explanation of the performance differences of Turks in the Netherlands and Germany: The case for a comparative political economy of integration' (2006) 97 *Tijdschrift voor Economische en Sociale Geografie* 69.

European Commission, *EU Citizenship Report 2010. Dismantling the obstacles to EU citizens' rights* (European Commission 2010).
——*EU Citizenship Report 2013. EU Citizens: Your Rights, Your Future* (European Commission 2013).
——'Report from the Commission to the European Parliament, the Council, the European Economic and Social Committee and the Committee of the Regions under Article 25 TFEU on the Progress towards Effective EU Citizenship 2011–2013' COM (2013) 270 final.
Euwals R., Dagevos J., Gijsberts M. and Roodenburg H., 'Immigration, integration and the labour market; Turkish immigrants in Germany and the Netherlands' (2006) CPB Discussion Paper no 75.
——Dagevos J., Gijsberts M. and Roodenburg H., 'The labour market position of Turkish immigrants in Germany and the Netherlands; reason for migration, naturalisation and language proficiency' (2007) CPB Discussion Paper No. 79.
Extra G., *De omgang met taaldiversiteit in de multiculturele samenleving* [Dealing with language diversity in a multicultural society] (valedictory lecture, Tilburg University, Tilburg 2011).
Fabbrini F., 'La Corte di giustizia europe e la cittadinanza dell'Unione: Corte di giustizia dell'Unione europea, grande sezione, sentenza 2 marzo 2010, Causa C-135/08 (Commento)' (2010) 7 *Giornale di diritto amministrativo* 702.
Fagan A., *Human Rights: Confronting Myths and Misunderstanding* (Edward Elgar 2009).
Faist T. (ed.), *Dual Citizenship in Europe. From Nationhood to Societal Integration* (Ashgate 2007).
Faist T. and Gerdes J., *Dual Citizenship in an Age of Mobility* (Transatlantic Council on Migration 2008).
Faist T., Fauser M. and Reisenauer E., *Transnational Migration* (Polity 2013).
Fox G.H. and Roth B.R. (eds.), *Democratic Governance and International Law* (CUP 2000).
Franck T.M., 'The Emerging Right to Democratic Governance' (1992) 86 *American Journal of International Law* 46.
Frindte W., Boehnke K., Kreikenbom H. and Wagner W., *Lebenswelten junger Muslime in Deutschland* (Bundesinnenministerium 2012).
Fukuyama F., *The Origins of Political Order: From Prehuman Times to the French Revolution* (Farrar, Straus and Giroux 2011).
Gaay Fortman B. de, *Political Economy of Human Rights: Rights, Realities and Realization* (Routledge 2011).
Gauchet M., *La Révolution des droits de l'homme* [The Human Rights Revolution] (Éditions Gallimard 1989).
Gearty C., *Liberty and Security* (Polity 2013).
Gerards J., *Het prisma van de grondrechten* [The Prism of Fundamental Rights] (2012) 8 *European Constitutional Law Review* 173.
Gerstenberg O., *Bürgerrechte und deliberative Demokratie. Elemente einer pluralistischen Verfassungstheorie* [Citizens' Rights and Deliberative Democracy: Elements of a Pluralist Constitutional Theory] (Suhrkamp 1997).
Giltaij J., *Mensenrechten in het Romeinse recht?* [Human Rights in Roman Law?] (Wolf Legal Publishers 2011).
Goldfarb M.M., *Emancipation: How Liberating Europe's Jews from the Ghetto Led to Revolution & Renaissance* (Simon & Schuster 2009).
Goldin I., Cameron G. and Balarajan M., *Exceptional People: How Migration Shaped Our World and Will Define Our Future* (Princeton UP 2011).
Goldston J., 'Epilogue' in Brad K. Blitz and Maureen Lynch, *Statelessness and Citizenship: A Comparative Study on the Benefits of Nationality* (Edward Elgar 2011).
Goodall C., 'The coming of the stranger: asylum seekers, trust and hospitality in a British city' (2010) UNHCR Research Paper 195.
Goodhart D., *The British Dream. Successes and Failures of Post-war Immigration* (Atlantic Books 2013).

Goudappel F., *The Effects of EU Citizenship: Economic, Social and Political Rights in a Time of Constitutional Change* (T.M.C Asser Press 2010).

Gozzini G., *Le migrazioni di ieri ed oggi, Una storia comparata* [Migrations in the past and present: a comparative history] (Bruno Mondadori 2005).

Grimm D., *Die Zukunft der Verfassung II. Auswirkungen von Europäisierung und Globalisierung* (Suhrkamp 2012).

Groot G.R. de, *Nationaliteit en rechtszekerheid* [Nationality and security under the law] (inaugural lecture University of Aruba, Boom 2008).

—— 'Wijzigingsvoorstel Rijkswet op het Nederlanderschap; Terug naar af' [Proposed amendment to the Dutch Nationality Act: Back to where we started] (2012) 4 *Asiel- & Migrantenrecht* 180.

—— and Doeswijk N., 'Nationaliteitsrecht en het internationale recht' [Nationality law and international law] in F.J.H. van der Velden, G.-R. de Groot and N. Doeswijk, *De nationaliteit in internationaal en Europees perspectief. Mededelingen van de Nederlandse Vereniging voor Internationaal Recht no. 129* (TMC Asser Presss, 2004).

—— and Vink M., *Meervoudige nationaliteit in Europees perspectief: een landenvergelijkend overzicht* [Multiple nationality in a European perspective: a comparison between countries] (ACVZ 2008).

Habermas J., *Strukturwandel der Öffentlichkeit. Untersuchungen zu einer Kategorie der bürgerlichen Gesellschaft* (Luchterhand Verlag 1974) or *The Structural Transformation of the Public Sphere: An Inquiry into a Category of Bourgeois Society* (Thomas Burger and Frederick Lawrence trans., MIT Press 1991).

—— *Die Einbeziehung des Anderen. Studien zur politischen Theorie* (Suhrkamp 1996) or *The Inclusion of the Other. Studies in Political Theory* (Ciaran P. Cronin and Pablo de Greiff trans., MIT Press 1998).

—— 'Citizenship and National Identity: Some Reflections on the Future of Europe' (1992) 12 *Praxis International* 1; included in Richard Bellamy and Antonino Palumbo, *Citizenship* (Ashgate Publishing 2010).

—— *Zur Verfassung Europas. Ein Essay* [On the European Constitution: an essay] (Suhrkamp 2011).

—— 'Über den internen Zusammenhang von Rechtsstaat und Demokratie' [On the internal relationship between the constitutional state and democracy] in Christoph Menke and Francesca Raimondi (eds.), *Die Revolution der Menschenrechte. Grundlegende Texte zu einem neuen Begriff des Politischen* [The Human Rights Revolution: Basic Texts for a New Concept of the Political] (Suhrkamp 2011).

Hailbronner K., 'Germany' in Rainer Bauböck, Eva Ersbøll, Kees Groenendijk and Harald Waldrauch (eds.), *Acquisition and Loss of Nationality: Policies and Trends in 15 European States. Vol. II: Country Analyses* (Amsterdam UP 2006).

Halberstam D., 'Local, global and plural constitutionalism: Europe meets the world' in Gráinne de Búrca and J.H.H. Weiler (eds.), *The Worlds of European Constitutionalism* (CUP 2012).

Halper S. and Clarke J., *The Silence of the Rational Center: Why American Foreign Policy is Failing* (Basic Books 2007).

Härle W., *Würde. Groß vom Menschen denken* [Dignity: thinking of mankind magnanimously] (Diederichs Verlag 2010).

Hart B. de, *Onbezonnen vrouwen. Gemengde relaties in het nationaliteitsrecht en het vreemdelingenrecht* [Impetuous women: Mixed relationships in nationality law and aliens law] (Aksant 2003).

—— 'The End of Multiculturalism. The End of Dual Citizenship? Political and Public Debates on Dual Citizenship in the Netherlands 1980–2004' in Thomas Faist (ed.), *Dual citizenship in Europe. From nationhood to societal integration* (Ashgate 2007).

—— *Een tweede paspoort. Dubbele nationaliteit in de Verenigde Staten, Duitsland en Nederland* (Amsterdam UP 2012).

Hartmann M., 'Dulden oder Anerkennen? Varianten der Toleranzkritik' [Toleration or rec-
ognition? Variations of the criticism of tolerance] in Matthias Kaufmann (ed.),
Integration oder Toleranz? Minderheiten als philosophisches Problem [Integration or tol-
erance? Minorities as a philosophical problem] (Karl Alber 2001).
Heeswijck G. van, *Tolerantie en actief pluralisme. De afgewezen erfenis van Erasmus, More en
Gillis* [Tolerance and Active Pluralism: The Rejected Heritage of Erasmus, More and
Gillis] (Pelckmans 2008).
Heitmeyer W. (ed.), *Deutsche Zustände. Folge 10* [German conditions. No 10] (Suhrkamp
2012).
Heyde L., 'Behoefte en vrijheid. Hegels begrip van het economische in de Grundlinien der
Philosophie des Rechts' [Need and freedom: Hegel's concept of economy in Elements of
the Philosophy of Right] (1977) 39 *Tijdschrift voor Filosofie* 286.
Hirsch Ballin E.M.H., *Het grondrecht op vrijheid en de wet* [The Fundamental Right to
Freedom and the Law] (Samsom H.D. Tjeenk Willink 1989).
―― 'Werking en verwerkelijking van grondrechten' [The operation and realization of fun-
damental rights] in L. Heyde and others (eds.), *Begrensde vrijheid. Opstellen over mensen-
rechten* [Limited freedom: Essays on human rights] (presented to Prof. D.F. Scheltens on
his retirement as Professor at the Catholic University of Nijmegen, W.E.J. Tjeenk Willink
1989).
―― 'Object en methode van de wetenschap van het staatsrecht en het bestuursrecht'
[The object and method of the study of constitutional law and administrative law] in
Rechtsstaat & beleid: een keuze uit het werk van mr. E.M.H. Hirsch Ballin (W.E.J. Tjeenk
Willink 1992).
―― *Wereldburgers. Personen in het internationale recht* [World Citizens: Persons in
International Law] (inaugural lecture Tilburg University, W.E.J. Tjeenk Willink 1995).
―― 'The Italian Republic' in Lucas Prakke and Constantijn Kortmann (eds.), *Constitutional
Law of 15 EU Member States* (Kluwer 2004).
―― *Law, Justice, and the Individual* (Thomas More Lecture, Brill 2011).
―― 'De rechtsstaat, wachten op een nieuwe dageraad?' (2011) 87 *Nederlands
Juristenblad* 71.
―― (ed.), *A Mission for his Time. Tobias Asser's Inaugural Address on Commercial Law and
Commerce, Amsterdam 1862* (Asser Press 2012).
―― *Christianity and the Future of Christian Democracy* (2013 Annual Lecture Christianity
and Society, Tilburg University School of Catholic Theology 2013).
―― *De Koning. Continuïteit en perspectief van het Nederlandse koningschap* [The King:
continuity and perspective in the Dutch monarchy] (2nd edn, Boom Juridische uit-
gevers 2013).
―― 'Voorwoord' [Foreword] in Laura Coello, Jaco Dagevos, Chris Huinder, Joanne van der
Leun and Arend Odé (eds.), *Het minderhedenbeleid voorbij. Motieven en gevolgen*
[Beyond the Minoritypolicies. Motives and consequences] (Amsterdam UP 2013).
―― *Een verbond van vrijheid* (Nationaal Comité 4 en 5 mei/Stichting Collectieve
Propaganda van het Nederlandse Boek 2013), English translation *A pact of freedom*
<http://www.4en5mei.nl/english/celebrating>.
Hobsbawm E.J., *Nations and Nationalism since 1780: Programme, Myth, Reality* (CUP
1992).
Hoeven J. van der, 'De waarde van de Grondwet' [The value of the Constitution] in
Staatsrecht en bestuursrecht, Opstellen van Mr. J. van der Hoeven [Constitutional law and
administrative law, essays by J. van der Hoeven] (W.E.J. Tjeenk Willink 1984).
―― *De plaats van de grondwet in het constitutionele recht* [The Place of the Constitution in
Constitutional Law] (first published 1958, 2nd edn with supplement, W.E.J. Tjeenk
Willink 1988).
Höffe O., *Democracy in an Age of Globalisation* (Springer 2007).
Honneth A., *Das Recht der Freiheit. Grundriß einer demokratischen Sittlichkeit* [The right to
freedom: outline of a democratic morality] (Suhrkamp 2011).
Huntington S., 'The Clash of Civilizations?' (1993) 72 *Foreign Affairs* 22.

—— *The Clash of Civilizations and the Remaking of World Order* (Touchstone 1997).

International Organization for Migration (IOM), *International Migration Report* (IOM 2010).

Jackson K., 'Cities' in Richard Bulliet (ed.), *The Columbia History of the 20th Century* (Columbia UP 1998).

Jackson T.F., *From Civil Rights to Human Rights. Martin Luther King, Jr., and the Struggle for Economic Justice* (University of Pennsylvania Press 2007).

Jacques M., *When China Rules the World. The End of the Western World and the Birth of a New Global Order* (Penguin Press 2009).

Jaghai S. and Vlieks C., 'Buitenschuldbeleid schiet tekort in bescherming staatlozen' [No-fault policy inadequately protects stateless persons] (2013) 5/6 *Asiel- & Migrantenrecht* 287.

Jaumc L., *Les Déclarations des Droits de l'Homme (Du débat 1789–1793 au Préambule de 1946)* [The Declarations of Human Rights (from the 1789–1793 debate to the 1946 Preamble)] (Flammarion 1989).

Jennissen R.P.W. (ed.), *De Nederlandse migratiekaart. Achtergronden en ontwikkelingen van verschillende internationale migratietypen* [The Dutch migration monitor. Backgrounds and developments of different types of international migration] (Boom juridische uitgevers/CBS/WODC 2011).

Jessurun D'Oliveira H.U., 'Europees burgerschap: dubbele nationaliteit?' [European citizenship: dual nationality?] in *Europees burgerschap* (Asser Instituut Colloquium Europees recht, 33ste zitting 2003, T.M.C. Asser Press 2004).

—— 'Multiple Nationality and International Law by Alfred Boll' (2007) 101 *The American Journal of International Law* 922.

Jessurun D'Oliveira H.U., Groot G.R. de and Seling A., 'Janko Rottman v. Freistaat Bayern C-315/08' [ECJ 2 March 2010] 7 *European Constitutional Law Review* 138 (Double note 'Decoupling Nationality and Union Citizenship?' and 'The Consequences of the Rottmann Judgment on Member State Autonomy – The European Court of Justice's Avant-Gardism in Nationality Matters').

Joas H., *The Sacredness of the Person. A New Genealogy of Human Rights* (Alex Skinner trans., Georgetown UP 2013).

Jong L. de, *Being Dutch, More or Less. In a Comparative Perspective of USA and Caribbean Practices* (2nd edn, Rozenberg Publishers 2011).

Kant I., 'Dritter Definitivartikel zum ewigen Frieden' in Immanuel Kant, *Zum ewigen Frieden und Auszüge aus der Rechtslehre: Kommentar von Oliver Eberl und Peter Niesen* (first published 1795, Suhrkamp 2011).

—— 'Metaphysik der Sitten, Erster Teil: Metaphysische Anfangsgründe der Rechtslehre. Das öffentliche Recht' in Immanuel Kant, *Zum ewigen Frieden und Auszüge aus der Rechtslehre: Kommentar von Oliver Eberl und Peter Niesen* (first published 1797, Suhrkamp 2011).

Kaplan R.D., *Balkan Ghosts. A Journey Through History* (first published 1993, Picador at St. Martin's Press 2005).

Kesby A., *The Right to Have Rights: Citizenship, Humanity, and International Law* (OUP 2012).

Kissinger H., *On China* (Penguin Press 2011).

Klein A. and Heitmeyer W., 'Demokratie auf dem rechten Weg? Entwicklungen rechtspopulistischer Orientierungen und politischen Verhaltens in den letzten zehn Jahren' [Democracy on the right track? Developments in right-wing populist movements and political behavior in the last ten years] in Wilhem Heitmeyer (ed.), *Deutsche Zustände. Folge 10* [German conditions. No 10] (Suhrkamp 2012).

Kochenov D., 'Mevrouw De Jong gaat eten: EU Citizenship and the culture of Prejudice' (2011) European University Institute Working Papers RSCAS 2011/06 <http://ssrn.com/abstract=1765983> accessed 30 July 2013.

—— 'Double Nationality in the EU: An Argument for Tolerance' (2011) 17 *European Law Journal* 323.

—— 'Who is "'One of Us"? The Nexus between Naturalisation, Language, and Minority Protection' (2012) forthcoming in Karin Jóhanna Knudsen, Hjalmar P. Petersen and Káriá Rógvi (eds.), *Four or More Languages for All: Language Policy Challenges of the Future* (Novus 2012) <http://papers.ssrn.com/sol3/papers.cfm?abstract_id=2063800> accessed 31 July 2012.

Koja F., *Allgemeine Staatslehre* [General Political Science] (Manz Verlag 1993).

Koopmans R., 'Trade-offs between equality and difference: Immigrant integration, multiculturalismn and the welfare state in cross-national perspective' (2010) 36 *Journal of Ethnic and Migration Studies* 1.

Kop P.C., *Mens en Burger. Een geschiedenis van de grondrechten* [Man and Citizen: A History of Fundamental Rights] (Walburg Pers 2009).

Kretzman N. and Stump E. (eds.), *The Cambridge Companion to Aquinas* (CUP 1993).

Kriesi H., Grande E., Lachat R., Dolezal M., Bronschier S. and Frey T., *West European Politics in the Age of Globalization* (CUP 2008).

Krisch N., *Beyond Constitutionalism: The Pluralist Structure of Postnational Law* (OUP 2010).

Kymlicka W., *Multicultural Citizenship: A Liberal Theory of Minority Rights* (Clarendon Press 1995).

—— 'The rise and fall of multiculturalism? New debates on inclusion and accommodation in diverse societies' in Steven Vertovec and Susanne Wessendorf (eds.), *The Multiculturalism Backlash. European discourses, policies and practices* (Routledge 2010).

—— *Multiculturalism: Success, Failure, and the Future* (Migration Policy Institute 2012).

Lakebrink B., *"Die Europäische Idee der Freiheit". 1. Teil: Hegels Logik und die Tradition der Selbstbestimmung* (Brill 1968).

Lammy D., *Out of the Ashes?* (Guardian Books 2011).

Lesaffer R., *European Legal History: A Cultural and Political Perspective* (CUP 2009).

Lewis B., 'The Roots of Muslim Rage: Why so many Muslims deeply resent the West, and why their bitterness will not easily be mollified' *Atlantic Magazine* (Washington, 1 September 1990) <www.theatlantic.com/magazine/archive/1990/09/the-roots-of-muslim-rage/4643/6/> accessed 1 August 2010.

Lijphart A., *Thinking about Democracy: Power Sharing and Majority Rule in Theory and Practice* (Routledge 2008).

Logemann A., *Grenzen der Menschenrechte in demokratischen Gesellschaften. Die "demokratische Gesellschaft" als Determinante der Grundrechtsschranken in der Europäischen Menschenrechtskonvention* [Limits of human rights in democratic societies: The 'democratic society' as a determinant of human rights limitations in the European human rights convention] (Nomos 2004).

Lucassen L. and Lucassen J., *Winnaars en verliezers, Een nuchtere balans van vijfhonderd jaar immigratie* [Winners and Losers, A Rational Review of Five Hundred Years of Immigration] (Bert Bakker 2011).

Maas W., 'Migrants, states, and EU citizenship's unfulfilled promise' (2008) 12 *Citizenship Studies* 583.

MacMillan M., *Peacemakers: The Paris Conference of 1919 and Its Attempt to End War* (John Murray 2001).

Magnette P., *La Citoyenneté Européenne. Droits, politiques, institutions* [European citizenship: rights, policies, institutions] (Éditions Européennes 1999).

Mak G., *Een kleine geschiedenis van Amsterdam* [A Short History of Amsterdam] (Atlas 2005).

Maihofer W., *Rechtsstaat und menschliche Würde* [The constitutional state and human dignity] (Vittorio Klostermann 1968).

Mann D.J. and Purnhagen K.P., 'The Nature of Union Citizenship between Autonomy and Dependency on (Member) State Citizenship: A Comparative Analysis of the Rottmann Ruling, or: How to Avoid a European Dred Scott Decision?' (2011) Amsterdam Law School Research Paper no 2011-46; (2011) Amsterdam Centre for European Law and Governance Research Paper no 2011-09 <http://papers.ssrn.com/sol3/papers.cfm?abstract_id=1964269> accessed 24 July 2013.

Mansel J., Christ O. and Heitmeyer W., 'Der Effekt von Prekarisierung auf fremdenfeindliche Einstellungen. Ergebnisse aus einem Drei-Wellen-Panel and zehn jährlichen Surveys' [The effect of precarization on xenophobic attitudes: results from a three-wave panel and ten annual surveys] in Wilhelm Heitmeyer (ed.), *Deutsche Zustände. Folge 10* [German conditions. No 10] (Suhrkamp 2012).

Mazauric C., 'La Déclaration des Droits de l'Homme et du Citoyen et la Révolution Française' [The Declaration of Human Rights and Citizens' Rights and the French Revolution] in Guy Braibant and Gérard Marcou (eds.), *Les Droits de l'Homme: Universalité et Renouveau 1789–1989* [Human Rights: Universality and Renewal 1789–1989] (Éditions l'Harmattan 1989).

McGoldrick D., 'Multiculturalism and its Discontents' (2005) 5 *Human Rights Law Review* 27.

Meier C., *A Culture of Freedom. Ancient Greece and the Origins of Europe* (OUP 2009).

Meijer F., *De Middellandse Zee. Een persoonlijke geschiedenis* [The Mediterranean Sea: A Personal History] (Athenaeum – Polak & Van Gennep 2010).

Menke C. and Raimondi F. (eds.), *Die Revolution der Menschenrechte. Grundlegende Texte zu einem neuen Begriff des Politischen* [The Human Rights Revolution: Basic Texts for a New Concept of the Political] (Suhrkamp 2011).

Menocal M.R., *The Ornament of the World: How Muslims, Jews, and Christians Created a Culture of Tolerance in Medieval Spain* (Little, Brown & Company 2002).

Merle J.C., 'Kulturelle Minderheitenrechte im liberalen Staat' [Cultural Minority Rights in the Liberal State] in Matthias Kaufmann (ed.), *Integration oder Toleranz? Minderheiten als philosophisches Problem* [Integration or Tolerance? Minorities as a Philosophical Problem] (Verlag Karl Alber 2001).

Merz F., 'Einwanderung und Identität' *Die Welt* (Berlin 25 October 2000) <www.welt.de/print-welt/article540438/Einwanderung-und-Identitaet.html> accessed 28 May 2012.

Metz J.B., *Christliche Anthropozentrik* [Christian Anthropocentrism] (Kösel-Verlag 1962).

Miller D., 'Immigrants, Nations, and Citizenship' (2008) 16 *Journal of Political Philosphy* 371.

Mitteis H., 'Über den Rechtsgrund des Satzes "Stadtluft macht frei"' [On the Legal Foundation of the Dictum 'Stadtluft macht frei'] in Erika Kunz (ed.), *Festschrift Edmund E. Stengel zum 70. Geburtstag am 24. Dezember 1949 dargebracht von Freunden, Fachgenossen und Schülern* [Festschrift in honour of Edmund E. Stengel presented by friends, colleagues and pupils on the occasion of his 70th birthday on 24 December 1949] (Böhlau 1952).

Neiberg M.S., *Dance of the Furies: Europe and the Outbreak of World War I* (The Belknap Press of Harvard UP 2011).

Neves M., *Transconstitutionalism* (Hart 2013).

Norton A., *On the Muslim Question* (Princeton UP 2013).

Novak D., 'Maimonides and Aquinas on Natural Law' in John Goyette, Mark S. Latkovic and Richard S. Myers, *St. Thomas Aquinas and the Natural Law Tradition: Contemporary Perspectives* (The Catholic University of America Press 2004).

Oers R. van, *Deserving Citizenship. Citizenship Tests in Germany, the Netherlands and the United Kingdom* (Wolf Legal Publishers 2013).

Olsen E.D.H., 'European Citizenship: Mixing Nation State and Federal Features with a Cosmopolitan Twist' (2013) 14 *Perspectives on European Politics and Society* 1.

Perabo B., 'The Proportionate Treatment of Enemy Subjects: A Reformulation of the Principle of Discrimination' (2008) 7 *Journal of Military Ethics* 136.

Peters A., 'Extraterritorial Naturalizations: Between the Human Right to Nationality, State Sovereignty and Fair Principles of Jurisdiction' (2010) 53 *German Yearbook of International Law* 623.

—— 'Les Changements Collectifs De Nationalité' [Collective Change of Nationality] (2011) in The Société Française pour le Droit International, *Droit International et Nationalité* (Editions A. Pedone 2012) <http://ssrn.com/abstract=1971860> accessed 31 July 2012.

Pierik R. and Werner W., 'Cosmopolitanism in context: an introduction' in Roland Pierik and Wouter Werner (eds.), *Cosmopolitanism in Context: Perspectives from International Law & Political Theory* (CUP 2010).

—— 'Can cosmopolitanism survive institutionalization?' in Roland Pierik and Wouter Werner (eds.), *Cosmopolitanism in Context: Perspectives from International Law & Political Theory* (CUP 2010).

Pinto-Duschinsky M., *Bringing Rights Back Home. Making human rights compatible with parliamentary democracy in the UK* (with a foreword by Leonard Hoffmann, Policy Exchange 2011).

Prakke L., *Pluralisme en staatsrecht* [Pluralism and constitutional law] (inaugural address University of Amsterdam, Kluwer 1974).

Prij J., 'Theedrinken als kern van het politieke' [Tea-drinking as the core of politics] (2010) 32 *Filosofie & Praktijk* 19.

Raad van State, *Jaarverslag 2006* [Annual report 2006 of the Council of State] (Raad van State 2007).

Raad voor Maatschappelijke Ontwikkeling [Council for Social Development], *Tussen afkomst en toekomst, Etnische Categorisering door de overheid* [Between Origins and Future: Ethnic Categorization by the Government] (Raad voor Maatschappelijke Ontwikkeling 2012).

Raimondi F., 'Einleitung' [Introduction] in Christoph Menke and Francesca Raimondi (eds.), *Die Revolution der Menschenrechte. Grundlegende Texte zu einem neuen Begriff des Politischen* [The Human Rights Revolution: Basic Texts for a New Concept of the Political] (Suhrkamp 2011).

Roberts J.M., *A History of Europe* (Allan Lane/The Penguin Press 1996).

Rodrigues P., *'De facto* staatloosheid of de uitdaging van onuitzetbaren' (2013) 5/6 *Asiel- & Migrantenrecht* 281.

Roex I., Stiphout S. van and Tillie J., 'Salafisme in Nederland: Aard, omvang en dreiging' [Salafism in the Netherlands: Nature, Scale and Threat] (Instituut voor Migratie- en Etnische Studies, Universiteit van Amsterdam 2010).

Rosenberg R., 'The "Woman Question"' in Richard W. Bulliet (ed.), *The Columbia History of the 20th Century* (Columbia UP 1998).

Rosenfeld M. and Sajó A., 'Spreading liberal constitutionalism: an inquiry into the fate of free speech rights in new democracies' in Sujit Choudhry, *The Migration of Constitutional Ideas* (CUP 2006).

Rubenstein K. and Lenagh-Maguire N., 'Citizenship and the Boundaries of the Constitution' in Tom Ginsburg and Rosalind Dixon (eds.), *Comparative Constitutional Law* (Edward Elgar 2011).

Rutjes M., *Door gelijkheid gegrepen. Democratie, burgerschap en staat in Nederland 1975–1801* [Seized by Equality. Democracy, Citizenship and State in the Netherlands 1975–2012] (Vantilt 2012).

Sachs A., *The Strange Alchemy of Life and Law* (OUP 2009).

Sadiq K., *Paper Citizens: How Illegal Immigrants Acquire Citizenship in Developing Countries* (OUP 2009).

Safferling C., *Internationales Strafrecht. Strafanwendungsrecht – Völkerstrafrecht – Europäisches Strafrecht* [International criminal law: sentencing law – international criminal law – European criminal law] (Springer 2011).

Sandvik K.B., 'A Legal History: the Emergence of the African Resettlement in International Refugee Management' (2010) 22 *International Journal of Refugee Law* 20.

Sarrazin T., *Deutschland schafft sich ab* [Germany abolishes itself] (Deutsche Verlags-Anstalt 2010).

Sassen S., *Globalization and Its Discontents* (The New Press 1998).

Saunders D., *Arrival City: How the Largest Migration in History is Reshaping our World* (William Heinemann 2010).

Scheffer P., 'Het multiculturele drama' [The Multicultural Tragedy] *NRC Handelsblad* (Rotterdam, 29 January 2000) <http://retro.nrc.nl/W2/Lab/Multicultureel/scheffer .html> accessed 10 January 2011.
—— *Immigrant Nations* (Polity Press 2011).
Scherner-Kim K., 'The Role of the Oath of Renunciation in Current U.S. Nationality Policy – To Enforce, to Omit, or Maybe to Change' (1999–2000) 88 *Georgetown Law Journal* 329.
Schmitt C., *Der Begriff des Politischen. Text von 1932 mit einem Vorwort und drie Corollarien* [The Concept of the Political: 1932 text with a preface and three corollaries] (8th edn, Duncker & Humblot 2009).
Schnepf R., 'Zum Problem der Staatenlosigkeit' [On the problem of statelessness] in Matthias Kaufmann, *Integration oder Toleranz? Minderheiten als philosophisches Problem* (Verlag Karl Albert 2001).
Schrauwen A., 'European Union in the Treaty of Lisbon: any change at all?' (2008) 25 *Maastricht Journal of European and Comparative Law* 55.
—— *Burgerschap onder gedeeld gezag* [Citizenship under Shared Authority] (inaugural adress University of Amsterdam, oratiereeks.nl 2013) <www.oratiereeks.nl> accessed 30 July 2013.
Schütze R., *European Constitutional Law* (CUP 2012).
Scientific Council for Government Policy, *Identificatie met Nederland* [Identifying with the Netherlands] (Amsterdam UP 2007).
Sen A, *Inequality Reexamined* (Russell Sage Foundation/Clarendon Press 1992).
—— *Development as Freedom* (Alfred A. Knopf 1999).
—— *Identity and Violence: The Illusion of Destiny* (W.W. Norton & Company 2006).
—— *The Idea of Justice* (The Belknap Press of Harvard UP 2009).
Senghaas D., 'Die Wirklichkeiten der Kulturkämpfe' [The Realities of Cultural Conflict] in Hans Joas and Klaus Wiegandt (eds.), *Die kulturellen Werte Europas* [The Cultural Values of Europe] (Fischer 2005).
Sengupta A., 'Development Co-operation and the Right to Development' in Morten Bergsmo (ed.), *Human Rights and Criminal Justice for the Downtrodden. Essays in Honor of Asbjørn Eide* (Martinus Nijhoff Publishers 2003).
Shachar A., 'Should Church and State be Joined at the Altar? Women's Rights and the Multicultural Dilemma' in Will Kymlicka and Wayne Norman (eds.), *Citizenship in Diverse Societies* (OUP 2000).
—— *The Birthright Lottery: Citizenship and Global Inequality* (Harvard UP 2009).
—— 'Earned Citizenship: Property Lessons for Immigration Reform' (2011) 23 *Yale Journal of Law & the Humanities* 110.
Shaw J., 'EU citizenship and the edges of Europe' (2012) University of Edinburgh CITSEE Working Paper 2012/19.
—— 'Citizenship of the Union: Towards Post-National Membership?' in Academy of European Law (ed.), *Collected Courses of the Academy of European Law, vol VI book 2* (Kluwer Law International, 1998).
Simmons W.P., *Human Rights and the Marginalized Other* (CUP 2011).
Skirbekk G., *Multiple Modernities. A Tale of Scandinavian Experiences* (The Chinese UP 2011).
Sommer T., 'Einwanderung ja, Ghettos nein: Warum Friedrich Merz sich zu Unrecht auf mich beruft' [Immigration yes, ghettos no: why Friedrich Merz wrongly cites me] *Die Zeit* (Hamburg 2000) <www.zeit.de/2000/47/200047_leitkultur.xml> accessed 28 May 2012.
Soysal Y.N., *Limits of Citizenship: Migrants and Postnational Membership in Europe* (The University of Chicago Press 1994).
—— 'Citizenship, immigration, and the European social project: rights and obligations of individuality' (2012) 63 *British Journal of Sociology* 1.
Spencer P. and Wollman H., 'Blood and Sacrifice: Politics Versus Culture in the Construction of Nationalism' in Kevin J. Brehony and Naz Rassool (eds.), *Nationalisms Old and New* (Macmillan Press 1999).

Spiro P.J., 'A New International Law Of Citizenship' (2011) 105 *The American Journal of International Law* 694.

Staples H., *The Legal Status of Third Country Nationals Resident in the European Union* (Kluwer 1999).

Steenvoorde R., *Regulatory Transformations in International Economic Relations* (Wolf Legal Publishers 2008).

Stern K., *Das Staatsrecht der Bundesrepublik Deutschland*, bd 1 [The constitutional law of the Federal Republic of Germany, vol 1] (2nd edn, C.H. Beck 1984).

Stiglitz J., *The Price of Inequality* (W.W. Norton 2012).

Stokkom B. van and Terpstra J., 'Neighbourhood, Youth, and Safety. A dissertation on social cohesion and active citizenship' in Ellen van den Berg, Emine Kaya, Max Kommer, Bert Niemeijer and Stavros Zouridis (eds.), *Justice = Social Cohesion* (Ministry of Justice 2010).

Strauss D.A., *The Living Constitution* (OUP 2010).

Stumpf J.P., 'Doing Time: Crimmigration Law and the Perils of Haste (2011) 58 *UCLA Law Review* 1705.

Stuurman S., *De uitvinding van de mensheid. Korte wereldgeschiedenis van het denken over gelijkheid en cultuurverschil* [The Invention of Mankind: A Short World History of Ideas on Equality and Cultural Difference] (Bert Bakker 2009).

Tambakaki P., *Human Rights, or Citizenship?* (Birkbeck Law Press 2011).

Taylor C., 'The Politics of Recognition' in Amy Gutmann (ed.), *Multiculturalism: Examining the Politics of Recognition* (Princeton UP 1994).

Teitelbaum M.S. and Winter J., *A Question of Numbers: High Migration, Low Fertility, and the Politics of National Identity* (Hill & Wang 1998).

Teubner G., 'Societal Constitutionalism: Alternatives to State-Centred Constitutional Theory?' in Christian Joerges, Inger-Johanne Sand and Gunther Teubner (eds.), *Transnational Governance and Constitutionalism* (Hart 2004).

—— *Verfassungsfragmente. Gesellschaftlicher Konstitutionalismus in der Globalisierung* (Suhrkamp 2012).

Thorbecke J.R., 'Over het hedendaagsche staatsburgerschap' [On Present-Day Nationality] in K.H. Boersema, *Johan Rudolf Thorbecke, Een historisch-critische studie* [Johan Rudolf Thorbecke, A Historical-Critical Study] (E.J. Brill 1949).

Tibi B., *Europa ohne Identität? Leitkultur oder Wertebeliebigkeit* [Europe without identity? *Leitkultur* or arbitrary values] (Siedler 2000).

—— *Fundamentalismus im Islam: Eine Gefahr für den Weltfrieden?* [Fundamentalism in Islam: a danger to world peace?] (Wissenschaftliche Buchgesellschaft 2000).

Tillie J. and Slijper B., 'Immigrant political integration and ethnic civic communities in Amsterdam' in Seyla Benhabib, Ian Shapiro and Danilo Petranović, *Identities, Affiliations, and Allegiances* (CUP 2007).

Tsagourias N., *Transnational Constitutionalism: International and European Perspectives* (CUP 2006).

Trincia F.S., 'Individuelles "Bedürfnis nach den Anderen", Universalität des Rechts und open citizenship' [The Individual 'Need for Other People', Universality of the Law and Open Citizenship] in Matthias Kaufmann (ed.), *Integration oder Toleranz? Minderheiten als philosophisches Problem* [Integration or Tolerance? Minorities as a Philosophical Problem] (Verlag Karl Alber 2001).

Tuck R., 'Asylum and the path to citizenship: A case study of Somalis in the United Kingdom' (2011) UNHCR Research Paper no 210.

United Nations High Commissioner for Refugees (UNHCR), 'Mapping Statelessness in the Netherlands' (2011) UNHCR <www.refworld.org/docid/4eef65da2.html> accessed 30 July 2013.

United Nations Department of Economic and Social Affairs (UNDESA) Population Division, 'World Urbanization Prospects: The 2005 Revision – Fact Sheet 1: World Urban Population' (2005) UNDESA <www.un.org/esa/population/publications/WUP2005/2005 WUP_FS1.pdf> accessed 4 February 2012.

Valadez J.M., 'Is immigration a human right?' in Roland Pierik and Wouter Werner (eds.), *Cosmopolitanism in Context: Perspectives from International Law & Political Theory* (CUP 2010).

Valk I. van der, *Islamophobia in the Netherlands* (Amsterdam UP 2012).

Vasak K., 'A 30-year struggle: The sustained efforts to give force of law to the Universal Declaration of Human Rights' (speech at the International Institute for Human Rights in Strasbourg 1977) XXX *The UNESCO Courier*.

Vermeulen B.P., Artikel 2 [Article 2] in A.K. Koekkoek (ed.), *De Grondwet. Een systematisch en artikelgewijs commentaar* [The Constitution: a systematic article-by-article commentary] (W.E.J. Tjeenk Willink 2000).

Vinogradoff P., 'Historical Types of International Law' in *Bibliotheca Visseriana Dissertationum Ius Internationale Illustrantium, Tomus primus* (Brill 1923).

Volpe G., *Il constituzionalismo del Novecento* (Editori Laterza 2000).

Vonk O., *Dual Nationality in the European Union: A Study on Changing Norms in Public and Private International Law and in the Municipal Laws of Four EU Member States* (Martinus Nijhoff Publishers 2012).

Waas L. van, *Nationality Matters. Statelessness under International Law* (Intersentia 2008).

—— 'Nationality and Rights' in Brad K. Blitz and Maureen Lynch, *Statelessness and Citizenship: A Comparative Study on the Benefits of Nationality* (Edward Elgar 2011).

Walker N., 'The migration of constitutional ideas and the migration of the constitutional idea: the case of the EU' in Sujit Choudry (ed.), *The Migration of Constitutional Ideas* (CUP 2006).

Weiler J.H.H., 'To be a European citizen – Eros and civilization' (1997) 4 *Journal of European Public Policy* 495.

Witte B. de, 'The European Union as an international legal experiment' in Gráinne de Búrca and J.H.H. Weiler (eds.), *The Worlds of European Constitutionalism* (CUP 2012).

Wolf C., 'Intergenerational Justice' in R.G. Frey and Christopher Heath Wellman (eds.), *A Companion to Applied Ethics* (Blackwell 2003).

Woud A. van der, *Koninkrijk vol sloppen. Achterbuurten en vuil in de negentiende eeuw* [A kingdom full of slums: back streets and dirt in the nineteenth century] (Bert Bakker 2010).

Young I.M., *Inclusion and Democracy* (OUP 2000).

Zakaria F., *The Post-American World* (W.W. Norton & Company 2008).

Zouridis S. and Hirsch Ballin E.M.H., 'A Legal and Justice Strategy towards Strengthening Social Cohesion' in S. Muller and S. Zouridis (eds.), *Law and justice: a strategy perspective* (TOAEP 2012).

Zypries B., 'Juristendeutsch: Handwerkszeug oder Herrschaftsmittel?' in Karin M. Eichhoff-Cyrus and Gerd Antos (eds.), *Verständlichkeit als Bürgerrecht? Die Rechts- und Verwaltungssprache in der öffentlichen Diskussion* (Dudenverlag 2008)

INDEX

acquisition of citizenship/nationality 24,
  38–9, 66–7, 74, 77, 81–5, 90–91, 93–4, 96,
  107, 111, 113, 119, 126, 131
active nationality principle 98
active personality principle 98–9
active pluralism 26
alien(s) 6, 11, 14, 17, 24, 42, 50, 58–9, 69,
  72–3, 77–9, 81, 83–4, 86, 89–90, 101, 111,
  134–5
  see also foreigners
allochtoon 22
antagonism 54
anthropocentrism 3
arrival cities 80, 84, 131
assimilation 26–7, 32, 37–8, 57, 87
asylum 86–7, 89, 109, 125, 135

change of nationality 77–8, 100, 126,
  133, 141
citizen(s) 1, 4, 6–9, 10–1, 14–6, 18–9, 25–6,
  36–8, 40, 47–8, 50, 52–54, 59, 60–1, 65–6,
  68–9, 71–6, 79–83, 86, 90, 96–7, 99–102,
  104–6, 111, 115–6, 120–5, 127, 130–3, 135–6,
  139–40, 142, 145–7
citizenization 28
citizens' rights 5–14, 16–7, 19, 24, 28, 31, 40,
  43, 46, 48, 51–2, 54–7, 61, 65, 72, 74–7, 79,
  82, 84, 86–7, 91, 100, 102–3, 105, 109–110,
  116–7, 119–23, 126–9, 131–6, 144, 147
citizens' sovereignty 126
citizenship xi, 4, 6–8, 10–13, 15–8, 23–31,
  33–4, 36, 38–45, 47–8, 50–1, 54, 56–7,
  60–3, 65, 69–76, 79–80, 82–6, 88, 90–2,
  94, 100, 102–3, 110, 112–27, 130–3, 135–6,
  139–42, 144–5, 147
citizenship of residency 84
citizenship rights 56, 72, 74
civil revolutions 8, 54, 136
civil rights 7, 71, 74, 76, 79, 87, 90, 115–6,
  120, 129, 141, 144
civil rights movement 5, 119
civil society 5, 60, 63, 74, 118–9, 137, 144
civilization 4, 18, 35
clash of civilizations 18, 32, 35, 58
coexistence 3, 13–4, 23, 39, 122, 132
co-nationals 103
constitution 9–12, 20, 24, 33, 41, 42, 48–50,
  52–3, 56, 66, 72–4, 80, 85, 96, 103, 115, 126,
  128, 132, 139–40, 142

constitutional change 15, 132
constitutional concept 53, 63, 132
constitutional context 31, 52, 118, 142, 146
constitutional democracy 49
constitutional idea 56, 118
constitutional interpretation 15, 53
constitutional law 28, 48, 50, 61, 66, 70–1
constitutional norms 27, 112
constitutional order 60, 63, 121
constitutional protection 21
constitutional questions 115
constitutional reform 108
constitutional relationship 63, 106,
  112, 125
constitutional rights 10, 66
constitutional setting 26, 132
constitutional state 36, 41, 48, 56, 76, 122,
  137, 142
constitutional system 8, 41, 51, 62, 115, 121,
  139, 141
constitutional thinking 41, 132
constitutional transformation 54
constitutionalism 49–50, 54
contrat social 54–5
cosmopolitan(s) 29, 62, 122–3, 125
cosmopolitanism 122–4
crimmigration law 38
cultural identity 27, 30, 114
cultural rights 63, 115–7

decision-making 41, 47–8, 50–2, 55–6, 85,
  122, 125, 132, 136, 140, 142, 146
*Déclaration des droits de l'homme et du
  citoyen* 8–9, 74, 126
deliberative politics 55
demarcation 13, 22, 24, 39, 65, 67
democracy/democratic 19–20, 26–7, 29,
  39–40, 42–3, 48–9, 51–2, 54–7, 60–1, 63,
  65, 107–8, 112–3, 116–9, 121–2, 125, 132, 134,
  136, 139, 141–7
democratic citizenship 41, 57–9, 61–3, 118
democratic constitution 115
democratic constitutional state 15, 27, 32,
  37, 41, 50, 52, 54, 61, 84, 134, 136, 145, 147
democratic constitutionality 121
democratic order/system 8, 13
democratic society 7, 43, 122, 132, 134, 136
democratic state 39–41, 51, 140
denationalization/denaturalization 126